To: D.

Best w...,

Allen Morris

Florida Gold

Robert Allen Morris

Orchid Springs Publishing, LLC

Orchid Springs Publishing, LLC
329 N. Park Ave., Floor 2
Winter Park, FL 32789

Copyright © 2013 Robert Allen Morris.
All Rights Reserved.
ISBN: 978-0-9960684-0-6

Also by Robert Allen Morris

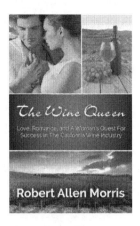

Available at www.amazon.com in paperback or on Kindle

Praise for The Wine Queen

"*The Wine Queen* is a very interesting book with a great story line. The writer is confident, intelligent, assertive, and obviously understands women. He takes us through the looking glass and into the pages by depicting this story from several points of view. He does this through love, happiness, manipulation, tragedy, and professional successes. The exploration of romance, love and tragic loss associated with it is extremely attention-catching and makes it almost impossible to put down. An absolute must read, particularly for women." - **Sumer Rohrs, Winner of Six National Championships in Track and Field, and the 2009 NCAA Division III Women's Outdoor Track Athlete of the Year.**

"In *The Wine Queen*, Allen Morris weaves the story of Ann Robinson from a tragic event in her childhood to a successful career. The reader learns about different industries as Ann works hard and climbs the corporate ladder. Ann's career choices take her from the Southeast United States to the Napa Valley of California. All the while, her quest for true love continues. The story held my interest throughout and I think others will enjoy it, too." **Candi Erick, Winter Park, FL.**

"Florida Gold" is a historical novel, comprised of fiction and nonfiction. It was originally published in 2011 under the title *"The Orange Juice King"*. In 2013 it was rewritten with 21 percent new content, retitled to reflect the broader content of the book, and copyrighted under the new title.

Critical Reviews of Florida Gold

"Robert Allen Morris, an agricultural economist with over 30 years of experience in the citrus industry, brings plenty of insider knowledge and passion to this fictional work, managing to make sequences featuring the main character, Jack Thomas' savvy with concentrate, cartons that don't leak, and other innovations quite engaging. His narrative gets a bit overripe at times, given the seemingly never-ending and near-superhuman heroics of his main character as well as a rather melodramatic string of family tragedies. Still, this novel is ultimately highly entertaining, and a surprisingly juicy account about a key segment of commerce in the Sunshine State." - *Kirkus Reviews*

"Florida Gold by Robert Allen Morris was one of those 'wow factor' books. An amazingly told story, with real feeling put into the words. It's an unforgettable story, one that I could read over again and still take something new away from it. The characters are real and fit the story, the plot was well thought out and researched, and the whole book flows properly. Robert Morris is clearly a natural born storyteller and I would love to read more from him." – *Readers' Favorite*
★ ★ ★ ★ ★

Florida Gold was inducted into the *Florida Citrus Archives* on September 24, 2014. The event was hosted by the Lawton Chiles Center for Florida History on the Campus of Florida Southern College in Lakeland, Florida.

Praise for Florida Gold

"*Florida Gold* is a historical novel that is very well written and captures the flavor of several industries that were central to the economic development of Florida in the early to mid-1900s. The characters are composites of people who were pioneers in the sense that they were the innovators and risk takers who were providing Florida with an economic base that exists today. Woven into the stories of the characters' lives is a sense of what it felt like to be poor and beaten down in early Florida and what it felt like to be wealthy and very successful.

The author, Allen Morris, grew up in a family that was similar to some of the characters in this novel and during his career he has met and known most of the leaders of the orange juice industry. He has carefully woven his understanding of the character of the industry into a very entertaining book and does a very good job of giving the reader the historical flavor of how orange juice became a large industry in the Americas. This history is still evolving as is the history of Florida.

The book is easy to read and very interesting. It may well be adaptable to a short TV series about the history of modern Florida and the impact of the orange juice industry.

Having been a part of the citrus industry for many years I understand and appreciate the depth of knowledge about the subject that Allen shows in this story. He is to be congratulated on researching and writing *Florida Gold*." - **M. Brent Gabler, Former Vice-President of Manufacturing and Engineering, Tropicana Products Inc.**

"If historical fiction is your genre, then *Florida Gold* is a must read. It is a delightful blend of the history of the citrus industry set in old Florida and the human intrigue of a multi-dimensional character, Jack Thomas. Robert Allen Morris carefully crafts a heart-warming story around interesting facts surrounding the citrus industry. Having been born and raised in Florida, the setting of old Florida is made believable through his personal experiences of life before tourism. Mr. Morris has taken the complex subject of Florida's citrus industry and presented it in such a fashion that the reader will come away with a deeper understanding and knowledge without having to crack a textbook." - **Rebecca Parmesano, Junior High History Teacher.**

"*Florida Gold* is phenomenal! It is a perfect blend of history and real life experiences, and I thoroughly enjoyed reading it. It's educational, descriptive, and I appreciated the depiction of old FL with the business aspect and personalization blended beautifully. The imagery allows the reader to vividly see the scenes painted by the author. You can almost hear Jack's strong southern tone as if you knew him growing up as a child and were reminiscing about the good ol' times. An excellent read for anyone wishing to gain knowledge about agricultural history and southern lifestyle, or for the individual who simply wants a swell love story with an awesome plot! I recommend this book for all ages." - **Sumer Rohrs, Winner of Six National Championships in Track and Field, and the 2009 NCAA Division III Women's Outdoor Track Athlete of the Year.**

"Allen Morris's *Florida Gold* is the saga of Jack Thomas, a young orphan who after escaping from a North Florida labor camp, rises to prominence as Florida's leading citrus magnate. A compelling story that carries with it both the ugliness and beauty that was Florida in the Twentieth Century—this novel chronicles the development of Florida's citrus industry from the 1930s to the present. Morris's characters are authentic and believable. This is great Florida fiction in the Patrick Smith vein." - **James M. Denham, Director, Lawton Chiles Center for Florida History and Professor of History, Florida Southern College.**

"I found *Florida Gold* entertaining, educational, and absorbing; not wanting to close the pages until I had completed the book. The author does a refreshing job of sharing with his readers a history of the forestry and citrus industries in Florida. He uses fact and fiction along with his obvious passion for life in rural Florida and the Florida citrus industry to develop an attention-grabbing story centered around his main character, Jack Thomas, Jack's family and peripheral characters. The story transitions smoothly using drama, tragedy, excitement, patriotism, and romance, while progressively developing a theme of character and family values." - **Richard Dicks, Licensed Citrus Fruit Dealer and Vice-President of L. Dicks, Inc., a company that provides harvesting, hauling and marketing services to citrus growers and also owns groves.**

ACKNOWLEDGEMENTS

I would like to recognize the late Brent Gabler, former Vice President of Manufacturing and Engineering at Tropicana Products, for his technical input about juice processing and his review of *Florida Gold*. Chip Bettle, former Senior Vice President of Technology at Tropicana Products, also provided helpful technical information about making orange juice that was sincerely appreciated. LaViece Smallwood's factual and vivid descriptions of life in rural north Florida in the early twentieth century in her book, *Once Upon a Lifetime in and Near Baker County, Florida* were a big help in writing about the main character, Jack Thomas's childhood. Finally, I want to thank each reader who sent me a testimonial describing his or her opinions of *Florida Gold*.

Cover design by Paul Schulz, www.Paulschulz.com.
Gutters and cup on turpentine face, courtesy *Pictorial Album of the Navel Stores Industry, Library and Archives*, Forest History Society, Durham, NC, USA; Aerial photo of citrus processing plant, courtesy Marcos Valim, Citrosuco; *Valencia Morning*, courtesy Paul Schulz.

INTRODUCTION

It was a brisk winter Central Florida morning in 1988. The long white limousine pulled onto the tarmac and drove up to the sleek Gulfstream jet. A uniformed driver opened the limousine door and Jack Thomas, the CEO of Tropical Juices Inc., stepped out. Jack stood over six foot two, with a mass of gray hair just beginning to thin. He was slender, with narrow hips, broad shoulders, prominent cheekbones, and blue eyes of startling clarity. Even at seventy-three, he was a handsome man with a compelling presence, the very image of integrity. He wore a blue pin-striped Brooks Brothers suit.

"Mr. Thomas," the uniformed pilot of the Gulfstream said as he extended his hand. "I'm glad you will be flying with us today, sir."

"Mornin', Corry," Jack said in a southern voice that was precise, graveled with age, but still charmingly formal. As Jack climbed aboard, he asked, "When do we land in New York?"

"ETA is 9:47 a.m., sir."

The aroma of leather was evident. The seats, sofas, and headrests were all hand-tooled Italian leather. The wood trim was mahogany, and light fixtures and control knobs were gold-plated. The cabin was spacious, more like a living room than the cabin of an airplane and there was a kitchen and bar onboard. "Will you be having breakfast this morning, Mr. Thomas?"

"Just coffee and buttered toast, Norberto."

"Yes, sir."

Jack went into the plane's private office, began spreading work papers around him and took out his calculator. As the plane ascended through seventeen thousand feet, Jack lifted the phone from its base on the desk in front of him and dialed the familiar number.

"Global Soft Drink Company, Roger Woods's office," a female voice said.

"Gloria, it's Jack."

"I'll connect you with Mr. Woods, sir."

"Are you in the air yet, Jack?" Roger, the CEO of GSDC, asked.

"Just took off. I take it that you were finally able to get the board's approval on revising our minimum price, or I would have heard from you."

"Yeah, but it was a close vote."

"Roger, Tropical Juices is worth every bit of $2.2 billion, and I won't agree to accept less. Tropical Juices is the largest, most profitable juice company in the world. Per my contract, I receive twenty percent of the selling price, and I intend to get the maximum for my family's inheritance. The same way I did when I sold Tropical Juices to GSDC for $500 million twenty-one years ago. Hasn't it been a profitable investment?"

"The most profitable we've owned, primarily because we had you to run it. But you're retiring, and with your son killed in that accident, you have no strong successor, and we don't think anyone else can manage it as profitably as you. Besides, a lot of board members and some of the largest stockholders believe that the citrus business is too commodity-like and risky, what with freezes that destroy supplies and volatile prices. It's no longer a strategic fit with the direction the company is taking."

"I know. That's what the bean counters tell us. But that's no reason to give it away. If the International Liquor Company

FLORIDA GOLD

won't pay $2.2 billion, there's the International Cereal Group, Morning Star Coffee, United Dairies, et cetera. We'll get our price."

"Ok, Ok, Jack. Get us our price, take your $440 million, and go spend the rest of your life enjoying your grandkids."

"That's just what I intend to do."

Jack thought back to when he'd sold his company to GSDC twenty-one years ago. He'd just turned fifty-two. He could have easily retired, but he wanted to continue to grow the business, both to create a career for his son, Jeb, and to increase his family's inheritance. And he loved the citrus business and the industry that supported it. But now he was seventy-three, Jeb was gone, and it was time to retire. He'd spend a lot of time with his grandchildren. He knew what it was like to grow up without a father, and even without a family for most of his childhood. Too much of his childhood had been a nightmare, and he intended to make sure that his grandchildren's was just the opposite.

3

CHAPTER ONE

Slap! Waaah! Awaaah!

"It a boy!" exclaimed the five-foot-nine 250-pound Molly, spitting tobacco juice into the brass spittoon as she held up the baby, a fire crackling in the large bedroom's fireplace. Molly was the Thomas family's black maid and also a midwife in the Amalgamated Land Company turpentine camp about twenty-seven miles into the woods north of Live Oak, Florida, a rural town of only 693 residents.

"My first grandchild! Born on February 22, 1915!" Margaret Thomas exclaimed.

"Yeah, to your unmarried daughter," said Irma Sue, Margaret's fifteen-year-old daughter. "I want to name him Jack, after my great grandfather." Then she began to weep softly while holding her baby, who was gradually falling asleep.

The Amalgamated turpentine camp north of Live Oak was fifteen miles from the nearest public road and could be reached only by a narrow company road winding through murky swamps and dense pine forests to the remote camp. It was a self-sufficient community. There were fifty-four families and sixty workers. The camp contained dwellings that housed the workers and their families, a house and associated buildings for general manager Pete Thomas and his family, a commissary or general store, a turpentine distillery, and a combination church and school. Pete was responsible for the entire turpentine operation. He directed field operations through his woods riders, who supervised chipping trees and dipping gum from horseback, and was enforcer of the law and order, director of the commissary and distillery, paymaster, and makeshift doctor.

The naval stores industry - whose principal products were tar, pitch, and turpentine produced from gum extracted from pine trees - derived its name from the use of tar and pitch for waterproofing the hulls of early wooden sailing vessels. The gum was distilled into rosin and turpentine and used in the making of soaps, axle grease, paint thinners, solvents, explosives, plasters, disinfectants, and the like. The industry was one of the oldest in the US, dating back to Jamestown in 1608. It was in its zenith in the abundant longleaf and slash pine forests of the southeastern United States from the 1830s until the 1930s. By the 1970s, increasing labor costs and development of new technologies and substitutes led to the end of the naval stores industry.

A strip of bark three-quarters of an inch wide (a streak) was cut from part of the trunk of a pine tree, called the face, with a tool called a hack. This was called chipping. The tree produces and secretes gum to heal its wound, and tin aprons were nailed to the tree to direct the flow of gum into cups or troughs. When cups filled with gum the gum was dipped from the cups into a wooden barrel hauled on a wagon. It was then hauled to the distillery where it was distilled into two products: rosin and turpentine. About every seven to ten days, another streak was cut into the face of the tree just above the last streak. This chipping process was continued until the face grew above head height, and a long-handled hack was used to extend the face about eight to feet high. After about four to six years, the trees would produce no

FLORIDA GOLD

more gum, and they were cut for wood. Then the turpentine camp moved to another location.

It was a primitive, hard, isolated, migratory, and unique way of life. But for those who endured it, it developed immense character and fortitude.

Pete carefully guided his Tennessee walking horse around the turpentine wagon, his leather saddle creaking with each step of the horse, and rode up to Forrest, one of his woods riders. The morning's chill was giving way to warmth as the sun's rays crept through the dense canopy of pine forest, the fragrance of alpine ever-present. The melodic voices of workers calling out their codes to signal the completion of chipping a tree to the tallymen could be heard in the distance. Pete Thomas stood over six feet and was a very powerfully built man of about forty-five, with longish curly dark hair lightly dappled with gray, and piercing brown eyes.

"How're we doing, Forrest?"

"We just may finish collecting scrape this week." Scrape was hardened residue on the face left from gum flowing into cups.

"Good, that means we can wrap up in about a month and head to Archer."

"I think we'll set the company yield record for 1914."

"Just shows what treating the workers fairly and with respect can accomplish. Negroes are no different than anybody else; they got to have pride in their work and know they'll get a fair day's pay for a fair day's work."

"There ain't one of our bosses that agree with that, Pete. All they know is that you can take a camp losing money and turn it profitable. They don't care how."

"But if they did care how, maybe the company would get more profitable."

"By the way, how's Irma Sue doing?"

"She's been in labor about five hours."

"You and Margaret still plan on telling folks the baby's yours?"

7

"Yeah. We don't come into contact with many folks way out here, and we'll soon be moving to another part of the state, so nobody but a few in this camp will know. This way, our grandchild will have parents who love it and our daughter will not have to live with the shame and rejection she would get if folks knew she got pregnant when she wasn't married."

"I admire what you and Margaret are doing. A lot of parents would have thrown her out of their house."

"We love our daughter, and we'll love our grandchild. Anybody who would not support their daughter in a situation like this ain't a good parent. Now I don't want to hear no more talk about it." Pete's stern tone indicated that this discussion was over as he rode off.

"Massa Tommy Lee, you done gots yoself another grandson," Dora, the black maid, told him.

Tommy Lee Dunaway, forty-six, stood five foot ten, was partially bald with a mustache, and had a growing round middle. He usually wore a long-sleeved Western-style shirt open at the neck that revealed a few curls of black chest hair, and a leather vest. Western boots covered his feet and he wore a Stetson hat. A .45 long Colt revolver that he would not hesitate to use rode in its shoulder holster just inside his vest.

Tommy Lee controlled most of the illegal moonshine business in North Florida, from the stills in the swamps that made it, to the fast-driving cars and trucks that hauled it, to the liquor stores and bars that bought it because, since no tax was paid on it, it was cheaper than other distilled spirits like bourbon. He also had a number of politicians on the take who made sure he was able to operate. Tommy Lee didn't know it, but when prohibition would be enacted into law five years later, his positioning in the moonshine business would enable him to become much wealthier than he currently was. And he was already a very wealthy and powerful man.

FLORIDA GOLD

"Where'd you hear that? None of my daughter-in-laws is expecting."

"He Massa Jerry's baby."

"Jerry? You must mean bastard baby."

"I mean yo grandson. Molly, who midwifes at one of the Amalgamated camps over in Live Oak, done told me. She delivered him yestiddy. Miz Irma Sue Thomas is his mama."

"I told him if he kept screwing around in them camps this would happen. And I told him to stay away from turpentine-camp girls. They're just a bunch of girls who'll do anything to get outta them camps. Why does he do that? He's got a beautiful wife."

"'Cause he like the challenge."

"What challenge? A bunch of desperate girls?"

"I don' know, Massa Tommy Lee. This camp run by Massa Pete Thomas."

"I've heard he's an honorable man, making lots of money for Amalgamated. What do they plan to do with the baby?"

"They name him Jack. Molly said Massa Pete an' Margaret gon tell folks he theirs and raise him theyselves."

"Good, at least he will have good parents." He turned to one of his foremen. "Bill, have Jerry come see me NOW!" Tommy Lee shouted.

The move to Archer, Florida, was a welcome change. It would be one of only a few times they had lived in town rather than in the turpentine camp Pete was managing. But with improved transportation enabled by the automobile, this was increasingly feasible. They bought a white wooden house in town, made friends with the neighbors, joined the local Methodist church, and settled into a pleasant life. The vast wilderness around them that included the massive Gulf Hammock meant that they could live in Archer for a long time, maybe until Pete could retire. In 1915, seventy years after Florida joined the Union as the twenty-seventh state, there were 1,866 people living in Archer. It was located about fifteen miles southwest of Gainesville, the new home to the University of Florida. By 1915 the town had four general stores, a drugstore, a bank, three saloons, a post office, hotel, blacksmith and the train depot.

In 1920, at age twenty, Irma Sue graduated from high school as valedictorian and also won the county beauty contest. She was older when she graduated because of the schooling missed from living in turpentine camps. Her parents had thrown a graduation party to celebrate, and most of the guests had arrived. Little Jack was playing with a toy truck on the floor, the brown ceiling fan above him creaking with its every revolution.

"Mama, where's Daddy?" Irma Sue asked.

"Now, honey, you know he's sometimes late because he's so busy."

"I know, but I'm worried. My intuition tells me he may be in some type of trouble."

"Pete Thomas can certainly take care of himself," Jim Lassiter, the local banker, observed. "Now about you, you're beautiful and smart too. Irma Sue, you're going to make some lucky man a fantastic wife."

"Do you plan to go on to college?" Reverend Austin, their minister, asked.

"Can't afford it, not even with the help of the scholarship I was offered."

"She's going to go to work at the drugstore and find her a nice man to marry," Margaret explained.

"I doubt if that will be hard for Irma Sue," Jim Lassiter remarked.

"Miss Margaret, sonthin' real bad done happened to Massa Pete!" Joe, one of the turpentine still operators, exclaimed breathlessly as he rushed into the room.

"What? Oh Lord, is he alright?"

"Don' know. Massa Forrest done rushed him to Doc Bentley's office."

FLORIDA GOLD

"Come on, Margaret, I'll take you there," Jim suggested. "Molly, please watch Jack," she yelled as she and Irma Sue ran to Jim's car. They jumped in and rushed out of the driveway.

Forrest met them just inside the doctor's office and said, "Pete's with Doc Bentley now, but it don't look good."

"What happened?" Margaret asked.

"Rattler spooked his horse and it threw him. He hit his head on a limestone boulder."

Dr. David Bentley emerged from the back and said, "Margaret, Irma Sue, I've done all I can for him. I gave him something to make him conscious, and you can see him, but he doesn't have long."

"Oh, Pete." Margaret wept, and Irma Sue knelt by his bed, gently holding his hand as she began to sob.

"How's my two girls?" Pete whispered weakly.

"We want you to get better," Irma Sue replied.

"I don't think that's going to happen. Margaret, you have been the love of my life ever since we met. And Irma Sue, you've turned your life around and made me proud. I love both...bo-...b-...." And then he was silent.

"No, no, don't die, Daddy!"

"Pete, I'll always love you. You are the rarest, most special man I have ever known."

His funeral was held in the First Methodist Church of Archer on Friday, June 13, 1920, where Pete, Margaret, and Irma Sue had been very active members. Their minister concluded the services by respectfully telling of the many good deeds of Pete, and the respect and admiration he commanded from his workers and the community, to a church filled by his many beloved friends and family, a weeping Margaret, Irma Sue, and Jack in the front row.

Jim Lassiter, forty-one, a balding man of medium height dressed in a dark blue suit, checked his pocket watch nervously, staring at the stack of financial papers on his desk. *I wonder how she will handle what I'm going to tell her,* he thought. *What will she do?* "Mr. Lassiter, Mrs. Thomas is here for your ten o'clock meeting."

"Thank you, Janice, please show her in."

"Margaret, how are you and Irma Sue doing?" he asked, standing and taking her hand as she entered the expansive office for their scheduled meeting a month after the funeral.

"We're OK, but it's hard," she replied, her voice breaking. "I still wake up thinking he's there."

"Pete was a good man, and he will be missed in many ways. Please, have a seat."

"Thank you," she replied as she sat down in a tall leather chair in front of the large mahogany desk. A wood-and-brass name-plate with the words JIM LASSITER, EXECUTIVE VICE PRESIDENT engraved into it sat atop the front of the desk.

"Margaret, I'm sorry to have to discuss this so soon after the funeral, but I need to go over your financial situation with you."

"Based on how profitable the camp has been, I assume there are no problems."

"That's not exactly true," Jim said uneasily.

"What do you mean?"

"Pete was nearly broke."

"What? I don't understand."

"He didn't want you to know. He's overextended on his debt and has borrowed heavily on your house. He really couldn't afford the new car he bought you recently. Once the debts are paid off there won't be much left."

"Why did he do this? He was paid well in his job."

"He wanted you and Irma Sue to have a nice house and nice things. You'd spent your life living in dingy turpentine camps in remote areas, and he wanted to make it up to you.

FLORIDA GOLD

One of the reasons he thought Irma Sue was mesmerized by Jerry Dunaway was that she wanted to move to a town and city and have a full social life and nice things. He was trying to give that to her and to you."

Tears welled up in Margaret's eyes as she tried to avoid crying. "I know he was just trying to make us happy. But we didn't need all those things. Our relationship with him was what was important."

"Pete was just being Pete. Margaret. Do you have any relatives that you, Irma Sue, and Jack could move in with?"

"I have a widowed sister in Mobile, but we've never been close. And she doesn't like children."

"I don't mean to sound insensitive, but the board is putting pressure on me to satisfy Pete's debts now that he's gone. You'll lose the house, most of the furniture, your car, and probably your jewelry."

"How much do I have?"

"Probably about $250 after the debt's paid off," Jim lied. The extra money in her account was there only because an anonymous benefactor had wanted to help.

When she got home, Margaret called her older sister Betty. Betty was sympathetic to her and Irma Sue's situation and said they could live with her while they got on their feet financially, but she said that Jack would not be able to come with them. She suggested that they find a family who would take Jack in until Margaret and Irma Sue were able to support themselves, and then they could bring him back to live with them.

With sadness, Margaret made herself some tea and began to recall the events of her life with Pete. One day Pete had ridden up to the buggy her father, Jim Henderson, was riding to town to get directions. Pete was in the area looking for turpentine land to lease on behalf of the Amalgamated Land Company. Her father and brothers knew him but she had never seen him before. She thought he was an exciting, good-looking young man. She formally met him later at a neighborhood party. After they'd met properly, he asked if he could drive her home in his horse and buggy. She said yes and he went off to borrow a lap robe. Everyone used lap robes to keep warm when they rode in a horse and buggy on cold days and nights. Her older sister Betty had to accompany her home, but it didn't matter. She was so smitten that she broke up with her boyfriend in spite of her mother's protests. "If this doesn't work out, don't come crying back to me," she'd said.

With her father's permission, Pete began courting her. It was called "sparking" in those days because the couple typically saw each other at night at the girl's parents' house. They would be up later than everyone else, and passersby could still see sparks coming out of the chimney where the fire had been kept going.

Pete was being sent to manage a turpentine camp in Valdosta, Georgia, and when he told her, he asked her to marry him. She happily accepted. They were married on December 10, 1895 at the Baptist church in Horseshoe, Alabama. She had been 18.

She was the new wife of the recently promoted Pete Thomas, who at age twenty-five was the new general manager of the Amalgamated Land Company's southern-most turpentine operation in Valdosta, Georgia. They had big plans. Pete was smart and talented, and he had some good ideas. He believed the key to profitability in turpentine operations was in the productivity of labor, which he believed would respond better to positive incentives rather than threats and force. If his camps could consistently be the most profitable in the company, he would be able to advance into senior management and move to the home office in Atlanta, they reasoned. Margaret would also play an important part in their plan. She would manage the camp general store, called the commissary, and keep the books for the turpentine operation. A well-managed store and accurate records were essential to

FLORIDA GOLD

a profitable operation. They agreed that it was best to delay having a baby until Pete could get promoted, because the rural life of a turpentine camp was no place to raise children.

Pete's ideas worked, and he soon developed a reputation of having the most profitable turpentine operations. However no promotion came. What happened was that the company sent Pete to manage its most troubled operations. Usually the problems were from mistreating workers, not keeping accurate records, or outright theft. Whatever the problems, the company knew it could depend on Pete to fix them and restore profitability. Pete had only a sixth-grade education, so by the time he was thirty he was pretty much limited to the navel stores industry for his career, and no other firm would consider him for anything but managing turpentine camps, which he was already doing.

He and Margaret decided to start their family, and she got pregnant with Irma Sue, who was born on January 21, 1900. Irma Sue was smart and kind, but like her father, she was too trusting. She had believed young Jerry Dunaway when he had said he loved her, had left his wife, wanted to marry her and take her to live with him in Atlanta, where his father's trucking company was headquartered. But when she got pregnant, Jerry had left for Atlanta with his wife. Pete had threatened to kill Jerry, but Margaret had calmed him down, reasoning that for Pete to throw his life away in prison would only add to their problems.

Irma Sue coming home from work jarred her back to the present. "Where's Jack?"

"Out back, climbing that tree you told him not to climb."

"I wish you wouldn't let him do things like that, especially things I've forbidden."

"And I keep telling you, you've got to let him experience things or he'll never grow up and be responsible."

"But he always wants to do such risky things."

"I guess that's part of his personality. Probably inherits it from Tommy Lee Dunaway."

"Jerry's father."

"Yeah. You've got to be a real risk taker to build the illegal moonshine empire that he has."

"Irma Sue, we need to talk," Margaret began nervously that evening at dinner.

"OK, what's up?"

Margaret explained their financial situation, the plan to go live with Betty, and that they would need to find a family to keep Jack until they could support themselves. "No way. Jack stays with us," Irma Sue replied angrily. "And why was Daddy so irresponsible?"

"Because he wanted to give us nice things and a life better than we'd had in the turpentine camps. Jim thought your dad felt that one reason you became close with Jerry was that you wanted a better life in town with him."

"Mama, Jerry was just my stupidity and nothing more."

"Maybe so, but we've got serious problems. They're going to take the house, the furniture, our car, most of our jewelry, and who knows what else. Your job at the drug store wouldn't even buy enough food, let alone anything else. And I can't find any work here in Archer. We only have $250 to our name. I don't know anything else we can do other than living with Betty for now."

"You're right, Mama. I just hate to leave Jack behind."

"We'll make a plan and a promise to each other. Our goal will be to be able to come and get him to live with us in a year."

"OK."

"Do you think the Robinsons that own the drugstore where you work would take him?"

"I don't know, maybe. They like children, and Roger, their youngest, is now a teenager. I'll explain the situation and ask Mr. Robinson tomorrow at work."

FLORIDA GOLD

The next morning Irma Sue was cleaning the soda fountain when Jesse Robinson walked in. "Irma Sue, you're doing a fine job here, and I'm glad we were able to hire you. How's your mother holding up since the funeral?"

"It's hard, but she's doing OK. Mr. Robinson, I need to talk to you in private."

"OK, as soon as Carey finishes in back, he can mind the soda and cash register and we'll talk back in my office."

"Mr. Robinson, is now OK?" Irma Sue asked as she entered the small, cluttered office behind where all the pills and medicines were stored forty-five minutes later.

"Is Carey out front?"

"Yeah." She told him about their financial situation, their plan to move to Mobile and move in with her aunt Betty, and about how they couldn't take Jack.

"That's terrible," Jesse said. "Does Margaret have someone to leave him with?"

"No, I wanted to ask you if you and Mrs. Robinson would take him. It will just be for a year, maybe less, until we can afford our own place."

"I need to talk to Emma about this, but I would be glad to. He's a well-behaved nice young boy. I'll let you know tomorrow."

"OK, thanks, Mr. Robinson."

"Dinner's ready," Emma Robinson said as she stuck her head out the screen door leading to the wide covered porch where Jesse and Roger were reading the newspaper and drinking iced tea.

"It sure smells good, love," Jesse observed as they entered the dining area next to the kitchen and took their customary seats around the oak table.

"Jenny wanted to try her new recipe for pear pie with the pears we put up last August."

"Those were some of the best pears I can remember from our trees," Roger observed as he heaped mustard greens onto his plate from the large bowl.

"Wait till you try my pie," Jenny said, passing the mashed potatoes.

"Margaret Thomas and Irma Sue are moving to Mobile to live with Margaret's sister, Betty," Jesse said as Emma passed him the platter of fried pork ribs.

"Why?" Emma asked, putting a biscuit on her plate.

"They're broke. Pete was highly in debt."

"That doesn't sound like Pete"

"I know, I was surprised too. Betty said they can't bring Jack with them."

"What? Why, that's awful. Do they have someone to take care of him?"

"Irma Sue asked me today if we would. She said it would only be for about a year."

"I'd love to take him. It will be wonderful to have a young child around again."

"What do you think about this, Roger and Jenny?" Jesse asked.

"I'd like a little brother to take huntin' and fishin', and play ball with. It would be great."

"Mom, we could teach him to cook," Jenny said.

"That's women's work," Roger replied.

"So you don't want us to teach him to make your favorite brownies?" Jenny asked.

"Well, when you put it that way..."

"I'll tell Margaret the good news tomorrow," Jesse said.

CHAPTER TWO

The bank handled the financial transactions to sell Margaret's house and car, while she sold their jewelry, radio and other personal items in order to settle her debts. After everything was sold she was several hundred dollars short in satisfying all of the debt. But the anonymous benefactor made up the deficit and increased the $250 to $303 to make this believable by Margaret, since the likelihood of exactly settling the debt was obviously small. As instructed, the bank kept this transaction confidential from her.

"Jim, where'd we end up?" Margaret asked when they met to discuss the status of her debt.

"Counting the $250 you had, you now have $303.[1] The extra $53 is being posted to your account today."

"That was close! Thanks for handling everything in the professional manner that you did, Jim."

"Margaret, it was a pleasure. Pete was a fine man and he will be missed. On behalf of the Farmers and Dealers Bank, I wish you well in your new pursuits."

"Irma Sue, that must be the Robinsons at the front door, would you let them in?" Margaret shouted from the bedroom where she was finishing her packing.

---

[1] The same as $3,529 in 2013.

Her words echoed in Irma Sue's head. The Robinsons, who were giving them a ride to the train station, were here. They were also here to pick up Jack. She promised herself she would not cry as she went to the front door at six a.m. on Friday, August 27.

Nobody spoke on the drive to the train station. Irma Sue clung tightly to Jack while Margaret prayed for the strength to leave Jack and be strong for Irma Sue. Five-year-old Jack, who knew he would be staying with the Robinsons and why, tried to be brave, but when a tear trickled down his little cheek, Irma Sue began to cry softly and held him closer. The Robinsons, sensing how traumatic this was for a family who had just lost a loving husband and father and were now going to be separated, respected their grief as they rode in a sad silence.

"Emma and I will load your luggage and check the train schedule," Jesse offered as they pulled into a parking space at the train station. "If it's on schedule, it's almost half an hour before the train leaves so you can have some time alone to say good-bye."

"Thanks, Jesse, Emma," Margaret replied. Irma Sue began to lose what little composure she had left, and Jack, sensing her sadness, also began to cry.

Margaret, who through the years had experienced many hardships, knew that as her family's leader, she had to pull them out of their depression. "Now I want both of you to listen to me," she began sternly, her voice shaky from grief. "We're Pete Thomas's family. And we're not going to let a few setbacks get us down. How do you think he feels, looking down on us from heaven and at the first problems we have, we're crybabies. Things are going to be fine. We settled our debts with a little money to spare, and we're going to get through this."

Somehow, Margaret's words calmed Irma Sue and she began to regain her composure. But Jack continued to cry.

FLORIDA GOLD

"Please Mama, take me with you. Tell Aunt Betty I won't eat much, and I'll sleep on the floor."

Jack's pleas almost tore Margaret's heart out and Irma Sue began to cry again. It took every ounce of strength Margaret had to keep from breaking down, but instead, she remembered something she had in her purse. "Jack, I want to give you something very important," she said as she looked through her bag.

"What, Mama?" Jack sobbed.

"This," she replied as she handed him a hand-carved ivory cross. On it were inscribed the words "𝔑𝔬 𝔥𝔞𝔯𝔡𝔰𝔥𝔦𝔭 𝔦𝔰 𝔱𝔬𝔬 𝔤𝔯𝔢𝔞𝔱 𝔱𝔬 𝔟𝔢𝔞𝔯 𝔞𝔰 𝔩𝔬𝔫𝔤 𝔞𝔰 𝔱𝔥𝔬𝔲 𝔥𝔞𝔰𝔱 𝔣𝔞𝔦𝔱𝔥."

"I've never seen that before, Mama, where did you get it?" Irma Sue asked.

"My grandmother gave it to me when my grandfather died. But there's much more to it than that." Jack stopped crying and began to listen. "My grandmother - my mother's mother - and my grandfather, Second Lieutenant Jack Henderson, a graduate of West Point from South Carolina, fell in love before he left to fight for the Confederacy in the Civil War as an artillery officer. When they were at the train station saying good-bye he gave this cross to her and told her to hold it to her heart and pray for strength when she needed it. She said it helped calm her fears, and she believes her prayers helped bring him back alive and safe."

"Is that who I was named after?" Jack asked.

"Yes it is," Irma Sue replied. "After the war, he became a very successful engineer, and started the New Orleans steam boat company that built Mississippi River boats. He was killed in an explosion in 1887, wasn't he, Mama?"

"That's correct. I was ten at the time and we were very close. He used to take me on riverboat rides. I was devastated by his death. There's more history to the cross, something I'll tell you and Irma Sue together, Jack, when you're old enough to understand. At this point suffice it to say that General

George Washington, who later became our first president, gave this cross to Jack Henderson's grandfather, John Henderson, just before they went into a major battle in the Revolutionary War. Jack, the cross is now yours. Keep it with you at all times. Whenever you're real worried or scared, or it looks like there's no hope, hold it to your heart and pray to God and Jesus. They will give you the strength you need."

"I'm OK now, Mama," Jack told her as he ran his fingers over the inscription on the cross. "You and Irma Sue go and make a place for us to live."

Their train arrived at the station in Mobile at 8:48 p.m., twelve minutes later than scheduled.

"Where do you want me to take these, ma'am?" the porter asked as he and another porter unloaded their luggage. It was starting to rain.

"Inside by that bench on the back wall would be fine," Margaret replied, gesturing to the waiting area that was visible through the large window.

"Where's Aunt Betty?" Irma Sue asked as Margaret tipped the porters, the rain pelting down now as people hurried into taxis. Those not under the covered loading/unloading area were holding newspapers or anything else they had over their heads to avoid getting wet. Automobile horns honked in the choked traffic, temporarily drowning out occasional shouts of "Taxi."

"Maybe she's running late," Margaret suggested. "Let's go inside and wait."

"Mama, there's one of those pay telephones, maybe we can call her," Irma Sue suggested after they had been waiting for about ten minutes.

"OK," Margaret agreed as she went to the phone beneath a sign that said GRAY PAY TELEPHONE. "Hello, Betty, it's Margaret."

"Where're you callin' from?"

FLORIDA GOLD

"We're at the train station. Are you coming to get us?"

"The Mobile Garden Club is meeting at my house for lunch tomorrow and I'm busy getting ready for it, but there's a bus stop only a couple of blocks from my house. Catch the bus."

"Betty, its pouring rain, we'll get soaked."

"Now I'm supposed to control the weather? You wanna stay with me or not? Because, if you don't, there's plenty of other people I can rent to."

"That's fine, Betty. We'll be there as soon as we can catch a bus."

"Aunt Betty wants us to take the bus in this weather?"

"She's busy getting ready for a social event tomorrow."

"She's busy being a cantankerous old grouch like she always is."

"Is there a bus that stops near 1570 Dauphin Street?" Margaret asked the clerk as she walked up to the barred ticket window.

"Let's see," the clerk said checking his schedule. "There's a bus stop at 1811 Dauphin, but that bus left about fifteen minutes ago."

"When will there be another one?"

"Not until eight thirty in the morning. But you can take a taxi."

Fine, Margaret thought. *At the rate we're spending we'd better to be able to find jobs soon.*

With a population of 60,777 in 1920, Mobile, Alabama, was located on the Mobile River and the Central Gulf Coast. It was the largest city on the Gulf Coast between New Orleans and Tampa. The port of Mobile, ninth largest in the US, has always played a key role in the economic health of this city. Mobile was home to art museums, a symphony orchestra, an opera, and a ballet company. The city is known for having the

23

oldest carnival celebrations in the US, dating back to the 1700s. It was also the birthplace of Mardi Gras.

Irma Sue got a job as a teller in the First Community Bank of Mobile and Margaret found work as a cashier in Hope's General Store. But even added together, their pay was not enough to support them unless they lived with Betty. Margaret began looking for a higher-paying job while she worked as a cashier. But money wasn't the only reason she was looking for another job. When she'd been working only about a month, her boss, Jim Hope, a short, middle-aged balding man with a pot belly and thick glasses, had come over to her register and said with a sneer, "You're one of those liberated women, aren't you?"

"What?"

"Yeah, prefer to work instead of being at home taking care of your family."

"My husband is dead and I have no family living with me but my daughter, who is twenty."

"Yeah, I heard you had a son, but left him with someone else. I guess he cramps your dating style."

"No, my sister wouldn't let us move him into her house," she said thinking, *Why is this any of his business*?

"Betty is one of the finest women I know, she'd never do that. Now as for dating, I'm available if you..."

"Mr. Hope, you're married!"

"That's OK. What Jane doesn't know won't hurt her."

"Well, I don't do that sort of thing."

"Yeah, I'll bet," he said angrily. And so it went. Margaret was afraid she'd lose this job, and she hadn't been able to find anything else that paid more.

"And who are you?" a handsome young man asked as he walked up to the coffee pot in the break room of the bank where Irma Sue was pouring a cup of coffee on Friday

24

FLORIDA GOLD

morning, December 3. He was tall, over six feet, with broad shoulders, a narrow waist, and a muscular, athletic look about him. He had thick, curly black hair that seemed always in his face, a quick, infectious smile, pronounced cheek bones, and an engaging set of hazel eyes that had caused female hearts from sixth grade onward to spontaneously flutter.

"Irma Sue Thomas, who are you?"

"Jeb Walker. My dad's George Walker, the bank president." He couldn't take his eyes off of her as he took in every detail about her. She looked taller than average, about five foot six or seven, and slender, with curves that even her modesty couldn't hide. Her hair was a fascinating blend of gold, brown, and colors in between, and flowed over her shoulders. Her eyes were crystal blue and tantalizing. Her face was narrow, its features distinct, with a creamy smooth complexion. All he could do was stare. And want.

"I haven't seen you around, where do you live?" asked Irma Sue.

"I'm in my senior year at the University of Alabama and just got home on Christmas break. Where are you from?"

"Archer, Florida. My daddy died recently and my mama and I moved here to live with my aunt Betty."

"Would you go out with me tonight? Say, supper at a very good French restaurant and a play at the opera house?"

"Jeb, we've just met, I need to get to know you better first," Irma Sue replied, blushing, but very attracted to the handsome, athletic-looking Jeb.

"Let's see, I play quarterback for the UA Crimson Tide, I'm majoring in finance in the School of Commerce, I work part-time in the bank summers, and over Christmas holidays, I have a neat car that was my high school graduation present, and I like to take pretty, smart girls on dates."

"You talked me into it," she giggled, impressed.

"Ok, I'll pick you up at six thirty."

"Great, here's my address," she replied, writing it on a slip of paper.

At 6:25 p.m., a well-dressed Jeb, three-piece suit, light-blue shirt, and charcoal tie with a bouquet of flowers in his hand, knocked on the door. Margaret answered.

"You must be Mrs. Thomas," Jeb replied.

"Yes, and you must be Jeb."

"It's good to meet you. It's obvious where Irma Sue gets her good looks."

"Thank you Jeb, Irma Sue will be right down, why don't you have a seat?" she suggested thinking, *Boy is he a charmer.*

"Irma Sue. You certainly look lovely," Jeb observed when she entered the room.

"Thank you, Jeb. The flowers are lovely." She was wearing a light town frock in soft blue wool, the blouse cut in a bolero effect, with an inset vest of white georgette matching the cuff bands of the flaring sleeve. The skirt had a circular cut with two inset box pleats in the front, and buttons at either side of the yoke. Her hat was a light-blue felt cloche with artificial flowers for trimming

"Here, I'll put them in some water," Margaret offered as she took the red roses.

"Mrs. Thomas, we should be home by eleven," Jeb said as they left.

"Oh, I like your car." It was a 1916 Studebaker convertible with whitewall tires and leather seats.

"Thank you."

He took her to Café du Monde, a French restaurant with a chef trained in Paris. The restaurant had a green awning out front partially obscuring a pair of formidable oak doors. Inside, the ceilings were high, the wood dark, the booths leather-backed, the white linens starched, and the napkins

FLORIDA GOLD

poufed up in cut crystal water glasses. As they were seated at a table Irma Sue said, "This is the nicest restaurant I've ever eaten in, Jeb."

"I hoped you'd like it. It's one of my family's favorites." The waiter brought menus.

"How are you this evening, Mr. Walker?"

"Fine, Wendell."

"And who's the lovely lady?"

"Irma Sue Thomas. She and her family are new in town."

"Well, welcome to Mobile, Miss Thomas."

"Thank you."

"I hear you've led the Crimson Tide to the national championships, Mr. Walker."

"Yes, Wendell, the game is in New Orleans on New Year's Day against Texas."

"And I know you'll win. You've made Mobile very proud, sir."

"Thank you, Wendell."

"You're a football star, I'm impressed," Irma Sue observed.

"I don't know how much of a star I'll be if we lose the game for the national championship."

"I'm sure you'll do just fine."

"So tell me about yourself," Jeb asked.

"There's not much to tell. My father, Pete, managed turpentine camps for the Amalgamated Land Company. He had a reputation for being able to turn a camp that was losing money into a profitable one, primarily by treating the labor with respect, paying them fairly, and keeping accurate records. Rather than incorporate that approach into their corporate strategy, Amalgamated simply sent him to turn around money-losing camps, so we moved around a lot. I was late graduating from high school because of that and the remote nature of the camps, which sometimes prevented me from attending classes. But I guess I made up for it because

27

when I graduated last June, I was valedictorian of my class. I have a little brother, Jack, who is five and staying with friends in Archer until my mother and I can get a place of our own. That's about it, now your turn."

She's the most beautiful woman I've ever dated, Jeb thought, *and smart, down-to-earth, not silly and overly flirtatious. I bet growing up in turpentine camps really gave her a strong sense of character.*

"Mr. Walker, are you ready to order?"

"Yes, Wendell."

"What will you have, Miss?"

"I'm afraid I don't understand much of this menu. Jeb, would you order for me?"

"Certainly. The lady will have *la soupe à l'oignon gratinée, la sallade César, magret de moscovie rôti a l'ail et risotto de pomme, l'assiette de legumes,* and for dessert, the crêpes Suzette."

"Excellent choices, sir. The duck is especially good this evening. And for you?"

"The same."

"Fine, sir."

"You speak French - I continue to be impressed. Now tell me what we're having."

"Baked onion soup, lettuce salad with croutons, roast duck, a vegetable plate, and pancakes with an orange sauce served flaming for dessert."

"I've always wanted to try roast duck. And a flaming dessert as well! I'm impressed again. Now you were going to tell me about you."

"I am an only child as well. Spend time hunting on our ranch and fishing in the gulf with my father and grandfather, who started the bank and has now passed away, and I also like to play golf and tennis. I played football in high school and was also valedictorian of my class. Then off to college. I plan

FLORIDA GOLD

to begin working in the bank as a loan officer in June, after my graduation from UA."

Every time he looked at her, she felt weak. *He's so good-looking and sexy, and so nice,* she kept saying to herself. *I'm really having a wonderful time. He's very easy to talk to.* Then he signaled a strolling violinist to come and play a song at their table, and while it was playing, he held her hand and said, "Irma Sue, I really enjoy spending time with you."

"I enjoy spending time with you too, Jeb."

They had a wonderful meal, and the duck with orange sauce was superb, as was the flaming dessert, which was impressive. They went to see Shakespeare's *A Midsummer Night's Dream.* During the intermission when they were mingling with the crowd, it was evident that Jeb's family was greatly respected, and his football accomplishments highly revered. Apparently a large group was going to the championship game in New Orleans to cheer him and their team on.

They really hit it off, and the chemistry between them was powerful. The play was over at ten thirty, after which he took her home. When they went to the door, he looked into her eyes and said softly, "I really had a good time tonight. I'd love to kiss you, but I know that would be too forward of me this soon, so instead, I would like to ask you to go out with me again tomorrow. I was thinking of horseback riding and a picnic, on our ranch."

"I'd love to," she managed to reply, even though she was trembling, her emotions raging.

"Ok, I'll be by at ten thirty."

"Goodnight," she said softly.

"Well, how was the date?" Margaret asked when Irma Sue came in the house.

"It was enchanting," she replied, with a glazed, faraway look in her eyes. "He's the most wonderful man I've ever met. I think I'm in love."

"So tell me all about the evening and about Jeb." Irma Sue recanted the evening's experiences to her mother, including the restaurant, the dinner, how polite Jeb was, that he was a football star, and how respected in the community he and his family were. "Well, just take things slow. Remember your last romantic experience."

"Mama, this is nothing like that. First, I'm older now and wiser. And second, he's not a married man who says he's leaving his wife. He's single, good-looking enough to get dates with any girl he wants, and well respected throughout the community."

"I realize all that. Just go slow and be sure. Has he asked you out again?"

"Yes, we're going horseback riding and having a picnic on his family's ranch tomorrow."

"Good."

"Tell us about this new girl," Amanda Walker asked her son curiously the next morning at their family breakfast, something they tried to do every Saturday and Sunday morning. Amanda Walker was beautiful in a distinctive Katharine Hepburn way. She was tall, with shoulder-length brown hair, shoulders that were marine straight, brown eyes, subtle cheek bones, and a soft, round nose.

"Yes, Son," his father, George, added. At forty-eight, George Walker's hair was just beginning to turn gray at the temples, which lent him a distinguished air. His eyes were gray and active, the angle of his chin blunt. His voice was deep, cultured, with a Southern accent. He wore three-piece suits, and favored pipe smoking over cigarettes. A graduate of Vanderbilt, he'd taken the banking business his father had started and grown it into an empire, with controlling interests in banks, department stores, railroads, textile mills, and timber land. They had vacation homes in West Palm Beach, Florida and Bermuda, and a townhouse on Park Avenue in

FLORIDA GOLD

New York, but chose to maintain a low profile as successful country bankers with a local ranch. Their only son, Jeb, was heir to one of the largest fortunes in the United States. "We'd like to know more about her. She's doing a great job at the bank, and our customers really like her. She goes out of her way to make sure their banking needs are met. And the men think she's the prettiest teller in town."

Jeb told them what he knew about Irma Sue, Margaret, and little Jack and told them how honest and open she'd been on the date, not pretentious or overly flirtatious.

"It's growing up in those turpentine camps. That can be a rough life, and I think it builds character. Every camp manager and woods rider I've ever made a loan to has been honest and willing to do whatever it took to pay off the loan," his father observed.

"It sounds like to me with Pete's death, these are some good, honest people just down on their luck," Amanda observed.

"I'm taking her horseback riding and on a picnic on the ranch today," Jeb offered.

"Why don't you invite her and her mother to have Sunday dinner with us, Son?" Amanda asked. Sunday dinner was basically lunch with a different name.

"OK, Mom, I think that's a good idea."

Jeb was at Irma Sue's door and knocking on time at ten thirty. "Hi, beautiful."

"Hey Jeb."

"How are you doing today, Jeb?" Margaret asked.

"Fine, ma'am. Do you have plans for today, Mrs. Thomas?"

"No, I normally work on Saturdays, but the owner is away visiting his daughter and grandson, so the store's closed."

"Then why don't you join us?"

"Oh, I wouldn't want to intrude."

"You wouldn't be Mama," Irma Sue offered, thinking, *What better way to show Mama what a fantastic guy Jeb is?*

"Why wouldn't I want to be with two beautiful women if I had the chance?" Jeb teased.

He's definitely a charmer, Margaret thought. "OK, can you give me about fifteen minutes to get ready?"

"Certainly."

The ranch entrance had the name "Spring Creek Ranch" across the archway. They drove for about two miles through beautiful scenery before arriving at a massive log house with outbuildings and a large horse barn. "This place is huge, Jeb," Margaret observed.

"We have twenty-one thousand acres. My grandfather, also named Jeb, acquired it after the Civil War, which he fought for the Confederacy in. He was one of the first bankers to finance the Reconstruction."

"Hey, Massa Walker," his dad's ranch assistant greeted him.

"Toby, this is Mrs. Margaret Thomas and her daughter, Miss Irma Sue."

"Good to meet you fine ladies," Toby replied. "Massa Walker, the horses are ready. And Noreen have a picnic lunch ready. It her fried chicken and them fine biscuits, black-eyed peas, and banana pudding."

"Great, Toby," Jeb replied as they walked into the barn.

They loaded the picnic lunch on Irma Sue's horse and all three mounted up.

"We'll ride to this spot on Spring Creek where we have a table set up for having picnics," Jeb explained. "It's about an hour's ride."

It was a beautiful day - sunny, blue sky, and warm for this time of year, about seventy degrees. The scenery was magnificent, ranging from pine forests to open pasture with

FLORIDA GOLD

contented cows grazing in the distance to shady oak hammocks.

A deer bounded out of a thicket and it spooked Irma Sue's horse, which bolted to run. But she quickly got control of him and calmed him down. "Where'd you learn to ride like that, Irma Sue?" Jeb asked, impressed.

"She used to help the turpentine woods riders out," Margaret explained. "That girl has been riding horses almost since she could walk."

They soon arrived at the picnic spot, and it too was beautiful, the creek gurgling in the background. "Want to catch a fish?" Jeb asked.

"What?" Irma Sue asked.

"We have fishing tackle in the shed," Jeb explained.

"Sure," Margaret replied.

Jeb rigged them up with rods and reels, and artificial lures. On the third cast, Margaret caught a bass, about two pounds.

"We are 'catch and release' unless we plan to cook them here," Jeb explained, releasing the fish. "That way, the fishing is usually good. I see you ladies are also no stranger to fishing."

"No, or to hunting," Irma Sue replied. "I killed my first deer when I was ten."

Jeb continued to be impressed. After catching several bass and large bream, they stopped fishing and laid out a table cloth on the picnic table for lunch. The fried chicken, biscuits, black-eyed peas, and banana pudding were superb. "I wish we'd had Noreen to cook for our camps," Margaret joked. "It would have been much easier to get woods riders and tallymen."

"I know what woods riders are, but what are tallymen?"

33

"They assist woods riders by keeping track of how many trees each worker completes. Sometimes we would fix lunch for the woods riders and tallymen," Margaret explained.

After lunch they took a walk along the creek and Margaret told Jeb about her life with Pete and described what a fine man he was. And how sad they'd been to have to leave little Jack behind, but were determined to get their own place soon so he could join them.

Some people can be so insensitive, he thought, understanding the situation that circumstances and an uncaring Betty had put them into.

Jeb told them of his family's background in banking, how his grandfather had led banking efforts in Alabama that helped finance the post-Civil War reconstruction, how they viewed the banker's role as one of helping the community grow, taking smart risks with honest, capable people. And about their charitable activities, like gifts at Christmas for underprivileged children, field days for the local orphanage on the ranch, etc. Margaret soon realized what a fine boy Jeb was, and what a fine family he came from.

On the way back home, Jeb explained that his mother and father would be honored if Margaret and Irma Sue would have Sunday dinner with them the next day. He would pick them up at noon.

"We'd love to," Margaret replied.

They got home about three thirty. "I hope I'm not being too forward, Irma Sue, but would you like to go out again tonight?"

"Absolutely," a mesmerized Irma Sue replied.

"Ok, I'll be here at seven."

When Jeb had left and they were inside, Margaret said, "Irma Sue, you were right, he's a wonderful young man and it sounds like he comes from a fine family."

"I don't want no boys coming around here, you hear?" Betty said loudly as she entered the parlor.

FLORIDA GOLD

"I understand, and he will not come in, only meet at the front door to go somewhere."

"Well, see that he don't," Betty scolded. "And I want my rent next Friday!"

"You'll have it on time," Margaret replied.

When Betty had left, Irma Sue whispered, "I hate that woman."

"Now Irma Sue, Betty has had a rough life and it's left her bitter."

"She's a bitch. She belittled and fussed at her kind husband until she drove him to an early grave. If he hadn't left her that inheritance, she'd be out in the cold like us."

"I won't judge my sister," Margaret replied.

They got a hamburger and fries at Joe's Diner, and went to see a movie - *Deliverance*. It was the story of Helen Keller, who lost her vision and hearing when she was two. Afterward, they drove down to the bay and walked along the waterfront. He took her hand, and butterflies came to her stomach.

"Jeb," she started, her voice barely more than a whisper as she looked up into his eyes, "I've had such a good time these past few days, I'm so glad we met, I..." and then he took her in his arms and she made a soft gasp as his lips slowly met hers with ravishing tenderness. Her mind whirled with the touch and feel of his lips on hers and her heart began to pound in great hammering leaps. Rings of pleasure expanded through her, shimmered, threatened to burst.

Her lips were soft, firm, sweet. He felt himself sink into her soft, lush mouth as it yielded under his, her fragrance whispering seductively around him. Their arms tightened around each other as their kiss deepened.

Instinctively she soothed her hands over his muscular shoulders and let herself sink into him. She should have

35

known it would be like this with him. Beautiful. Achingly beautiful.

The feel, the warmth, and beauty of her created a longing and a joy in Jeb that he had never felt. Then their lips separated, and he said, "I've wanted to do that all evening."

"Oh, Jeb, I've wanted you to ... so much." On their drive home they were like two high school kids with their first crush. She practically sat on his lap and rested her head on his shoulder, his arm around her.

They soon arrived at her aunt Betty's, and he walked with her toward the house in the crisp fall night. When they were outside her door, she looked up at the sky and said, "The moon's so white tonight. Its light gives everything a silvery glow."

"God, you're beautiful," Jeb said as he looked deeply into her eyes, gently trailing the back of his fingers across her cheek.

"Oh, Jeb," she said staring at him, her eyes wide and aware as he slowly bent closer. His lips met hers in a soft, exploring kiss as she moaned, her eyelids lowering. Her body pressed sensuously into his and he pulled her closer, their kiss growing more demanding. Then his lips left hers as he kissed her down her cheek, and on to her neck and throat, while her fingers caressed up and down his back. His mouth returned to hers and she made a soft innocent sound as her body shuddered, their kiss growing harder, more urgent, hungry. Her trembling hands skimmed over his face into his hair and locked there. She forgot about the past, the future and even the present - about everything, wanting him until she shook with it.

"WHAT'S GOIN' ON OUT HERE?" Betty wailed in a sharp, accusing voice.

"I'm giving Irma Sue a goodnight kiss," Jeb respectfully explained.

FLORIDA GOLD

"I'll bet," Betty replied angrily. "All you boys are the same, you just want one thing from a girl."

"Mrs. Harrington, I really respect..."

"I don't give a damn if your daddy is a rich banker. Now git!"

"Bye Irma Sue," Jeb said as he left.

Irma Sue burst into tears, stormed into the house, and fell on her bed sobbing. Margaret heard the commotion and lightly tapped on Irma Sue's door.

"Go away," she sobbed.

"What happened, did you and Jeb get into a fight?"

"No, Mama," she replied with a tear-stained face as she opened her door. Then she explained what happened.

"We're going to get our own place – now. I won't have her treat you and Jeb that way."

"How, Mama? Our combined pay is only twelve dollars a day."

"We'll see if we can find a boarding house and each rent a room. They'll provide our meals as part of the rent. I checked when we first got here, and most of the clean ones rent for fifteen to sixteen dollars per room per week."

"Why, that's not much more than Aunt Betty's charging us, plus we have to do all the housekeeping for her."

"I didn't want to do it then because we have more space and privacy where we are, but with Betty's attitude, I'm ready to leave if you are."

"I'm ready. Maybe we could bring Jack."

"No, that was why I checked out boarding houses in the first place. All I checked with specified no children."

When Jeb got home his father and mother were in the parlor by the fireplace reading. "Well how was the visit to the ranch and the date tonight, Jeb?" his mother asked.

"It was wonderful, Mom. Irma Sue and her mother, Margaret, are some of the finest people I've ever met, they're just down on their luck, that's all. They remind me of the way you said Grandfather and Grandmother were, with strong, enduring characters. And I think I'm falling in love with Irma Sue."

"Son, so soon?" George asked.

"Dad, you know I've dated a lot of girls in high school and college, but I've never met one I'm as attracted to as Irma Sue. Didn't you say it was love at first sight between you and Mom?"

"Yes it was," she said, blushing slightly.

"Well I think she might be the girl I'm going to marry."

"Not until you graduate," George replied.

"Of course not, Dad, but that's only six months away."

"Well, we need to meet them before I'll give my blessings," Amanda interjected.

"And you will, tomorrow, Mom."

CHAPTER THREE

The next morning Jeb was there to get them at noon. They drove to an upscale section of town on the water and Jeb stopped at the gate while the guard opened it. The asphalt drive was lined with magnolia trees, and various other colored shrubs and plants adorned the beautifully-landscaped lawn. He turned into the circular drive and parked in front of the house. Their house was a sprawling two-story structure of brick and stone. Irma Sue felt dwarfed by the giant white columns towering above her at the entrance.

When they entered they were greeted almost immediately by a uniformed maid. "Jenny, this is Mrs. Margaret Thomas, and her daughter, Miss Irma Sue."

"Pleased ladies," Jenny said as she curtsied.

"Mr. and Mrs. Walker will meet you on the terrace." As Jeb led them through the house, they looked at an interior that was breathtaking, with Persian rugs on rich brown hardwood floors and original paintings decorating the walls. The ceilings were tall, about twice as high as most homes, with carved beams, and there was a varnished oak spiral stair case. They arrived on the terrace to find a table laid out with hot coffee, tea, Coca-Cola, and snacks.

"Welcome to our home," Amanda Walker said as she walked up to meet them. Jeb's father, George was just behind her.

39

"Mom, Dad, this is Margaret Thomas and Irma Sue, my parents, George and Amanda Walker."

"It's so good to meet you," Amanda said warmly to Margaret.

"Yes," George agreed. "Jeb you were right, these are two very lovely ladies."

"Jenny will have dinner ready in about half an hour, so why don't we sit, have some refreshments, and get to know each other?" Amanda suggested.

The two families exchanged backgrounds and Margaret explained her responsibilities of managing the camp store and keeping the books.

"How big of a camp was it?" George asked.

"In Archer, we had sixty-two workers and forty-eight families, and tended almost six hundred thousand trees."

"That's pretty big," George observed.

Margaret fought back tears as she explained the circumstances around Pete's death, his funeral, their financial situation, and Pete's motivation for his debt.

"That's too bad. I take it he was able to pay it off as long as he was working?" George asked.

"Yeah, Mr. Lassiter, our banker, said Pete could afford the payments. But without his salary, well..."

"I think it's terrible that your sister wouldn't let you bring Jack with you," Amanda said.

"Well, that's the way it is. At least he's with a good close family and we're hoping to be able to afford our own place in a year so we can go get him."

"Let's talk about something more pleasant," Amanda suggested. "Did you enjoy the ranch yesterday?"

"Yes, it was wonderful," Margaret replied.

"They're both good with horses, Mom."

"You probably had lots of opportunities to ride in the turpentine woods," George observed.

FLORIDA GOLD

"Yes, we've both substituted as woods riders several times when one got sick or hurt," Irma Sue explained.

"Margaret, I don't know if Jeb told you, but he plays quarterback for the University of Alabama Crimson Tide," George said.

"He didn't but Irma Sue did. I hear the Crimson Tide is in the playoff against Texas for the national title."

"That's right," Amanda replied.

"We are strong supporters of the Crimson Tide and have front row seats on the fifty- yard line to watch the games from. Would you and Irma Sue like to join us at the upcoming title game?" George asked.

"That's very kind of you, George, but Irma Sue and I are hoping to go to Archer and see Jack at Christmas. We are all very close and we miss him terribly."

"Massa Walker, dinner is ready," Jenny said as she came onto the terrace.

On the way in to lunch, Amanda and George stopped just outside and talked quietly for a minute, then went in. Margaret and Irma Sue went into a formal dining room that was as impressive as the rest of the house. There was a five-foot long golden and lead crystal chandelier with numerous lights, suspended from the ceiling by a long golden chain. The dining table could seat twenty, and it was rich mahogany with elaborate carvings and inlaid medallions. Lunch was simple Southern cooking - fried pork chops, mashed potatoes, butter beans, corn bread, and apple pie for dessert.

"George, Amanda, I want to sincerely apologize for my sister Betty's behavior last night." Irma Sue and Jeb exchanged glances.

"What happened?" Amanda asked.

Margaret's respect for Jeb increased, for he hadn't told his parents of the belittling way he'd been treated by Betty. Margaret explained what had happened.

41

"Oh, I think it's terrible what your aunt did to you, Irma Sue," Amanda said sympathetically.

"And to Jeb," Irma Sue added.

"He's pretty thick-skinned, he can take it," George kidded.

"Unless it prevents me from seeing Irma Sue," Jeb added.

"Don't worry about that. Irma Sue and I have discussed it, and we're moving out and into a boarding house as soon as we can find one," said Margaret.

"I may have just the place," George began. "The lady that owns it borrowed the money from the bank to buy it, and she's fixed it up very nicely. There's one suite in the southern corner that is two connected bedrooms with a private bathroom. And it's walking distance from the bank."

"That sounds perfect, how much does she want?" Margaret asked.

"She had it at twenty-five dollars per week, but there were no renters, so I believe she's decided to reduce it to twenty dollars per week, George lied, intending to make up the difference himself. "Plus, if you sign a six-month lease, she'll reduce the fee to seventy-five per month," George lied again.

"Oh, Irma Sue, that's less than we're paying Betty and we won't have to do all the cooking and household chores!"

"You have to pay your sister rent and still do all the housework and cooking?" Amanda asked incredulously.

"Yeah," Irma Sue replied. "We just had no other choice at the time."

"Oh, thank you George and Amanda, you don't know what this means," Margaret said.

"You're more than welcome," Amanda replied.

"I think I've thought of a way you can see Jack and still watch the football game with us," George offered.

"How?" Margaret asked.

FLORIDA GOLD

"I am an investor in one of the companies that own the railroads throughout the Southeast. As a perk, I get unlimited free round-trip train fare anywhere in that region. So my suggestion is that either you or Irma Sue, or both of you, go to Archer and bring Jack back here. We'll have a big Christmas celebration on the ranch, big Christmas tree, toys, horseback riding, all that. Then after Christmas, you take Jack back to Archer, and get back here in time to go with us to the game."

"Oh, Mama, can we do that?"

"I'm still in shock," Margaret replied.

"Don't answer now, just let us know by tomorrow so we can be sure and get you a good travel schedule. You know how busy the trains get during the holidays," George said.

The rest of lunch and the conversation after were pleasant as the two families got to know each other better. George told Margaret if she wanted, he would take her to see the suite in the boarding house during her lunch break the next day and she agreed.

When they got home, Margaret said, "My God, Irma Sue, those are the most wonderful people I've ever met."

"I know, Mama, and I'm in love with their son."

"Do you think he's in love with you?"

"I don't know, but he acts like it."

"Oh, Irma Sue, I'm so excited and happy, and happy for you."

"Well, Mom, Dad, what do you think?" Jeb asked after he'd returned from taking Irma Sue and Margaret home.

"If you wait until you graduate, you definitely have our blessings," George replied.

"I thought I'd ask her to marry me on Christmas Eve."

"That's only about two weeks away, so it sounds to me like you need to start looking for a diamond," George teased.

The next morning, Margaret's boss, Jim Hope, came up to her and said, "I've thought about it and I've got to cut costs. Starting today, your pay will be reduced to sixty-five cents per hour."

"But Mr. Hope, we need that money to live on!"

"Hey, you know what you can do to prevent the pay cut," he said as he moved close to her.

"Never mind."

"OK, suit yourself."

Just before noon, George came into Hope's General Store. "Hey Margaret, ready to go?"

"Yeah, just let me get my purse."

"The cashier must be out today."

"I'm the cashier."

"What? Jim Hope has someone with over twenty years' experience in managing a store and keeping the books for an operation twice as big as this, and he has you working as a cashier?"

"Yes."

"I think your talents may be needed in a more responsible job."

"What do you mean?"

"When we get to Dorothy's I need to make a phone call. I don't want to get your hopes up yet."

"Hey, Mr. Walker, it's good to see you again. You must be Margaret," Dorothy said as she answered the door.

"Yes, it's good to meet you."

"Dorothy, why don't you show Margaret the suite while I use your phone, if that's OK."

"Sure, Mr. Walker, it's in the office down the hall."

As George left, Dorothy turned to Margaret. "Well, this is it."

"Oh, it's wonderful, and so spacious."

One bedroom was turquoise, with frilly curtains over the windows and a big comfortable bed. The larger bedroom was

FLORIDA GOLD

light green, with light-brown curtains, and the bed looked like it had a homemade quilt on it. Both had throw pillows, chairs, night stands, large mirrors, and rugs on the floor. The larger room also had a desk and chair. The bathroom was very clean.

"This is where the couple that owned it lived, along with their daughter. I live alone, and would rather rent out the space."

"How big is it?"

"I believe the repairmen said the two bedrooms and bathroom were about 650 square feet."

"And the rent is twenty dollars a week for both of us, or seventy-five dollars a month with a six month lease?"

"That's correct."

"Meals are included?"

"Breakfast, dinner, and supper."

"I'm ready to sign now and make the first month's deposit. When can we start moving in?"

"As soon as you sign the rent agreement and make the rent deposit."

"Great, let's go down to the office and get the agreement."

After they had finished their transaction, they walked out to the hallway and George was there with a big grin on his face. "When do you expect to start moving in?"

"Maybe tonight."

"We've got one more stop to make," George said.

"Where, and what are you grinning about?"

"How would you like to change jobs?"

"What do you mean?"

"One of our clients just opened a second department store on this side of town, actually not far from here. He's been looking for a store manager for several weeks but has been unable to find one, so he's been running back and forth managing both stores. I told him about your background and experience managing turpentine camp commissaries and

45

keeping the camp books and he wants to meet you. He'll probably hire you on the spot."

"George, you're being too kind, I can't let you…"

"Nonsense, this isn't a favor. I'm one of his investors. Believe me, I'd rather have someone with your experience and honesty managing my investment than anyone I can think of."

Margaret couldn't think of what to say - she was just struggling to hold back tears of joy. They pulled up in front of a store with a large sign that said BLALOCK'S DEPARTMENT STORE.

"Margaret, this in Ben Blalock. Ben, Margaret Thomas. I'll leave you two to talk."

Ben almost stumbled when he took her hand in greeting her. With a strikingly beautiful face, crystal-blue eyes, brownish-blonde hair, and ivory skin, at forty-three, Margaret was still a head turner when men were present. She was about five foot six, 125 pounds, and had an almost perfect hourglass figure. He realized that she was an incredibly beautiful woman.

"Come on in," Ben said, glad he could still speak, motioning her into a large, comfortable-looking office. "George tells me you used to manage turpentine camp commissaries."

"That's correct." Over the next twenty minutes she told him her background and situation and answered his questions. He then told her about their holiday and vacation policy, their commitment to treating and paying employees fairly, and their focus on quality products, quality services, and satisfied customers. The job of store manager had nine people reporting to it, seven sales girls and two stock boys.

"Mrs. Thomas…"

"That's Margaret," she corrected.

"Margaret, let me meet with George for a few minutes and then I will call you back in."

FLORIDA GOLD

"OK."

As Margaret walked through the store looking at the neatly laid-out merchandise and observed the busy employees, she could tell it was a well-managed store. *I wonder if he'll offer me the job,* she thought. *And I wonder what it would pay.* The store manager of Johnson's Mercantile in Archer made $3,800 a year, but it was a smaller store. She knew his salary because his wife was a good friend, and she'd been curious what she would have been worth managing the camp commissary. She certainly wouldn't have a problem with $3,800 a year. Her hourly pay, with the recent cut, now came to only $1,352 a year.

"George, is she for real?"

"She's for real, Ben."

"She's a perfect fit for this job! Do you think $5,000 a year is fair?"

"Make it $5,400[2] and I think you'll have your new store manager."

"Great, and just before Christmas too, our busiest time."

"Margaret, can you come back in?"

"Sure."

"I'm prepared to offer you a starting salary of $5,400 a year," said Ben. "In addition to that there will be a bonus, tied to sales and profits, of twenty percent of that salary. So if you achieve the maximum bonus your annual salary will be $6,480.[3] You'll get two weeks paid vacation and seven paid holidays."

Margaret almost fainted, but somehow regained her composure. "I accept," she replied, still in shock.

"When can you start?"

"I'll give one week's notice to Mr. Hope, so..."

"You work for Jim Hope?"

---

[2] The same as $62,900 in 2013.
[3] The same as $75,478 in 2013.

47

"Yes, I hope that's not a problem."

"Not at all," Ben said as he started to laugh. George joined him.

"What's so funny?"

"That greedy bas... sorry, I don't want to offend you," Ben apologized.

"Mr. Blalock, I've lived most of my life in turpentine camps, I assure you, you won't offend me."

"That's Ben. It's just that Jim Hope is so greedy and shortsighted, and treats his employees so badly, he deserves to lose a jewel like you. Do me a favor. When you give him a week's notice and he asks where you are going, tell him it's confidential."

He and George exchanged looks and began to laugh again.

"Now what's so funny?"

"The idiot will probably fire you when you won't tell him where you're going. He'll probably think you're holding out for higher pay given the busy holiday shopping season."

"I think I will go and be in the background and listen," said George. "I need to tell him the loan committee passed on making him a loan. Maybe I'll tell him after Margaret resigns and he fires her."

"Yeah, after you tell him she's coming to work for me." They both burst out laughing again. "George, if he fires her, you've got to come back and give me the details," he said, laughing again.

"You've got a deal, Ben."

They arrived at the store at 1:25, so she was late coming back from lunch. George went to the back of the store and disappeared behind some shelves of cloth. Margaret went to Jim's office. He saw her and strode outside.

"YOU'RE LATE, MARGARET!"

"I know, I'm sorry, but I..."

"Well, I'm docking your pay for an entire hour."

FLORIDA GOLD

"Mr. Hope, I just wanted to tell you that I'm resigning from my job and I'm giving you one week's notice."

"What, where are you going?"

"That's confidential."

"Why you bitch. You're just holding out for me to restore the cut I made in your pay this morning because this is my busiest time of year. OK, if that's the way you want it, you're FIRED!"

"Good job, Jim," George said as he walked out from behind the shelves.

"Mr. Walker, what are you ...?"

"Just came by to tell you your loan was rejected. We think with how badly you run this store, Blalock's will clean your clock. Especially now that he's found a new, very experienced and capable manager for the new store."

"Who did he...?"

"That's where Margaret is going to work. She's the new store manager. I doubt if you'll still be in business a year from now. Come on, Margaret, let's get out of here."

"Just let me get my things, George."

Jim was pale, and he looked sick.

They went back to Blalock's and after George and Ben stopped laughing, Margaret asked, "When do you want me to start?"

"Yesterday. Tell you what, I hear you're moving into a new place. I'll start your pay tomorrow, but between now and next Monday, you take your time getting settled, and only work whenever you want to. Call me tomorrow and let's schedule a time to hold an employee meeting where I can introduce you as the new store manager."

"OK, and thank you, Ben."

"Oh, and this will be your new office. I'll have my things out by next Monday."

"Thanks, Ben."

49

On the way to Betty's, Margaret was in a daze, too shocked to believe what had just happened. Then she looked at George and said, "George, you and Amanda are our guardian angels. You've done so much for us."

"Only given you opportunities. You did the rest yourself, Margaret. By the way, call and let me know how it goes when you tell Betty you're moving."

When Margaret got home, she found Betty on the back porch potting a plant. "Betty, we need to talk."

"If it's about my policy on visitors, I will not change my mind. NO VISITORS, ESPECIALLY MEN!"

"No, Betty, I just came to tell you we're moving out."

"WHAT? You can't afford your own place!"

"We're moving into a boarding house, and I just got a new, higher-paying job."

"You can't do that! I depend on your rent!"

"You never needed rent before."

"Well, there's been some new expenses."

"You mean the new dining room furniture and the jewelry. Take them back."

"Tell you what, Irma Sue can have her boyfriend over, OK?"

"No, I've already paid the first month's rent for the new place. We will be out of here by tomorrow night."

"Fine, you ungrateful BITCH. That's how you repay all my help?"

"What help? You charged us more rent than we're having to pay in the new place, and we won't have to do all the housework there."

"Go to HELL!" Betty shouted and stormed off.

As she promised, Margaret called George at the bank and told him what happened. "I'm not surprised," he said. "She took out a consumer loan to buy new furniture and jewelry and was using your rent to pay it off. I guess now

FLORIDA GOLD

she'll HAVE to take in a renter, and they won't do the housework, she'll have to."

The more Margaret got to know George, the more she liked and respected him.

Irma Sue got home at five thirty and Margaret was busily packing. "You won't believe what happened today, Irma Sue." Margaret then spent the next half hour telling her about the day's events in detail.

"I sure know one thing," Irma Sue observed. "These are the finest people I've ever met. I didn't know there were people like this."

"I feel the same way, Irma Sue."

"Maybe we'll be able to stick to our original plan and bring Jack to live with us by next summer."

"I hope so."

"Jeb came by and took me to lunch and we went to the train station to look at the schedules. We can get a train out of here on Friday, the 17th at 7:30 a.m. and it gets into Archer at 10:20 p.m. Then back on Sunday that gets here at 9:40 p.m."

"That sounds good to me."

"I take it you want me to go since you will be starting your new job."

"Yeah, that was my thinking."

"Mama, every time I am with Jeb, I just can't take my eyes off of him, and when I'm not with him, I can't stop thinking about him and wanting to be with him."

"That's real love. It was that way with Pete."

"Do you think he also feels that way?"

"The way I see him look at you when you're together, I'd be surprised if he didn't."

"I hope so, Mama."

"Are you going to tell him the truth about Jack?"

"Yes. But only if he asks me to marry him."

"That might ruin things between you."

51

"If it does, then it does, but I'll not have any secrets between us. That's not the way to have a good marriage. I'll be crushed and broken-hearted at first, but somehow I'll get over it. Because I'll know that Jeb isn't the kind of man I think he is."

"Did I ever tell you how proud of you I am, and how much I love you?" Margaret said as she hugged her daughter.

"Yeah, lots of times, but I still like you to tell me."

CHAPTER FOUR

During the following week, Jeb and Irma Sue seemed inseparable. He began taking her to their country club, Heron Lakes, and teaching her to play golf and tennis. They went to the museum, a movie, another play, had elegant dinners, casual dinners, went horseback riding, on a picnic, etc. She knew she'd found her soul mate and he felt the same way about her. Their parents were very happy for both of them.

George and Amanda invited Margaret and Irma Sue to go fishing with them on Saturday, and to dinner that night. They usually had friends over after a fishing trip and divided the day's catch among everyone, since fish were only good on ice for a few days. "Ready for a day at sea?" Jeb asked as he greeted Irma Sue and Margaret at their new place at seven a.m.

"I guess," Margaret replied.

"You sound uncertain."

"I've done all of my fishing from the bank or a small row boat. I'm not sure about this ocean thing."

"Oh, relax, Mama, you'll enjoy it."

They drove down to the Mobile Landing Marina, about twelve miles southwest of the city. Jeb took their bags and led them amid numerous sail boats and sport fishing boats to his family's boat, the *Sea Mist*.

"Oh, this is a really nice boat," Irma Sue observed.

The *Sea Mist* was a forty-eight foot cabin cruiser with twin 450-horsepower diesel engines. It had three carpeted teakwood-lined state rooms (bedrooms) on the bottom deck, with a private bathroom for the master bedroom and a center-way bathroom for the other two bedrooms. The middle deck, two steps up from the fishing deck, consisted of a full kitchen with stove and oven, ice box, dining table, and a living area with leather couch, reclining chairs, and a wet bar. The rear fishing deck had one swivel fishing chair, two stationary fishing chairs, an ice box for bait, and a bait preparation table. Two twenty-eight foot outriggers graced the sides of the vessel. The next level up was the flying bridge, from which the captain navigated the boat. It contained a circular U-shaped couch, small bar, and other chairs, and is where passengers could get the best view when cruising. The thirty-foot high tower was where the captain piloted the boat when trolling, because he could see all of the fishing activity.

George piloted while Jeb had the job of first mate, preparing the bait and fishing rods and tackle, helping land the fish, etc. It was a sunny, crisp day and the water was calm as they headed out to sea, Jeb preparing bait and rigging tackle on the way while Amanda got soft drinks and snacks for everyone.

"Oh, this is exhilarating!" Margaret exclaimed as they churned out into the open ocean, experiencing the aroma of the sea and a beautiful morning horizon.

"It sure is," Irma Sue agreed, taking in the sights and sounds, ecstatic to be at sea for the first time with the love of her life.

"We'll start out trolling for yellow fin tuna and king mackerel. Later we'll bottom fish for amberjack, grouper, and snapper," Jeb explained.

FLORIDA GOLD

"I don't understand what you just said, but I sure am having fun," said Margaret, sipping a Coca-Cola and munching on crackers.

"How far out are we going?" Irma Sue asked.

"About thirty-five miles. That's where the fishing is best. Mom brought sandwiches for lunch, but that's only as a backup. If we're lucky, we'll catch fish to prepare for lunch. Nothing is better than freshly caught fish eaten out here," Jeb explained.

Margaret again thought about how wonderful and special this family was, and how much she valued their friendship.

"Something just hit yours, Irma Sue," Jeb shouted over the roar of the engines as they were moving about five miles per hour, trolling. "Jerk the line like I told you."

Irma Sue stood from the swivel chair and jerked hard on the line. "You've hooked him!" Jeb shouted. The big fish erupted out of the water no more than fifty feet away, then headed to find the bottom. But there wasn't enough line on the reel for the fish to make it two hundred plus feet to the bottom. "It's a yellow fin tuna," Jeb shouted. Irma Sue fought the fish well, listening to Jeb's instructions and reeling in line when it went slack, and letting the fish take it off through the drag when he fought. It took almost half an hour, but the fish tired and she was able to get it into position for Jeb to gaff. "Damn, he's big!" Jeb said as he struggled to pull the fish on board. The scale read ninety-seven pounds.

Irma Sue and Margaret had never seen or imagined anything like this and were fascinated. "Congratulations on your first salt water fish, and your first yellow fin," Jeb said as he hugged Irma Sue.

"There's dinner," George remarked as he came down to admire the large yellow fin.

"They are very good to eat," Amanda commented.

55

About that time the line began to go out on Margaret's rig, and Jeb helped her. She had also learned from watching Irma Sue, and fought him perfectly, and there was soon another yellow fin on board. It tipped the scales at seventy-eight pounds.

"Dad, we've got plenty of yellow fin, let's try some bottom fishing," Jeb suggested.

"You're not going to try and catch a yellow fin?" Irma Sue asked

"No, we've got plenty to eat, and they'll only keep a few days. Besides I have more fun watching you and Margaret." Jeb rigged the rods for bottom fishing, using ballyhoo as bait. He then dropped the lines in the water. "When you feel a tug, jerk the rod to set the hook, but not nearly as hard as you did for the tuna."

In about fifteen minutes, Margaret felt a tug, and jerked upward. Then she felt pulling on the line. "Just like the tuna, Margaret, reel in when you can and let the fish take it when he pulls harder than the drag is set." In about eight minutes, Margaret had landed a black grouper. He weighed twenty-seven pounds. Over the next hour Margaret and Irma Sue landed seven more grouper, ranging from twenty-two to forty-five pounds.

"I'm exhausted and my arms feel like spaghetti," Irma Sue said.

"I am too," Margaret added.

"It's after twelve, so let's fix some lunch," Amanda suggested.

"Sounds good to me, I'm starved," Irma Sue replied. George idled the boat engines while Jeb cleaned one of the groupers and cut it into fillets. Amanda took out some breading she had in a paper sack and put a small amount of shortening in a pan.

"We'll roll them in seasoned bread crumbs and sauté them. Can't use too much shortening or it'll spill with the

FLORIDA GOLD

rocking of the boat," Amanda explained as she lit the kerosene stove. While they were doing that, George brought out some cornbread and baked beans they'd brought. Then he also brought out a bottle from the ice box and five wine glasses.

"Isn't that illegal now?" Margaret asked curiously.

"Only in the United States, but we're not in the United States."

"That's right, we're way past the three-mile boundary," Jeb explained.

"Can I interest you ladies in a fine Chardonnay?"

"You bet," Margaret replied. He poured four glasses of wine, took the fifth to Amanda, then brought out crackers for them to snack on while lunch was being made. He opened another bottle of wine and they were soon enjoying freshly caught grouper, cornbread, and beans for lunch, out at sea. It was a perfect day, sunny, blue sky, only a slight breeze, calm waters, and about seventy-one degrees.

"I think this is the best food I've ever had," Margaret said.

"Me too," Irma Sue replied with a mouth full of grouper and cornbread, taking a sip of wine.

"Catching those fish made you work up an appetite," Jeb explained. "Plus, I think food just tastes better out here."

"You're certainly right about that," Margaret added as she stabbed another large grouper fillet with her fork.

They arrived back at the dock about three thirty. They unloaded the rest of the fish onto two large tables, both under faucets and George began sharpening his fillet knife. Amanda was cleaning up the boat. "I'll be back and help you as soon as I take them home," Jeb said. "I'll come and get you at six-thirty for tonight's get-together," Jeb told them when he dropped them of at their place. He gave Irma Sue a kiss, and headed back to the marina.

"I don't think I've ever had that much fun," Margaret observed when they were in their room.

"I know I haven't," Irma Sue agreed. "I got the bathroom first," Irma Sue shouted as she dashed into the bathroom to take a bath.

They arrived at the Walkers' a little past seven as other guests were arriving. Everyone was in the expansive living room where there was a large, crackling fire in the fireplace. Toby, who they'd met at the ranch, was bringing out baked oysters on the half shell, crackers, toast, boiled shrimp, and chunks of broiled yellow fin from their catch for hors d'oeuvres.

George introduced Margaret and Irma Sue to their guests. It was a virtual who's who of Mobile. There was Jim Raymond, head of surgery at Providence Hospital, and his wife, Judy; Robert Jones, their Lutheran minister, and his wife, Katharine; Ray Staley, the district attorney, and his wife, Jennifer; Ron Burns, Mobile's chief of police and his wife, Betty; Jason Browning, superintendent of the local schools, and his wife, Carolyn; Ed Butler, the mayor, and his wife, Lynn; Peter Helms, a US Senator, and his wife, Helen; and Ben Blalock, Margaret's new boss.

"I see beauty runs in this family," Ben said as he gently squeezed Irma Sue's hand when they were introduced.

"Your wife couldn't make it?" Margaret asked.

"Ben's a widower," George replied.

"Yes, my wife, Carol passed away a little over two years ago, from cancer."

"Oh, I'm sorry to hear that," Margaret replied.

"I'm expecting great things out of your mother," Ben said to Irma Sue, changing the subject.

"She can do them," Irma Sue replied. About that time Amanda came in and announced that dinner was served.

George sat at the head of the table and Amanda was next to him to his right. Jeb was at the other end and

FLORIDA GOLD

Margaret and Irma Sue were on either side of Jeb. Ben Blalock sat next to Margaret. "Before we begin our meal, I want to introduce everyone to our new friends, Irma Sue and Margaret Thomas," George said. "Since our son, Jeb and Irma Sue became romantically involved, Amanda and I have gotten to know her and Margaret, and they are both delightful people. They are new to Mobile, coming from Archer, Florida. Please join me in giving them a warm welcome." Everyone stood and clapped while Irma Sue and Margaret blushed.

Then Margaret stood and said, "Thank you. You are all warm and friendly, and the Walkers are wonderful friends. I can't imagine anyplace I'd rather live than here." Everyone clapped, and the meal was served.

Jenny and Toby had both been trained in gourmet cooking by a chef in New Orleans, and their culinary skills were obvious in the meal. First was conch chowder, then there were two gourmet offerings with portions small enough that everyone could have both of them: citrus-glazed grouper with tarragon sauce, roasted garlic potatoes, and steamed carrots and Brussels sprouts; and blue crab-crusted yellow-fin tuna, mango blanc, roasted asparagus, and jasmine rice. In addition, there were chunks of fried grouper and smoked yellow fin on the side with freshly baked sourdough bread. It was a feast.

"I hear you plan to bring your son, Jack, here for Christmas," Ben said.

"Yes, we both miss him so, we can't wait to see him," Margaret replied.

"I'm planning to be at the train station early on Friday so I can be sure I get a good seat. It's a fourteen-hour hour trip," Irma Sue said.

"You won't need to worry about that. George has his own private rail cars on several of the lines, and they're very elegant."

"What?"

59

"Yeah, he didn't tell you? He owns the controlling interest in the Southern Atlantic Railroad."

"He just said he was an investor that got free travel."

"That's George," laughed Ben. "You probably think he's just a successful country banker like the rest of the town does."

"That was our impression," Irma Sue replied curiously.

"George and Amanda want to maintain a low profile. It's one reason they stayed here to live after George built one of the largest business empires in America. Not many people other than those in this room know who George Walker really is. In addition to the Southern Atlantic Railroad, George either outright owns or owns controlling interest in many of the banks in Alabama, the Southern Resin Chemical and Timber Company, Fields' department stores in Chicago, and textile mills throughout the South. He's one of the wealthiest men in America. He and Amanda have vacation homes in West Palm Beach and Bermuda, and a townhouse on Park Avenue in New York."

Margaret and Irma Sue were stunned.

"Hey, George, I just told Margaret and Irma Sue your big secret," Ben said, laughing.

"George, they don't know who you really are?" Peter, the senator, asked.

"Amanda and I were going to tell them, it just never seemed to be the right time, plus we didn't want to scare them away. We wanted them to get to know us better first."

"Well, consider them told," Ben replied.

George and Amanda got up and walked over to where Margaret and Irma Sue were seated, and George said, "I'm sorry we didn't tell you about us sooner, it was just that..."

"George, Amanda, please, you don't have to apologize. Irma Sue and I are very impressed, both at your modesty and your accomplishments." At that, the group clapped, showing their approval.

FLORIDA GOLD

"Jeb, are you going to lead the Crimson Tide to its first national championship on New Year's Day?" Mayor Butler asked.

"I'm sure going to try." At that the conversation turned to the Crimson Tide, Jeb's football accomplishments, and the upcoming game, that most in the room were planning to go see.

Dessert was hand-churned vanilla ice cream and strawberry compote with pastry layers, and freshly ground coffee. Everyone seemed to enjoy the meal and to have a good time. When people were getting ready to leave, George told them that there were twenty-pound packages of fish for each couple to take home with them, and he had Toby and Jenny at the door so everyone could voice their satisfaction to them about the wonderful meal as they were leaving.

On his way out, Ben came up to Margaret and said, "Why don't you go with Irma Sue to get Jack?"

"I'd love to but I thought you needed me in the store."

"Oh, believe me I do. But I'll manage to cover for you. It will give you some time alone with just Jack and Irma Sue," he explained.

"Are you sure?"

"Absolutely, and you will still be paid. You are salaried, not paid by the hour, and if I know you, you'll be thinking about ways to improve our profitability no matter what you are doing."

Margaret threw her arms around him and kissed him on the cheek saying, "Oh, thank you, Ben." But when she did that, she felt something - a romantic twinge. So did Ben. Both tried to ignore it, but both also knew there was something there. Margaret had never really looked at Ben Blalock before now. Now in his mid-forties, he was taller than average, about six feet, with a deep chest and brown hair with specks of gray just beginning to show. His powerful build was evidence of a youth spent working in logging operations that harvested

61

pine trees after they had been tapped out for turpentine. He had a commanding, yet gentle presence that immediately put Margaret at ease.

Because of his "head for numbers," Ben was promoted to book keeper for the timber company he worked for when he was in his mid-twenties. The resulting reduction in costs and increase in profits got the attention of the timber company's lender, Preston Walker, George's father. Ben went over the now more accurate books with Preston and answered his questions, pointing out why the management changes had increased profitability. Preston was impressed and hired Ben to work at his bank as a lending officer. Ben and George were about the same age and became friends. When Preston decided to add a new department store to his businesses, he asked Ben to manage it. Ben did so, very successfully. When Preston died, he left Ben ownership of the department store.

Ben was now wealthy. In addition to the department stores, he was an investor in many of George's companies. He had a standing offer from George to buy him out for $9 million.[4] Ben had been wanting to retire and travel the world - to cruise to the major ports of Europe, bicycle across Italy, hike in the Swiss Alps, safari in Africa, raft down the Amazon, fish for marlin in Costa Rica, sail to Puerto Rico. But he didn't want to travel alone. He wanted a wife to enjoy these things with him. He hadn't taken George's offer because if he wasn't traveling, he'd be bored without the challenge of managing his stores. George didn't retire because he wanted to keep building his empire for Jeb to run.

Everyone was soon gone but George, Senator Helms and his wife, Jeb, Amanda, Margaret, and Irma Sue. George was in the foyer talking to Senator Helms. "Would you like go into the living room and sit next to the fire?" Amanda asked.

"Yes, sure," Margaret replied.

---

[4] The same as $104.9 million in 2013

FLORIDA GOLD

"We have to go, but thanks for inviting us," Helen, the senator's wife, said.

"I'll be there in a minute," George told Amanda.

When they were seated, Amanda again apologized for not telling Margaret and Irma Sue who they really were.

"Like I said, no apology is needed," Margaret replied. "I'm impressed with your modesty and accomplishments."

"George is a very special man. This is something almost nobody knows, except maybe Ben, his best friend. Each year George goes to work for a week in each of his companies. He works as a bank teller in one of the banks away from Mobile, as a conductor on one of the trains, as a sales clerk in Fields department store, as a woods rider in the resin and timber company, and as a line supervisor in one of the textile mills. He does that to see what is really going on at the level where the work is being done, and to make sure the employees are happy and being treated fairly. I think it's one of the reasons for his success."

"And while he does that, my mother volunteers at various orphanages," Jeb replied.

"Well, how did you like the supper?" George asked as he came into the room. "I believe Toby and Jenny really outdid themselves tonight."

When they were back home, Margaret and Irma Sue marveled at the day's events. "Irma Sue, I'm more impressed with these people every time I meet them. I didn't even know there were people like them."

"They are definitely special, and very rare."

"How are things going with you and Jeb?"

"It's hard for us to stay out of the bedroom, but neither of us believes in sex before marriage."

"Good thinking. Do you think he is going to propose?"

"I don't know, but I think so. And I sure hope so."

Jeb took them to the train station on Friday morning. As he helped them with their luggage he said, "Irma Sue, my dad

63

and I will be in New York on business and I won't be back until next Wednesday."

"Oh, I'll miss you," Irma Sue replied, giving him a passionate kiss and hug good-bye.

"I'll miss you too," Jeb replied.

They boarded the private Pullman car and were awestruck. This was the first time Margaret and Irma Sue had ever seen anything like it. The car was eighty feet long, with a living room, two bedrooms, kitchen, bathroom, and servants' quarters. The elegant interior included inlaid mahogany, ornate moldings, and stained glass. There were books and magazines on shelves; that day's editions of the *New York Times, the Wall Street Journal* and the *Mobile Register* on the coffee table; and a large radio.

"Ladies, my name Sarah," a black woman said coming out of the kitchen as they were sitting down. "Would you like some breakfast?"

"Yes, that would be nice," Margaret replied. The train soon left the station.

They were served bacon, eggs, grits, toast with jelly, fresh-squeezed orange juice, and coffee. "Now this is the way to travel," Irma Sue observed as the train raced along, while Margaret began searching for a radio program to listen to. She soon settled on a musical variety show. They arrived twenty-five minutes ahead of schedule, at 9:55 p.m.

"I guess they aren't here yet since we're so early," Margaret observed.

The porter helped them get their luggage into the train station and they sat down to wait.

In about ten minutes, they saw Emma Robinson and Jack come through the door. "Mommy! Irma Sue!" Jack shouted as he ran to them. The three of them hugged tightly and Irma Sue and Margaret began to cry softly. Emma's eyes became red as she watched, struggling to hold back tears at this special reunion.

FLORIDA GOLD

On the way to their home Emma said, "Jack has been a wonderful boy. We really enjoy having him stay with us."

"We're very glad you could keep him, Emma," Margaret said.

The next morning at breakfast, Margaret said, "You won't believe the wonderful friends we've made in Mobile." She and Irma Sue then spent the next half hour telling the Robinsons about the Walkers (omitting the part about how wealthy they were), about Irma Sue and Jeb, and about Margaret's new job. "I think we'll be able to take Jack to live with us by next summer," Margaret said.

"It sounds like this move has been good for both of you. We'll miss Jack, but we're certainly happy for both of you," Emma replied.

"Is there anywhere you'd like to go today?" Jesse asked.

"Not really. We'll be happy just to stay here and relax."

"OK," Emma replied. "We have planned a small get-together here tonight for you and Irma Sue, sort of a chance to fill your old friends in on what's happening in your lives. We expect Jim Lassiter, and June with their daughter Sarah, who really wants to see you, Irma Sue, Reverend Austin and Sandra, and Doc Bentley and Judith."

"Great! It will be good to see old friends."

It was a wonderful visit, and all were happy about the life Margaret and Irma Sue had started to make for themselves in Mobile, and the new friends they had made.

Margaret and Irma Sue were glad to be headed back to Mobile on Sunday. Jesse dropped them off at the train station at six thirty Sunday morning. All said a warm good-bye, and Margaret, Irma Sue, and Jack boarded the private Pullman car.

"Boy, riding on trains is neat," Jack observed as he looked around.

"Most people don't have a private coach," Irma Sue explained. "We're just lucky."

65

ROBERT ALLEN MORRIS

After pancakes, sausage and eggs, Irma Sue read a novel while Margaret began reading the newest issue of *The Saturday Evening Post* and Jack busied himself with a coloring book and crayons that Emma had given him for the trip back.

They got into the train station at 9:35 p.m. and Amanda was there to meet them. "So you're Jack," she observed as she shook his hand.

"You must be Mrs. Walker," Jack replied. "My mama and sister have told me a lot about you, Mr. Walker, and Mr. Jeb."

"Jenny should have supper on the table when we get there," she told Jack. "Do you like fried chicken?"

"YES MA'AM!"

"I think we'd better make it a quick supper, Amanda, because both of us have to be at work first thing in the morning."

"No you don't, George and Ben are giving you both off tomorrow with pay. They figured you'd be tired after your trip and would want some time to get Jack settled in. So sleep in and we'll have a leisurely breakfast in the morning."

Jack was up by seven and exploring the large back yard. When they saw he was up, Irma Sue and Margaret also got up. Amanda was already awake and doing some knitting in the living room.

At breakfast Amanda asked, "Have you made arrangements for Jack during the day?"

"Yeah, Dorothy, our landlady is going to keep him."

"I've got a better idea. Why don't I keep him? We can go fishing and horseback riding at the ranch, he can play with Jeb's old toys, and there are lots of other fun things we can do."

"Are you sure?" Irma Sue asked.

"Absolutely, it's been a long time since I've had a little boy to do things with."

"Thank you, Amanda," Margaret replied.

FLORIDA GOLD

On Tuesday morning, Amanda took Jack to the ranch and Toby saddled up horses for them. Jack had begun riding with his grandfather in the turpentine woods when he was four, but it had been awhile since he'd been on a horse. They rode to the picnic spot and Jack went fishing while Amanda watched. When she felt comfortable that he was OK, she built a fire in the fire pit, got a frying pan out of the shed, and took out shortening and meal from her knapsack. She'd also brought biscuits and honey, and Coca-Colas that were cooling in the creek.

She'd given Jack a stringer to put the fish he caught on, and told him to keep two or three of the bigger ones and she'd cook them for their dinner. Once the fire was going, she went back to where Jack was fishing, and he showed her a bass that looked to be about two pounds.

"See what I caught?" he said, proudly holding his fish up.

"He's a nice one," she said admiringly. Over the next hour, Jack caught six fish: four bass and two bream. One of the bass was about three pounds. This they cleaned and filleted, then Amanda dredged it in cornmeal, put a fire grate over the hot coals, and fried it. She put the biscuits on a tin plate next to the coals to warm. Soon the fish was ready, and Jack went to retrieve the Coca-Colas while Amanda put a table cloth over the picnic table and put fried fish, hot biscuits, and honey on more tin plates.

"This is real good," exclaimed a hungry Jack.

"It's hard to beat freshly caught fried fish cooked outside," she remarked.

After lunch was finished and the plates and utensils had been rinsed off, they took a walk. Soon they came up on about two acres of planted cedar trees of various ages and sizes. "Want to pick out a Christmas tree?" she asked.

"YEAH!"

They found one about ten feet tall that they liked, and Amanda tied a piece of red ribbon on it to mark it. They got back to the ranch house about two thirty, and Amanda told Toby where to go and cut the tree. "We'll be coming out tonight for supper and to decorate the tree," she explained. "We should get here about six thirty and there'll be four of us, counting Jack."

"Yessum. I'll tell Noreen to fix some o' her poke chops and gravy, with biscuits, collard greens, butter beans, and banana puddin'."

When they got home, Amanda called Irma Sue and Margaret and told them she planned to decorate the Christmas tree that night at the ranch, and that she'd pick each of them up from work.

They arrived at the ranch house at 5:50. Neither Irma Sue nor Margaret had seen the inside of the ranch house or barn, since their horses had been saddled when they arrived and they'd eaten at the picnic spot. When they entered through the huge wooden double doors, Irma Sue and Margaret were again awe-struck. Amanda gave them the grand tour so they'd know their way around, since they would be staying there two nights, Christmas Eve, and Christmas Day. With views from every window, the ranch house gathered natural light and played it off its stone, tile, and rich-wood interior. The living room was dominated by a double-opening stone fireplace that warmed both the living and dining rooms. The cathedral ceilings with exposed log rafters had a wall of arched windows that looked out toward the ranch. There was also a billiard table in the large living room, and a built-in gun cabinet with a glass door that held numerous rifles, shotguns, and pistols that George, Jeb, and Amanda hunted with. The spacious kitchen had Italian marble counter-tops with tile accents, and custom blue-mountain-pine cabinets. The house had six bedrooms - four on the second floor, and the master bedroom suite and another bedroom on the ground floor. There was also a large office with a cherry wood desk and leather chair on the second

FLORIDA GOLD

floor. There were two bathrooms on the second floor and two on the ground floor, one of which was in the master bedroom suite that also had its own fireplace. All bathrooms had artistic concrete counters designed by a French sculptor.

The sturdy timber-frame barn smelled of fresh hay and horses, with stalls for six of them, a spacious tack room, and a large overhead hay loft. A 180-foot well and state-of-the-art filter system guaranteed plenty of fresh, delicious water for the house and adjacent vegetable garden. In a separate wood-frame building adjacent to the barn was a three-car garage with a cement floor and a carriage that seated six.

Toby and Noreen Reid, now in their late forties, were husband and wife. They had two grown children, a boy and a girl. They lived in a three bedroom frame cottage about a half mile from the ranch house. In addition to providing free housing, the Walkers provided food, medical services, and a salary to the Reids. Their children, both married with children of their own, lived in Mobile.

After a delicious supper, they all busied themselves with decorating the Christmas tree. They finished about nine o'clock, happy with their work.

69

CHAPTER FIVE

George and Jeb's business trip to New York was both to select and buy a diamond for Jeb to present to Irma Sue when he asked her to marry him on Christmas Eve, and to arrange for George to acquire controlling interest in a company. It was the same jeweler George had purchased Amanda's engagement ring from, and he'd also purchased other jewelry there over the years.

"Hello, Mr. Walker, this must be Jeb," Tony Rossi said in a heavy Italian accent as he greeted them.

"It's a pleasure to meet you, Tony," Jeb said as he shook his hand.

"Congratulations on your upcoming engagement. I'll bet she's something."

"Yes, she is," Jeb replied.

"I got your telegram, and I've picked out several stones I think you'll like."

"Good, let's see them," Jeb said.

Tony went into a back room and came out with a small velvet bag. He laid out a black velvet cloth on top of the glass case and laid out four beautiful diamonds. "Jeb, four things, called the 'four C's,' determine the quality and thus the value of a diamond," Tony began. "They are cut, color, clarity, and carat weight. These range from 2½ to 3¾ carats. Here, look at them under the microscope," Tony offered.

Jeb peered at each of the stones, then said, "There's a tiny bubble or something in the 3¾ carat one."

"You have a sharp eye, Jeb. Most customers simply choose the largest stone, thinking it's the best. I put that slightly flawed one in the group to see if you were judging them correctly."

"You did the same thing with me twenty-four years ago, Tony."

"I like the 3¼ carat the best," Jeb told them.

"Excellent choice, Jeb. Just tell me her ring size and I'll set it for you."

"Mom got her ring size when she told her that Dad wanted to get her a ring with her birthstone for Christmas. It's a seven."

"Great, now do you want white or yellow gold?"

"White."

"Tony, I also need to get Irma Sue a ring with her birth stone. It's an opal, and I need to pick out diamond earrings and a pearl necklace," Jeb told him.

Tony went into the back room and brought out some opals. "Pick one out while I set the diamond. Then we can look at the rest."

After they'd bought the jewelry, they went to Wall Street to meet with one of George's bankers at Chemical Bank.

"How've you been, George?" Douglas Archer greeted them as his secretary escorted them to his large corner office.

"Fine, Doug."

"And this must be the football star. I hear the Crimson Tide is competing for the national championship against the Texas Longhorns this year, Jeb."

"Yes, sir."

"Well I hope you win. Can I interest you in something to drink?"

"Coffee would be fine," George replied.

"I'd like a Coca-Cola," Jeb said.

FLORIDA GOLD

When they'd been served, Doug asked, "What can I do for you, George?"

"I want to buy controlling interest in the West Virginia Coal Company."

"Fifty-one percent of the outstanding shares?"

"That's right. Stan will be contacting you to arrange the funds for payment."

"He's with F.J. Lisman?"

"Yeah, he's my broker. I thought you met him last summer at our Fourth of July party at the townhouse."

"I remember him now. Young guy, late twenties, Harvard man."

"That's him."

"George, coal mines now?"

"Yeah. The coal business is a good diversification from my other businesses. But the main reason I'm interested is the situation with the coal miners and their families. I don't like the way their workers are treated or the safety conditions in their mines. Company stores are charging outrageous prices and there's no place else for workers and their families to go. Workers must lease the tools they use from the company, and although they're paid based on how much coal they mine, it isn't weighed. Each car brought from the mines is supposed to hold two thousand pounds of coal, but many of the cars have been altered to hold more than two thousand pounds, so they're being paid for less than they're bringing in. The support infrastructure down in the shafts needs to be upgraded and reinforced as well. In only the last eighteen months two shafts partially caved in. Luckily nobody was hurt."

"So with controlling interest, you're going to change all that."

"That's the plan. The changes will increase costs and reduce profits, which will make the value of the stock decline. Once it levels out at say, about half its current price, I'll buy up the rest of the stock and take the company private. At its lower value, I'll have a company earning a good return on my investment."

"But not as good as it did before, considering the cost of the fifty-one percent you acquired initially," said Doug.

"But he will have improved the incomes and working conditions for hundreds of workers," Jeb replied.

"I think philanthropy needs to be added as one of your corporate goals," Doug observed.

After they'd finished their meeting with Doug, they went to the townhouse to spend the night. George wanted to be sure it was ready for when he and Amanda would come to see plays on Broadway in January and February.

That night during dinner at the Colony Club, their private dining club, George asked, "Jeb you look deep in thought. Worried about the big game?"

"No, I just hope telling Irma Sue and Margaret about our wealth didn't put them off or intimidate them. So many wealthy people are snobs, I'm not sure how they might react."

"They seemed fine after the party on Saturday night. And they know us well enough to know we aren't snobs. The way Irma Sue looks at you, I seriously doubt she'll turn you down. Anyone can tell she's deeply in love with you. Stop worrying!"

Their train arrived back in Mobile on Wednesday morning. George and Jeb went straight to the bank - George to work and Jeb to see Irma Sue, after which he was going to work as well. When they walked in, Irma Sue jumped up and ran to Jeb, throwing her arms around him and hugging him tightly, saying "Oh, Jeb, I missed you so."

"I missed you too, Irma Sue." George shot Jeb an amused glance with his thumb in the air.

Amanda had planned a large supper for everyone that night, giving George and Jeb a chance to meet Jack. They got

FLORIDA GOLD

there at six and when they went inside, Jack was in the living room, playing with toy horses that had been Jeb's. "So you're Jack," George said as they walked up to the boy.

"Yes, sir, you must be Mr. Walker and Mr. Jeb."

"Yes we are. Welcome to our home, Jack," Jeb said.

"Hey, dear, I'm so glad you and Jeb are back," Amanda said as she hugged them both. "How was New York? Were you successful in your meeting with Tony?"

"Yes, very," Jeb replied.

At dinner, George said, "I guess we'd better make some plans. Christmas is only three days away."

"Jack and I found a nice cedar Christmas tree in the tree farm on the ranch, and Toby cut it down and put it up," Amanda explained. "Last night we all had supper in the ranch house, decorated the tree, and prepared the house for Christmas."

"I helped," Jack added.

"You were a lot of help," Amanda added.

"Your ranch house is fabulous!" Irma Sue exclaimed.

"It sure is," Margaret agreed.

"I'm glad you like it," George replied. "My father built it, and we've added things since then like the pump and filter system on the well, the garage, etc."

That night in their bedroom, Amanda said, "George I've watched Irma Sue's behavior around Jack, and I think she's his mother, not Margaret."

"Really, what makes you think that?"

"Oh, just little things, how she looks at him, how she acts around him. A mother can sense these things."

"Do you think she'll tell Jeb after he asks her to marry him?"

"I think so. She's very honest and has a strong character."

"And if she doesn't?"

"Then we'll tell him well in advance of the wedding and he can decide what he wants to do after he knows."

75

"I agree," George replied.

"What will you think of her if she did have Jack out of wedlock?"

"As long as she's honest about it, I'm fine. Things like that happen, especially to naïve young girls looking for a white knight to take them out of the turpentine camp. There are bastards out there who prey on girls like that. I think they ought to be shot."

Everyone would be off from work starting at noon on Christmas Eve. That's when the town of Mobile pretty much shut down in observance of the holiday. Nothing much would be open until the following Monday morning. George, Jeb, and Irma Sue would go get Margaret from the department store, and Amanda would already be at the ranch, fixing dinner (lunch). They always gave Toby and Noreen a generous Christmas bonus and Christmas Eve and Christmas Day as paid holidays to be with their families. Amanda did the cooking for them at the ranch.

That night, Irma Sue was going to prepare their supper. She had not been able to cook for Jeb at the boarding house and wanted to cook for him and everyone else. On Christmas day, Ben Blalock would be their guest, as he had for the last two Christmases, since his wife passed away. She had been unable to have children, and the Walkers didn't want him spending Christmas alone.

They got to the ranch house just before one and Amanda had a light lunch of ham sandwiches and fruit prepared. They were eating light because of the large supper they were having.

That afternoon, Jeb and George took an excited Jack out to their shooting range to shoot a single-shot .22 rifle, something he had not done yet, while Amanda and Margaret planned the next day's Christmas dinner.

Irma Sue began baking a chocolate cake that was to be that night's dessert, and cleaning freshly harvested mustard

FLORIDA GOLD

greens and carrots from the garden. She planned to prepare prime rib roast, roasted garlic potatoes, greens, steamed carrots and home-made biscuits for their supper, which she planned to have ready at six thirty.

The men got back just after three and went into the parlor to set up an electric train set George had bought when Jeb was nine. Margaret and Amanda were sitting in the living room next to the fireplace reading and Irma Sue was putting the roast in the oven and cleaning up the kitchen.

Supper was ready just after six thirty and they all sat down and George said a prayer.

"Irma Sue, this is great! Where did you learn to cook like this?" Jeb exclaimed.

"She cooked a lot of lunches in the turpentine camp for the woods riders and tally men, but not any prime rib," said Margaret. "That was one of Pete's favorite dishes."

"Well, it's sure superb," George said, taking a fork-full of beef.

"I agree," Amanda said as she buttered a smoking, flaky biscuit.

"She always was good in the kitchen," Margaret added. Jeb didn't say anything else. He was busy gobbling down Irma Sue's excellent cooking.

When they had finished their fluffy, rich chocolate cake, Jeb said, "I'm stuffed. I couldn't hold another bite."

"You better pay attention, Son - beauty, brains, and an excellent cook. I wouldn't let this one get away."

"I won't, Dad."

When Amanda, Margaret, and Irma Sue finished cleaning up the kitchen, they joined George, Jeb, and Jack in the living room. Then George said, "Margaret, we usually like to take a family buggy ride along Spring Creek on Christmas Eve. We bring lap robes, blankets, and feet warmers to keep warm. But tonight it's not that cold, probably because a front is moving in and we'll have rain tonight or tomorrow. Would

77

you, Irma Sue and Jack like to join us? The buggy seats six so there will be plenty of room." George and Amanda both knew what would happen next.

"Dad, I think Irma Sue and I would like to stay here while the rest of you go. I have to go back to Tuscaloosa for football practice day after tomorrow, and I would like Irma Sue and I to have some time alone."

"We understand, Jeb, and we'll see you in a couple of hours."

Jeb waited until George had hitched the two horses to the carriage, then said, "Irma Sue, I'll be right back."

A clearly shaken Jeb was soon back in the living room. *I wonder why he's so nervous?* thought Irma Sue.

Jeb went over to her, and knelt before her. He took the black velvet case that held the engagement ring out of his pocket and laid it on her lap. She thought, *OH MY GOD! He's going to propose to me now!* A giddy excitement began to overwhelm her.

Irma Sue was trembling as Jeb took her hand, looked deeply into her eyes, and said, "Irma Sue, you are the most wonderful and special person I've ever known and I love you so much. I thank God every day for bringing you into my life. You are my soul mate, and the woman I want to spend the rest of my life with. Will you marry me?"

She threw her arms around him and exclaimed, "Oh yes, yes, darling!" And they kissed, passionately, tenderly. The feel of being in each other's arms and knowing that they were going to share the rest of their lives together filled each of them with a joy that they had never known. Then he carefully took the diamond engagement ring out of its box and gently placed it on her finger. She was laughing and crying at the same time. They had never experienced so much emotion as they held each other and kissed.

Then she remembered Jack, and had to blink back tears as she said nervously, "Jeb, there's something I need to tell

FLORIDA GOLD

you. And if you change your mind about marrying me after I tell you, I will understand."

"What is it?" Then a tearful Irma Sue told him the story about how Jerry Dunaway had told her he loved her and would marry her, and they would move to Atlanta where he would manage his father's trucking business. About how he wanted nothing to do with her after she told him she was pregnant. About giving birth to Jack when she was fifteen, and that her parents claimed him as their own to prevent her from suffering from the stigma of having a baby out of wedlock.

"Come here," Jeb said as he pulled her to him. "Do you know how special you are, and how much I love you?"

"I - I think so," a relieved Irma Sue replied.

"It takes very strong character and honesty to tell me what you just did, and I admire you and love you even more for telling me."

"Oh, Jeb, I love you so much."

"I think we should tell my parents. I know they will understand."

"Whatever you suggest, darling," she replied blissfully.

The group returned from their ride about nine and entered the house to find a blissful Irma Sue and Jeb sitting on the couch listening to Christmas music on the phonograph - he with his arm around her and she with her head on his shoulder.

"You're the happiest couple I've ever seen. "What's going on?" Amanda asked.

"I asked Irma Sue to marry me and she accepted!" Jeb explained.

"Congratulations, Son, and to you, Irma Sue," George replied.

"Yes, congratulations to both of you," Amanda and Margaret replied.

"Jack, it looks like you are going to have a brother-in-law," Margaret said.

"Oh boy!"

"Jack, can you come with me into the kitchen? I bet you'd like some more of that chocolate cake," Irma Sue suggested.

"YEAH!"

"When we get married, Jack will have the father he deserves," Jeb explained.

"What?" Margaret asked excitedly. George and Amanda exchanged glances.

"Irma Sue told me all about how Jack was really her baby and you and Pete claimed him to protect her and Jack."

"It must have taken a lot for her to tell you about that just after you proposed," Amanda offered.

"Yeah, and it just made me love and admire her more."

"You've really found yourself a wonderful wife, Jeb. I'm proud for both of you," George added.

"Let's go in the kitchen and tell her how proud we are of her, and how happy that she'll soon be our daughter-in-law," Amanda suggested.

They all went into the kitchen, and Jeb said, "I told them, Irma Sue."

Amanda went over to Irma Sue and hugged her. "I'm getting the best daughter-in-law in the world," she said.

"I second that," George added as he hugged Irma Sue.

Margaret stood in astonishment, convinced that these people were saints from heaven. When she regained her voice, she said, "And I'm getting the best son-in-law in the world." Then she began to cry with joy, realizing that Jack would have the father he deserved and a loving family around him.

When Irma Sue was drifting off to sleep that night, she knew she had never been this happy in her entire life. Margaret felt the same way.

FLORIDA GOLD

Jack was up first, at six thirty, eagerly wanting to see what Santa Claus had brought him, and Irma Sue got up with him. She explained that they needed to let everyone else sleep. They went downstairs and Jack used restraint about going to the Christmas tree, and played with the electric train while he impatiently waited for everyone to wake up and come down stairs.

After what seemed like an eternity, but was only about forty-five minutes, Jeb came in the parlor. He walked up behind Irma Sue, gave her a passionate kiss, and said, "Merry Christmas! How's my fiancé doing this morning?"

"Happy as a clam. How about my fiancé?"

"The same."

"Is it time to go open the gifts yet?" an impatient Jack pleaded.

"It will be, very soon," Jeb replied.

In a few minutes, everyone came in. Amanda yawned, and said, "I wonder what Santa brought?"

"Let's go, sport," Jeb said, and Jack charged into the living room.

Under the tree were a lot of toys. There was a bicycle with training wheels, a fishing rod and reel, a BB gun, a pocket knife, a football and football uniform, a pair of cap pistols in a belted holster, a cowboy hat and outfit with cowboy boots, and several other things.

"Oh boy, Santa sure was good to me this Christmas!" Jack exclaimed as he began to open his gifts. Margaret looked at George and Amanda and mouthed a silent Thank-you, but you shouldn't have.

"Now what would Christmas be without toys?" George kidded.

After Jack had opened everything, sat on the new bike, and shot the cap pistols, Jeb said, "Jack, you still have another surprise outside. It was too big for Santa to bring in the house."

81

They all went outside and Jeb led them to the barn, and led out a pony. "Merry Christmas, Jack."

"Mama, it's a PONY!"

"I see that," Margaret said, once again nearly in shock.

"We'll keep Skeet out here and take care of him. And you can come ride him whenever you want to."

"Oh, thank you, Mr. Jeb. Can I put on my cowboy outfit, my cap pistols and go riding?"

"After we grown-ups have opened our gifts, I'll go riding with you," Jeb promised.

"OK,"

Once they were seated, Jeb handed out the gifts. Irma Sue began by opening her opal birthstone ring from George and Amanda. "It's beautiful and I love it!" Irma Sue exclaimed as she turned the stone, its blend of yellow, orange, blue, and green colors changing in the light.

Amanda opened her diamond earrings next and said, "George, how'd you know I've been wanting these ever since we visited Tony last year?"

"A little elf told me," George kidded.

Next, Jeb opened a long package. "Dad, it's the Fox Double!" It was a side-by-side double-barreled sixteen-gauge shotgun made by the A.H. Fox Gun Company that Jeb had been dreaming about. The balance, weight and feel of Fox shotguns were unsurpassed. Most of the gun was made by hand, requiring a skilled master craftsman for the polishing, rust bluing, engraving, stock checkering and custom fitting. These requirements dictated that newly made A.H. Fox shotguns would never be available in great quantities. Only about twenty-five a year were produced. No amount of labor or expense was spared to make it perfect. The best mechanical principles known in gun making were combined with the finest workmanship and materials obtainable, absolutely regardless of cost. The A.H. Fox was built for the sportsman who was satisfied by only the best. It was in every

FLORIDA GOLD

sense a "work of art." The engraving was a revelation in the ornamentation of guns, consisting of gold inlays surrounded by beautiful scroll work and engraved game scenes. The stock was selected from richly figured four star Turkish Circassian walnut. The checkering was explicit, being the finest diamond pattern on the grip, panels and forearm. It was in a high-quality fully accessorized leather trunk case that came with the gun.

"Get ready to do some quail hunting," George replied.

"I guess," a mesmerized Jeb replied.

"We'll have to go outside again for the next gift," George explained. Everyone followed him outside and he opened the door to the garage. There was a brand-new 1920 Ford Model T center-door sedan. "Merry Christmas, Margaret!" George and Amanda said together. "Now you and Irma Sue won't have to walk to work," George told her. It was too much for her, and she began to cry softly. "What's the matter, Margaret?" George asked.

"It's just that you're such wonderful people. I don't know what we did to deserve friends like you."

"We're no longer just friends. You're part of our family now," Amanda explained. "Margaret, you've led a hard life, but it's built a character in you and Irma Sue that anyone would admire."

"I work as a woods rider for a week each year in one of the Southern Resin Chemical and Timber Company's camps. Of all the places I work and the people I meet, if my life depended on it, I'd rather have someone from a turpentine camp in my corner than anyone else," George observed. "They're the most honest, brave, hardworking, trustworthy people I know, and you and Irma Sue certainly live up to that ideal."

"I think that you, Amanda, and Jeb are saints from heaven," Margaret replied.

"No, we're just good citizens that enjoy exposing you and Irma Sue to things you might not otherwise get to experience, and helping you get back on your feet financially. And like Amanda said, you're family now," George explained.

They went back inside, and finished opening gifts. Jeb had bought his father a .30-06 bolt-action Remington hunting rifle, his mother a new leather purse, Irma Sue a pearl necklace, Margaret a pair of pearl earrings, and Jack the BB gun from earlier. Irma Sue and Margaret had bought George and Amanda a set of stainless steel German-made knives for the kitchen, Jeb a fishing rod with one of the new Shakespeare reels, and Jack a new baseball and bat. It was a great Christmas morning, and everyone was euphoric about Jeb and Irma Sue's engagement.

The women went to work fixing the Christmas dinner while Jeb and George took Jack horseback riding. At eleven thirty there was a knock on the front door that Amanda answered. Ben Blalock said, "Merry Christmas," as Amanda gave him a hug.

Jack, George, and Jeb came in a few minutes later, and then Amanda announced, "Christmas dinner is ready." They had roast turkey, cornbread stuffing with giblet gravy, cranberry sauce, a green-bean casserole, scalloped potatoes, sweet-potato casserole, corn fritters, yeast rolls, and pumpkin and pecan pies.

"Ben, Jeb has some wonderful news," George said.

"An angel told you that the Crimson Tide was going to win the national championship," Ben joked.

"I wish. Irma Sue and I became engaged to be married last night!"

"Why, that's wonderful! Congratulations Jeb, Irma Sue!"

Everyone stuffed themselves on the wonderful meal until they were cross-eyed. Then they went into the living room to have coffee and talk. Ben kept stealing glances at Margaret, and when he did, she smiled at him, captivating his thoughts.

FLORIDA GOLD

Ben left around three and everyone took a nap. As she was drifting off to sleep, Margaret wondered what was going to happen with Ben, knowing that his being her boss complicated things. But she was definitely attracted to him.

They had leftovers for supper at seven. Afterward, Jeb took Jack out to the barn to feed and groom his new pony.

"George and I had a discussion about Jack," Amanda began as she joined Margaret, Irma Sue, and George in the living room. "We'd like to suggest that you send for his things in Archer, and let him move in with us."

"We have lots of space, he'd have his own room, and he needs to be with his family," George suggested.

"What about the fact that he's really Irma Sue's son?" Margaret asked.

"As you know, we're fine with that. But I doubt if the community would be, and the result would be unfair treatment of you, Irma Sue, Jeb, and us," Amanda explained. "It might even cost George some banking customers and Ben some store customers. We think it would be best just to stay with the story you always have - that he's yours, Margaret."

"Of course when Jack is old enough to understand the situation and its ramifications, we'll tell him," George explained.

"Obviously you can visit Jack as often as you like, and he can spend weekends and holidays with you and Irma Sue or with all of us if we're together," Amanda added.

"What about when Jeb and Irma Sue get married?" Margaret asked.

"That's their decision," said George, "but our suggestion would be that Jack live with them, and visit you as often as you like. The reason given to those who ask is that you have to work every day and Jack would be alone when not at school if he lived with you. It will be Irma Sue's decision, but we assume she'd quit her job when she and Jeb become married, get active in a number of social and charitable organizations, and start their family."

"What do you think, Irma Sue?" asked Margaret.

"I like it. I think it's perfect."

"So do I. And again, thanks for everything you are doing for us," Margaret added.

"You're very welcome, and like I said, we're all family now," Amanda replied. George and Irma Sue went to the barn to see Jack, Jeb, and Jack's new pony. When they'd left, Amanda asked, "What's up with you and Ben Blalock?"

"What?" Margaret asked, blushing.

"Every time I looked at him, he was stealing glances at you and you were smiling back."

"Was it that obvious?"

"It was to me, but I doubt if it was to George."

"I don't know, I'm just attracted to him. When I lost Pete, I didn't think I'd ever be romantically attracted to any man. Now I'm not so sure."

"Well, Ben is a very fine man. He was absolutely devoted to Bess, his wife, and they were close. They couldn't have children, but they enjoyed doing things with them. Ben was a Boy Scout leader and Bess was a Girl Scout leader for years. Ben also used to take boys from the local orphanage camping on our ranch. It almost killed him when Bess died of cancer. I think he'd make some lucky woman a great husband. He's also open-minded enough to accept the truth about Jack."

"None of that surprises me. I could sense that he is a good man."

"Tell you what, if you want, I'll talk to George about this and get him to talk with Ben, to help break the ice given the situation with Ben being your boss."

"Oh would you? That would be great."

When everyone came back inside, Margaret asked, "Jack, how would you like to move to Mobile and live with Mr. and

FLORIDA GOLD

Mrs. Walker? Irma Sue and I would visit you a lot and we could spend weekends and holidays together."

"Yippee!" Jack shouted, as he jumped with excitement and joy.

"I think you've got a new boarder," Irma Sue added.

On Sunday morning they got up early, had a light breakfast, and headed back to Mobile. Irma Sue rode with Jeb and his mom and dad, and Margaret followed in her new Ford. When they got to the Walkers' house, Irma Sue kissed Jeb and got in the car with Margaret. "Remember, be at the Lutheran church at 10:50," Amanda reminded them.

"I think that was the best Christmas I've ever had," Margaret observed.

"It certainly was for me. The man of my dreams asked me to marry him and my son will be able to live with us."

Jeb packed for his trip back to school. He would catch the train at 2:30 p.m. They would have football practice on Monday, Tuesday, and Wednesday in preparation for the game, travel to New Orleans on Thursday, have one practice there on Friday, and the game would be on Saturday. He hated being away from Irma Sue, but was looking forward to seeing his team mates, telling them about his new fiancé, and winning the national title.

Margaret and Irma Sue arrived early at 10:40 and people were just leaving Sunday school classes. George, Amanda, and Jeb soon arrived, and they were all seated together. As the minister opened the ceremony, he asked if anyone had any news or announcements. One lady told everyone that her husband was out of the hospital, and thanked everyone for their prayers. A man thanked the congregation for taking up a collection to help pay for his son's operation. Then George stood up and said, "Reverend Jones, I'd like to come to the front if I may."

"Certainly, George."

When he was on the stage standing next to the reverend, George said, "Amanda and I have wonderful news. Our son, Jeb, has asked Irma Sue Thomas to marry him and she accepted. I'd like to ask that my newly expanded family all come up here so I can introduce them."

Amanda, Jeb, Irma Sue, Margaret, and Jack all went up and the group stood next to George.

"Everyone knows Jeb and Amanda. This is Irma Sue, Jeb's new fiancée, who also works in my bank, and her mother, Margaret Thomas, the new general manager of the recently opened Blalock's Department Store. And the little guy in front of me is Margaret's son, Jack. They are new to Mobile and moved here from Archer, Florida, last September after Margaret's husband, Pete, passed away. Please extend them a warm welcome."

Everyone shouted welcomes to Irma Sue, Margaret, and Jack.

After the sermon, the three stood next to Reverend Jones and greeted people as they left. A number of couples suggested they get together for a meal and that they would come see Irma Sue at the bank or Margaret at the store to determine when to get together.

Jeb was leaving for the train station from church, but asked Irma Sue to come back with him into one of the now-empty Sunday-school rooms. Once they were inside, he put his arms around her and kissed her passionately, longingly, his lips massaging hers until they both shook with desire. His kiss gripped her like a powerful drug. "We'd better stop," she said breathlessly.

"Yeah," he agreed reluctantly. They went back out front. Margaret was taking Jeb to the train station, and he and Irma Sue soon left with her.

They arrived a few minutes early, and Margaret gave them these last few minutes alone while Irma Sue walked

FLORIDA GOLD

with Jeb to the rail car and stood near him at its steps. "Oh Jeb, I don't want you to leave."

"I know. I don't want to, but we'll see each other after the game and have dinner together that night. That's only six days from now."

"It seems like six years to me," she said, her voice breaking with sadness.

Jeb held her until the last minute, and then he kissed her and said good-bye.

"Good-bye, darling," she said, her voice breaking with emotion, and then she hurried out of the train station, tears streaming down her cheeks.

CHAPTER SIX

The next morning, George called Ben Blalock and asked if he had time for lunch. Ben said he did and they agreed to meet at the Circle Grill. "What's up, George?" Ben asked after they'd ordered.

"Apparently Amanda had a conversation with Margaret about what she thought was a potential romantic interest you and Margaret have for each other."

"What?"

"I don't really understand. I probably should have brought Amanda to explain but she took Jack out to ride his pony and shoot his BB gun this morning."

"What did she tell you?"

"I guess she saw you and Margaret exchanging glances and smiling at each other during Christmas dinner so she asked Margaret about it and Margaret said she was attracted to you, but worried about pursuing it because you were her boss."

"George, I admit, I'm very attracted to Margaret. She's doing a great job at the store, her employees like her, and she's one of the smartest women I've ever met. She's also very beautiful."

"Well, what are you going to do about it?"

"Until now, I wasn't sure, because of my being her boss. Now that I know she's interested in me, I think I'll ask her on a date."

"Good man. Now on to other important things. Are you going to be able to join Jeb and me at the quail-hunting lodge in Albany the first weekend in February?"

"That's right, our annual quail hunt is coming up. Count me in. I guess Jeb will be trying out that fine A.H. Fox you got him for Christmas."

"He sure will."

"Great."

"Are you going to bring Jack?"

"Absolutely. He may not be old enough to shoot, but he can certainly enjoy the hunting trip."

It was about four o'clock when Ben came to Margaret's store and asked to see her in her office. "Is everything OK, Ben?"

"With the store? Things couldn't be better. You're doing a great job. This visit is of a more personal nature," he said uneasily.

Amanda must have talked to George who talked to Ben, she thought. "What is it, Ben?"

"I don't want you to get the wrong impression since I'm your boss. But would you go out with me this Friday night? If you don't..."

"I'd love to, Ben."

"You would?"

"Yes."

"Great. I'll pick you up at your place at seven. I thought we'd have supper and go see that new movie, *Deliverance*, about Helen Keller."

"That sounds good to me."

Soon after Ben left, the phone rang. "Blalock's Department Store, Margaret Thomas speaking."

"Hey, Margaret. This is Amanda."

FLORIDA GOLD

"I was getting ready to call and thank you. Ben just asked me on a date for Friday night."

"Wonderful! George's talk must have been effective. I hope things work out with you two."

"I do too. I'm looking forward to Friday night."

"Margaret, we plan to leave for New Orleans at seven thirty Saturday morning. That gives us time to check into the hotel and have lunch before the game starts at two."

"I'm sorry, but I won't be able to go. I just need to be here with the store. Things are real busy now."

"I understand."

Ben was on time, and they went to a diner and had hamburgers and fried potatoes before going to the movie. Afterward, during the ride back to her place, Ben said, "Seeing that movie reminds me that if you try hard enough, anything is possible."

"I agree. I've seen people accomplish some pretty impossible things in my life." They soon got to her place and Ben walked her to the door.

"Since we can't travel to the championship football game, would you like to go with me tomorrow to my country club, have lunch, and listen to it on the radio?"

"Sure."

"Good, I'll come get you at twelve. That gives us time to have lunch before the game starts at two."

"Goodnight, Ben, I had a wonderful time."

"Good night."

When Margaret was inside, she sat on the bed, trying to sort out the events of the last few weeks. Irma Sue had met the man of her dreams and was engaged to marry him, she'd become friends with two of the most wonderful people in the universe, she and Irma Sue were getting Jack to live close enough to them that they could see him regularly, she had the job of her dreams, and now she'd been out with a wonderful man. Moving to Mobile had definitely been the best decision she'd ever made. She couldn't know that it would soon turn into her worst nightmare.

The next day, Ben came by at twelve and they went to his club, Heron Lakes - the same one Jeb had taken Irma Sue to for golf and tennis lessons. They had tuna salad sandwiches and potato salad for lunch, then went into the game room to hear the football game on the radio.

Irma Sue, Jack, Amanda, and George left on the train at 7:30 Saturday morning for the championship football game in New Orleans. They arrived at 11:20. "The Roosevelt Hotel," George told the cab driver as he was loading their luggage into the back. They arrived about twenty minutes later, and as she entered, Irma Sue was taken with the beauty. The spacious lobby was adorned with crystal chandeliers, potted palms, a giant clock, original paintings, and model-size recreations of famous ships. George checked them into their two adjoining suites and the bellman took their luggage up.

"Let's meet in the lobby for lunch in fifteen minutes," George suggested as they went into their rooms. Irma Sue and Jack's suite consisted of polished marble floors, walk-in closet, a private balcony, living room, bedroom with two large beds, and a marble bathroom with gold fixtures.

They had jambalaya, fried oysters, and cornbread for lunch. Then they took a cab to Tulane Stadium, where thirty-five thousand fans were finding their seats. Theirs were in the front row, near the fifty-yard line. Irma Sue and Jack had never watched a football game or been in a stadium before, and were eagerly taking in all the sights and sounds around them. The players soon came running out, with Jeb leading the Crimson Tide team onto the field. He looked toward the seats and smiled and waved when Irma Sue waved.

The University of Alabama Crimson Tide opened up the national championship game against the University of Texas Longhorns by finding the end zone first on a twenty-three-

FLORIDA GOLD

yard pass from Jeb to Tim Murphy. John Jackson's extra point brought the CT ahead 7-0.

It took a 2:13 drive for UT to answer two and a half minutes later when quarterback Sam Morris hit Texas wide receiver Jermaine Green with a nine-yard touchdown reception. The Longhorns drove 65 yards for the score to bring the margin 7-7 all.

Junior Ted Davis led the CT defense on UT's next possession, rallying for a key fourth-and-one stop that prevented the UT from jumping ahead after a twenty-six-yard pass that put Texas on the Alabama four yard line. Jeff Greene capitalized on the momentum with a forty-six-yard run that brought the CT to midfield.

While the CT punted on the possession, the CT defense sustained on the UT ensuing drive, ending the drive on Alabama's three-yard line when junior Bud Wright intercepted a Morris pass.

When Jeb hit CT wide receiver Jim Morrison with a seventeen-yard pass, he exploded through a gap and ran fifty-five yards to the UT twenty-five. Three plays later, Jeb's nine-yard touchdown strike to Tim Hammond gave the CT a seven point lead, making the score 14-7 and taking both teams to the locker rooms at the half.

After CT and UT swapped possessions to open the second half of the game, the CT jumped out of the gates, stringing together a seventy-five-yard scoring drive when Jeb found the end zone on a six-yard score with 5:22 to go in the third quarter. Jeb rushed for forty-nine yards on the drive and Jackson found the uprights to bring CT ahead 21-7.

Following a CT punt, Texas narrowed Alabama's lead when Morris connected with Greene for his second touchdown of the game, an eleven-yard pass to cap off a sixty-seven-yard drive and bring the score to 21-14.

An interception by CT cornerback Jeremy Williams put the CT on the Longhorns' twenty-two-yard line, and on the next play, Jeb ran the twenty-two yards for a touchdown. Although Jackson missed the extra point, Jeb's touchdown gave the CT a commanding 27-14 advantage, and the momentum. The CT fans were going nuts and chanting "Walker! Walker!"

As Irma Sue watched the game, she realized how talented an athlete Jeb really was. Yet he'd never bragged, nor had his parents. They'd only said that he played quarterback for the Crimson Tide and was going to compete for the national championship.

A forty-three-yard field goal by UT's Tony Pitt, his longest of the season, cut CT's lead to 27-17 with just over four minutes to play. However, passes from Jeb to sophomore tight end Aaron Hines, junior David Nettles and senior Josh Nelson composed a seventy-six-yard game-winning scoring drive by the CT when Jeb ran for a four-yard touchdown, giving the CT a 34-17 lead, the final margin of the game.

When it was over and the announcer broadcast the final score, fans and the press poured onto the field, running toward Jeb. He sprinted over to the fence in front of where his family was seated and said, "Come with me, Irma Sue." Before she could respond, he nimbly lifted her over the fence as hundreds of fans and the press surrounded them.

"You're on the national radio news, Jeb. As undoubtedly one of the best quarterbacks in college football, can you tell us how it feels to lead the Crimson Tide to their first national championship?"

"It was a team effort. No one person can claim this great victory."

"But you did score the most points of any player."

"Yeah, thanks to good protection by the line, good wide receivers, and a good team."

"What about professional ball, Jeb? The scouts have been after you since the beginning of this season and a number of them are waiting to talk to you now."

FLORIDA GOLD

"As I've said before, I'm not interested in playing professionally."

"Jeb, is there anything you want to say to the thousands of fans out there?"

"Yeah. This is Irma Sue Thomas, my fiancé and the love of my life."

"Miss Thomas, how does it feel to be engaged to a national football star?"

"It feels great! But Jeb's my soul mate and would be whether or not he was a football star."

As the many fans came up to Jeb, congratulating him, and she listened to his humble responses, Irma Sue knew she was marrying the finest man in the world, and even though it didn't seem possible, her love for him grew deeper.

After a brief locker room celebration with his teammates, Jeb showered, dressed and met his parents outside the stadium. Irma Sue ran to him as he walked up and gave him a big kiss and hug.

"Great game, Son!" George said.

"Thanks, Dad. It looks like all that backyard football practice you put me through when I was a little boy paid off."

"That and having a football star for a father who led Vanderbilt to a national championship twenty-four years ago," Amanda added.

"Like father like son," George replied proudly.

"Can I play football when I grow up?" Jack asked.

"With George and Jeb to teach you, I would be surprised if you didn't," Amanda replied. No one could know at the time, but not only would Jack not go to college, he wouldn't even get the chance to graduate from high school.

They went to Broussard's in the French quarter for supper. They entered a stunning lobby of hand-painted tiles surrounding a fountain, and George said "Walker party." They were led through a spacious and beautiful courtyard to the second of two elegant private dining rooms. As they entered, everyone stood and clapped, with several saying, "Congratulations, Jeb." The same people Irma Sue had met at dinner after the fishing trip were here, except Ben Blalock. There were also several other couples, which George introduced her to. There was Andrew McShane, the recently elected mayor of New Orleans, and his wife, Jean; Braxton Comer, the governor of Alabama, and his wife, Virginia; and Xen Scott, Crimson Tide's head football coach, and his wife, Jackie.

When everyone was seated, George said, "Jeb has an announcement."

"You mean that Irma Sue is his fiancée?" Braxton Comer replied. "That was on tonight's radio news." At that everyone stood and clapped again.

Dinner was elegant. Irma Sue had shrimp roulade for an appetizer, which was shrimp tossed in red-and-white roulade served with celeriac salad; the New Orleans bouillabaisse for the main course, which was fish, shrimp, scallops, and mussels in a savory saffron tomato broth finished with crabmeat and croutons; and bananas Foster for dessert, which was bananas sautéed in a brown sugar sauce, butter, and cinnamon, and served flaming over vanilla ice cream.

About fifteen minutes after Ben and Margaret settled into the comfortable leather chairs in the game room, the radio began broadcasting pre-game information. The broadcast was soon describing the game on a play-by-play basis. "...The ball is snapped and Jeb Walker is in the pocket, waiting, waiting,.., and it's a forward pass from Walker to Tim Murphy! TOUCHDOWN! The Crimson Tide makes the first score in this closely matched game."

"Walker just ran twenty-two yards for another touchdown, bringing the score to 27-14 - a commanding lead. Fans, no one knows what has gotten into Jeb Walker tonight, but he's on fire! He seems invincible!"

FLORIDA GOLD

Ben and Margaret listened to the whole broadcast on the edge of their seats, cheering whenever the Crimson Tide scored. At the postgame interview, Margaret was very impressed. Here Jeb was using his special moment on national radio to introduce Irma Sue as his fiancé. "Pretty special young man, isn't he?" Ben observed.

"He certainly is. The whole family is special."

"Can I interest you in dinner?"

"Certainly."

There was a band at the club and a number of couples were dancing. A nice-looking gentleman came up and asked Ben, "Do you mind if I ask the lady to dance?"

Before Ben could respond, Margaret replied, "Sorry, I've already promised all my dances this evening to Ben, my date." The man nodded, and walked away. Then Margaret said in a teasing and flirtatious tone, "Well, Ben, you don't want to make me a liar to that man, do you?"

"No, I certainly don't," Ben said as he got up and walked with her to the dance floor. They began a fast dance to the up-tempo music. Then the band began to play another arrangement, and Ben remembered a Latin hustle he'd learned that seemed just right.

"Want to try something I learned in a dance class once?"

"You bet!" Margaret picked up the steps and moves quickly as they whirled, turned, and dipped to the music. Noticing that they were just getting warmed up, the band chose another similar arrangement. Suddenly, they were the only ones dancing and the other couples were watching them. When the music stopped, everyone applauded. "That sure was fun!" she said breathlessly.

"Yeah, and you make a great dance partner." Then the band put on a record of slow romantic music while they were packing to leave.

Ben started to leave the floor with her and she said jokingly, "Oh no, Ben, you're not getting off that easy."

They danced to many of the popular romantic pieces of the time: "Whispering," "Hold Me," "Girl of My Dreams," "Barefoot Trail," and more. And then it was midnight and the club was closing. On the ride back to Margaret's place neither of them spoke, preferring instead to ride in silence with their thoughts.

He walked with her to the door, and said, "I really enjoyed tonight, Margaret."

"I did too."

Then he turned her toward him, pulled her against him and tenderly kissed her, their arms encircling each other. The same butterflies came to her stomach as when Pete kissed her, and like with Pete, she couldn't turn off her desire to be his.

"Would you have dinner with me tomorrow night?"

"Of course."

"Good, I'll be by to get you at six thirty, if that's OK."

"That sounds good to me."

On Sunday, Margaret busied herself with doing laundry and cleaning their two bedrooms and bathroom.

At three, Dorothy tapped on Margaret's door and said, "Amanda Walker is on the phone for you."

"Well, how did the date with Ben go?"

"Great. We went out Friday night, listened to the game at Heron Lakes yesterday, went to dinner and dancing last night, and we're going to dinner tonight."

"So what do you think of Ben?"

"He's a wonderful man."

"Oh, that's great, Margaret. I'm so happy for you both. Why don't you meet me tomorrow at the Circle Grill for lunch? I'd like to get all the details."

Ben took Margaret to Pellegrino's, an Italian restaurant with low lighting and intimate, well-spaced tables, and travel posters of Italy decorating the walls. She had another great time, and was itching to tell Amanda the next day.

FLORIDA GOLD

"I want to know everything," Amanda said excitedly as Margaret met her at their table.

Margaret described their time together briefly, then said, "The only other time I ever felt like this was when Pete and I first met."

"Ben's a fine man. I'm glad you and he enjoy spending time together. You'll be good for each other, particularly since both of you lost your spouses."

Margaret and Ben began dating. Both were too tired at the end of their day to go out more than once or twice a week. The store, like the other retail outlets in Mobile at the time, was closed Thursday afternoon and all day Sunday, and was open the rest of the week from nine until six. As managers, Margaret and Ben could take off during store hours, but preferred not to. So they settled into a dating routine of going to see a movie or a play or just having dinner together on Thursdays, going to the club on Saturday nights, and to church together followed by lunch at the club on Sundays.

George and Ben's train pulled into Albany just before Jeb's, and Fuller, one of the servants at the Open Meadows plantation where they were headed, met the three of them in the car that Friday afternoon just after four o'clock. "Massa Walker, Massa Blalock, it good to see you! Massa Jeb, you done good in that football game."

"Thanks, Fuller."

"An' who this little man?" he asked as he shook Jack's hand.

"I'm Jack."

"Well, Jack, you ready to go bird huntin'?"

"I sure am."

They arrived at the plantation just before dark. Open Meadows was the plantation house on a twenty-nine-thousand-acre operation owned and operated by the

Southern Resin Chemical and Timber Company, of which George owned 55 percent, and Ben another 10 percent. There was also the overseer's house, the stables, the main barn, the kennels, and the gardening shed. As they walked through the columned entrance, Lena Mae, the cook, greeted them.

"Who yo little guest?" she asked looking at Jack.

"He's my fiancé's brother," Jeb replied.

"That's right. I heard you was gittin' married soon."

"Yes."

"You-all ready fo' some good fried sweet taters an poke chops?"

"I've been looking forward to your cooking all week," Ben replied.

They were up and out early the next morning. George, Jeb, Ben, and Jack were riding Tennessee walking horses, while up ahead, Patrick, the hunting guide and dog trainer was riding another walking horse. Jack was too young to shoot, but he would be able to enjoy the hunt. Patrick signaled the dogs with a low-pitched, drawn-out whistle he somehow produced from deep in his throat. George could just make out two of his prize pointers, King and Duke, ranging through the golden sea of sedge, trying to get wind of quail coveys. Quail was considered the aristocrat of American game birds. It was what the grouse and the pheasant were in Scotland and England – only better. With the grouse and pheasant, men had to literally beat the bushes and to drive the birds toward the shooters. With quail, the hunters had to stay on the move. They had to have great dogs, great horses, and great shooting skill. Only the quail exploded upward into the sky and made the hunter's heart bang away so madly in their rib cage.

Jeb, Jack, George and Ben rode on in silence for a while, waiting for some signal from Patrick, listening to the creaking of the wagons, the clip clopping of the mules, and the snorts

102

FLORIDA GOLD

of the horses. One wagon was a rolling dog kennel, containing cages for two more pairs of pointers to take turns in the ceaseless roaming of the sedge for birds. A team of mules adorned in brass-knobbed yokes and studded harnessing pulled the wagon, and two of George's dog handlers, both of them black, adorned in thorn-proof yellow overalls, drove them. The other was the buckboard, rebuilt with shock absorbers and rubber tires and upholstered with rich tan leather. Two more black employees drove the buckboard and served food and drink from ice boxes built onto the back. Off to the side were two more black employees on horseback, wearing the yellow overalls, whose main job it was to hold the horses of the shooters when they dismounted.

By now they were almost two miles away from Open Meadows and deep into the plantation's seemingly endless fields of broom sedge. The sun was strong enough by eight a.m. to make the ground mist lift like wisps of smoke and create a heavenly green glow in the pine forests and light up the sedge with a tawny gold.

Up ahead, Patrick, the dog trainer, stopped and looked back. "Pooooiint!" he yelled. There was Duke in the classic pointer's stance, his nose thrust forward and his tail sticking up at a forty-five degree angle like a rod. Out beyond Patrick, King was in the same position, backing Duke's point. The wagons came to a halt, everyone grew quiet, and George and Jeb dismounted. For safety, there would be only two shooters at the time and Ben was going to let father and son have the first shots. Jeb withdrew his new Fox sixteen-gauge from its leather scabbard, slipped two shells into the twin barrels, closed the action, and began walking through the sedge with George. His heart was thumping away. No matter how many times you went quail hunting, you were never immune to the feeling that came over you when the dogs went on point and you approached a covey hidden somewhere in the tall grass. Jeb took a position off to George's left. The understanding

103

was that an imaginary line ran between them, and George would go after any birds to the right of it, and Jeb to the left. It was so quiet Jeb could hear his own breathing, which was rapid. With an extraordinary pounding of the air, the covey exploded up and out of the grass, the sound startlingly loud. Jeb raised the stock to his shoulder and swung the shotgun to the left, moving the barrels just ahead of a gray blur and fired. The bird came tumbling out of the air. He quickly found another gray-and-white bird, swung the barrels almost straight up and fired again, and the second bird came peeling down out of the sky.

"Wow!" yelled an excited Jack.

Jeb turned toward George and asked, "How'd you do, Dad?"

"I got one, but missed the second one. It looks like that Fox fits you pretty good."

"It sure does, and it's a dream to shoot." Soon the dogs had fetched all three quail from the underbrush and brought them to Patrick, who in turn brought them to Jeb and George, who examined them briefly, then put them in one of the ice boxes on the buckboard.

They broke for lunch and a rest in a shady oak grove at noon, then started again at two. By four o'clock they had forty-two birds and had fired about ninety shots, a pretty good shooting average. They had been hunting their way back toward Open Meadows most of the afternoon, and were back at the plantation house by five. Jeb, George, and Ben went inside while Patrick and Jack got the four drivers and took the birds to the barn to clean.

"How many y'all git?" Lena Mae asked.

"Forty-two," Ben replied.

"Lawd, we's a' goin' to have fried quail tonight. An' buttermilk biscuits with quail gravy, mustard greens, an' black-eyed peas." The hunters' mouths were already watering

FLORIDA GOLD

at the thought of her wonderful cooking, particularly as hungry as the day's hunting had made them.

While George, Jeb, Jack, and Ben were away quail hunting, Amanda, Margaret, and Irma Sue got together at the country club with for lunch on Sunday.

"So how are things with you and Ben?" Amanda asked.

"Fine. We've settled into this routine of going out on Thursdays and Saturday nights, then to church on Sundays."

"I think that's great." Amanda observed. "Take things slowly."

CHAPTER SEVEN

February 22 was Jack's sixth birthday. Amanda planned a party at their house for the following Saturday and invited ten of Jack's new friends from his Sunday-school class. They all came, and there were also three mothers that stayed for the party.

The party began at eleven with the clown they'd hired. He did magic tricks and made animals out of balloons, which the children really enjoyed. Then the Mobile fire chief showed up, complete with truck and firemen. Everyone got to ride in a "real fire truck" with the siren blaring away.

Lunch was hot dogs, popcorn, and fruit punch. Margaret and Irma Sue brought out a large birthday cake they'd baked with six candles on it for dessert. After making a wish and blowing out the candles, the gifts were brought out. In addition to the toys Jack got from his guests, there was a new Winchester single-shot .22 rifle from Jeb, and a fishing rod and reel from Margaret and Irma Sue. After the gifts were given, everyone enjoyed birthday cake with chocolate ice cream.

Then it was party games - the bean bag toss, with prizes for those who put the bean bag through the target hole about fifteen feet away; a lollipop draw, where lollipops with a colored dot on the end entitled the one who drew it to get a prize; and finally the collection game, where the kids went around seeing who could collect the most party rubbish in bags they were given. There were popped balloons, bits of candy wrappers, cups, wrapping paper, etc. Whoever collected the most got a party bag of goodies to take home. A good time was had by all, and after everyone had left, Jeb took Jack to shoot his new .22 rifle. Jack was a very happy boy when he went to bed that night. It was the last happy childhood birthday he would ever have.

On Sunday afternoon, Amanda called Margaret. "We've got a wedding to plan!"

"I know! I'm so excited."

"Could you and Irma Sue join me for lunch tomorrow at the Circle Grill so we can start planning it?"

"I don't see why not."

The group met, and after lengthy discussion, it was decided that the wedding date should be July 16. There simply wasn't time to organize a formal wedding for any earlier date. They also assigned tasks among them - key things like the guest list, choosing the florist and flowers, the design of the invitations, registering for gifts, choice of flower girl and ring bearer, bridesmaid and flower girl dresses, choice of baker and wedding cake, choice of menu for the reception, and choice of photographer would be a group decision, with approval of George and Jeb.

Other tasks were assigned to each of them. Irma Sue would choose the color theme, the hairdresser, the bridesmaids, and the music, she and Margaret would shop for the wedding dress, and register for gifts. Amanda would choose the caterer, the wedding rehearsal dinner restaurant and menu, and wedding favors for the maid of honor, bridesmaids, best man, and ushers; send invitations for the rehearsal and rehearsal dinner; and arrange transportation for the bride and groom to and from the wedding and to the hotel where they would spend their wedding night.

FLORIDA GOLD

Amanda and Margaret would choose the guest book, toasting glasses, ring bearer pillow, and flower girl basket. Jeb would choose the hotel where he and Irma Sue would spend their wedding night, plan the honeymoon, and choose tuxes for himself, the best man, and the ushers. Jeb and George would decide where the reception would be held. Amanda and Margaret would plan the bridal shower. It would be the social event of the year in Mobile.

Jeb chose the Battle House Hotel in Mobile for them to spend their wedding night. It opened in 1852 and had been the site of many Mardi Gras balls, debutante presentations, and gatherings of prominent politicians and captains of industry. They would take a forty-five-day cruise to Europe for their honeymoon, departing from Savannah. Transportation for the bride and groom on their wedding day would be by horse-drawn carriage.

Although Irma Sue and Margaret were assigned choosing the wedding dress, they asked Amanda to join them in such an important task. She suggested they use a custom dressmaker she knew well, who had designed dresses for two governor's balls and numerous wedding gowns.

"Is Jenny working tonight?" Jeb asked as he walked through the door into his father's study with Jack following.

"No, she's off. You two must going rabbit hunting," George observed, noticing that Jack was carrying Jeb's .410 shotgun, and also knowing how much Jeb liked Jenny's hasenpfeffer.

"Yeah, I told Jack when he got good enough with my .410 I'd take him rabbit hunting with it. Has Toby told you whether he's seen any lately? They should be out feeding on all this spring growth."

"He said he's seen several in that meadow just south of the swimming hole in Spring Creek."

"Great, that's where we'll go. By the way, have you heard from Mr. Johns since he left?"

"Actually, he called me yesterday afternoon."

109

"How's the new job treating him?"

"He says he feels right at home in the new bank. Apparently they really appreciate what he brings to their management team."

"Just shows you were right to give him a chance, Dad."

"Character. It's all about judging character."

As they were driving to the ranch in Jeb's car, Jack asked, "What were you and Mr. Walker talking about just now when you said he gave Mr. Johns a second chance and he said it was about judging character?"

"When Mr. Johns – Jeremy - was a senior at Alabama Tech, he got arrested for conducting policy games, a type of gambling, with students. His father, a prominent lawyer in Birmingham, got so mad at him he refused to get him out of jail or talk to him. Jeremy had worked at our bank the summer before and had Dad's phone number, so he called him. Dad felt he had good character and had just made a mistake, primarily because of the influence of a couple of his non-student friends that had questionable reputations. Anyway, Dad bailed him out of jail and talked to his father. But his father refused to talk to Jeremy and cut him off financially. So Dad loaned him the money to finish his senior year and graduate, then gave him a job here to pay off the loan. Jeremy became a successful loan officer, and this past January accepted a position as vice president of farm loans at Citizens and Southern Bank in Savannah."

"So Mr. Walker saved him and made a good man out of him?"

"Not exactly. Jeremy was already a good man, and my dad knew it because he had gotten to know him when he worked at our bank that summer. But everybody makes mistakes. My dad just gave him a second chance, and it was a good decision."

"I guess knowing how to judge character is important to being a successful man like Mr. Walker, huh?"

FLORIDA GOLD

"Jack, I think it's one of his most valuable talents."

"Irma Sue's fried rabbit is real good, so if we get some, maybe you won't miss Mrs. Jenny's cooking," said Jack.

On Sunday, July 10, after George, Amanda, Margaret, Irma Sue, Jack, and Jeb had finished a wonderful dinner of fried pork chops, butter beans, collard greens, and cornbread, George said, "Let's all go for a ride." They drove about a mile, and into a relatively new, upscale neighborhood. Most of the residents were young well-to-do couples and families. Soon they pulled up to a nice brick house on a large lot.

"Who are we going to see, Dad?" Jeb asked.

"You're going to see your new house! It's a wedding present from your mother and me!"

"What? A new house?" Jeb asked excitedly.

Irma Sue was too surprised to speak. "Come on, let's go in," George gestured. It was a four bedroom with a fireplace in the oak-paneled living room. There was a cathedral ceiling in the large master bedroom, tiled bathrooms, a walk-out basement with laundry room, ceiling fans throughout, and a large wraparound porch, complete with rocking chairs. "If you don't like it, I can cancel my offer, which I made subject to your approval," George explained.

"It's perfect," Irma Sue said, still in shock. She and Jeb had planned to rent an apartment until they were able to save enough for a house.

"I agree, Mom and Dad. Thanks!" an excited Jeb said.

"Thanks, Mr. and Mrs. Walker!" Irma Sue replied.

"Now what did we tell you?" George asked.

"I'm sorry, I keep forgetting. Thanks, Mom and Dad."

"That's better."

Margaret touched Amanda's arm, her eyes glassy with emotion, and said, "Thanks to both of you. You continue to make our lives so special."

As the wedding date approached, Irma Sue grew increasingly nervous. "I don't know what your problem is. You're marring the man of your dreams and into a family we adore," Margaret observed.

"It's just all those prominent people, the governor, all those senators. We even have the vice president of the United States coming."

"And they'll all adore you."

"Well, I just hope I'm not a disappointment to Jeb or his parents."

"Look at me, Irma Sue. Jeb loves you very much, and so do his parents. That's all that counts."

"I know. But I'm still nervous."

Finally it was the day before the wedding - the day of the rehearsal and the rehearsal dinner. The practice went smoothly, and there were only a couple of slips. Jeb said "to keep and to hold" rather than "to have and to hold." He also put the wedding ring on the right hand instead of the left. Other than that, things went as planned. The dinner, which was held at Café du Monde, also went well. The food was good, the conversation interesting and everyone had a nice time.

Jeb and his ushers, all but one of whom were on the Crimson Tide football team, went to his best man Jim's house, to celebrate his "last night of freedom." Jim had been a close friend since boyhood. They were all sons of captains of industry, destined to take over their family's business at some point. Jim had obtained some illegal bath-tub gin, and the group was soon feeling no pain. "Well, you depraved reprobates, here's to the downfall of a great man," Wilford said, raising his glass in a toast.

"No more sorority girls, no more wild women, old boy. It's time to settle down and be domesticated," Dean teased.

"Well, if I had to settle down, someone like Irma Sue would be my choice. Boy, is she good-looking!" Dan said.

FLORIDA GOLD

"Guys, I'm marrying the woman of my dreams and the most beautiful woman in Alabama. What else could any man want?" Their party broke up around one a.m. Jeb went home and crashed onto his bed, asleep before he could even remove his clothes.

Irma Sue and her wedding party were staying at the Battle House Hotel. She went to bed early, lost in her thoughts. How would her new life with Jeb be? Had she made the right decision? But for such doubts, it was too late. Instead, she dreamed of watching romantic sunsets from the deck of their cruise ship, their arms tightly around each other, having breakfast in bed with him, dancing under a glimmering starry sky. She managed to soon fall asleep.

Early in the morning she took a hot bubble bath. Coffee and toast with orange marmalade were brought to her room. But she sipped just a little coffee. Her heart was pounding! Could not everyone in Mobile hear it? The hairdresser came and fixed her hair. Then Margaret and Irma Sue's maid of honor, Janet Jones, whom Irma Sue worked with, came in with a case full of makeup, powder, and rouge. They applied just a little color on Irma Sue's face, and mascara. She should appear fresh and innocent at the altar. Soon it was time to get into the elegant wedding dress.

The bridal gown was ivory silk taffeta with a large portrait swathed neckline set off with a single strand of pearls. The full skirt had interwoven tucking bands and tiny wax flowers. A rose point lace veil was attached to the bride's hair with orange blossoms amid a tiara of lace.

The spacious church was decorated with pink gladioli and white chrysanthemums. The ushers, dressed in black tuxedos, began escorting the 307 guests to their seats. The wedding party soon assembled. George, who would give Irma Sue away, was in the back waiting to escort the bride to the Alter. The five bridesmaids wore pink silk faille gowns with Tudor caps. Margaret was wearing a formal ballerina-length gray satin evening dress with a black velvet hat and ostrich feather. Amanda was wearing a full skirted dress that showed off her waistline. Her hat was a light-gray felt cloche with artificial flowers. Both women were wearing corsages on their shoulders.

Irma Sue walked to the church's entry and stood next to George, who was awed by her beauty. Jack walked through the entry with the rings on a velvet pillow, the flower girl walking beside him, tossing rose petals into the isle. They soon reached the wedding party and Jack gave the rings to the best man.

Then Jeb saw her, and gasped at her breathtaking beauty, as did everyone in the room. The solemn ceremony ran without slips. Then the minister said, "I now pronounce you husband and wife, Jeb, you may kiss the bride." He gently lifted her veil, tilted her chin up to him, and put his arms around her as they kissed tenderly, sweetly, the realization that they were finally married filling each of them with an indescribably sweet joy.

Their guests sensed how incredibly special this moment was to them and the room was very silent while they enjoyed their tender kiss. Then Reverend Jones said, "Ladies and gentlemen, I present to you Mr. and Mrs. Jeb and Irma Sue Walker." The room broke into applause and Irma Sue noticed that her mother was crying, obviously very happy for them. The following coach ride to George and Amanda's home, and the waving to the guests, Irma Sue completed as though in a trance. However, she soon realized that the pressure was finally off and really began to have a good time.

The wedding reception was held in a white tent on the lawn of George and Amanda's home. The menu consisted of pea soup with mint, shrimp, and apples; roast chicken with rice; sirloin of beef; and a six-tiered yellow-butter wedding cake with chocolate filling and white icing, and vanilla, strawberry, and chocolate ice cream.

FLORIDA GOLD

They opened their reception with a waltz that they had practiced just for this occasion. When they finished, the guests applauded, and Jeb noticed his mother-in-law was crying again. While Irma Sue danced with George, Jeb asked Margaret to dance with him. "What's wrong, Margaret?"

"Oh, Jeb, you and Irma Sue are such a beautiful couple and it's obvious that you're both very deeply in love. For many years I've wished for her to have the happiness that she deserves and now that it's happening, I'm overjoyed for both of you. I'm sorry I can't help being so emotional."

"That's OK, Margaret," Jeb said as they continued to dance. Everyone seemed to have a great time at the reception, which was still going strong when, after changing their clothes, Jeb and Irma Sue left about three hours later. Their bags were already packed and loaded into the car, so they headed straight to the Battle House Hotel. They were scheduled to board the train the next morning at 11:15 and go to Savannah, where they would depart on their forty-five-day cruise to Europe.

After the bellman had brought their luggage to their suite, Jeb tipped him and he left. Then Jeb lifted Irma Sue into his arms and carried her over the threshold. Their lips met in an urgent and devouring kiss, each of them caressing the other in the most intimate way as they hurriedly undressed. With a soft, eager sound, she melted against him as he carried her to the bedroom and put her gently on the bed. "Jeb, I want you so badly," she moaned in a voice thick with desire.

"I want you too," he said, his voice cracking with passion.

This was the happiest Irma Sue had ever been. Neither she nor anyone else could have known that she would never get to celebrate her first anniversary, or any other anniversary, with Jeb.

CHAPTER EIGHT

October, 1921. Three months after the wedding.

"Jack, how would you like to go to a dove shoot?" Jeb asked on a Friday night after dinner.

"Boy, would I!"

"I didn't know you knew what a dove shoot was, Jack," said Irma Sue, winking at Jeb.

"I don't, but I bet I'd have fun."

"Dad is organizing one at the ranch. Remember that twenty-five- acre corn field we planted last spring for cattle feed?"

"The one with the watermelons in it?" Jack asked, remembering going out and cutting and eating the tasty melons in the field with Jeb the past July before the wedding.

"Yep. Toby and his crew just finished pulling corn and the birds are coming in. Dad has invited twenty of his friends, and Toby will be barbecuing a pig. We'll eat about one-thirty, and go to the field around three or three thirty. Each of us takes stands throughout the field, and we shoot the doves when they fly over."

"Can I use your .410?"

"That's the plan. When a feller can hit a running rabbit, he's ready to try and hit a flying dove."

"Thanks, Mr. Jeb."

The next morning Jeb, Irma Sue, and an excited Jack loaded their gear into their new car and headed to Spring Creek Ranch. As they turned off the main dirt road onto a rutted one, Irma Sue said, "I don't believe I've been back here before."

"They grow good watermelons in the cornfield," Jack remembered.

"I thought those melons came from Noreen's garden?"

"Some do, but Dad always has a few rows of watermelons planted with the field corn so we can have good melons after the ones in the garden are finished. The field corn is planted about three weeks after the melons in the garden, so those melons ripen later."

The rutted road soon opened up onto the edge of the twenty-five-acre corn field. In the distance under a shady grove of pecan trees there were several cars and trucks, smoke rising from a barbecue pit, and people standing in groups sipping iced tea and talking while others went about various tasks. Southern dove shoots were part social event, part feast, and part ritual. "A dove shoot is the only way to welcome the fall," Jeb remarked as they parked amid the other vehicles.

"Irma Sue, is that your sweet potato pie?" her friend Janet asked as she took the large cloth-covered platter out of the back seat of their car.

"Why, of course. Did you bring your spicy black-eyed peas?"

"Yeah, and Donna brought her crackling cornbread."

Toby and a helper were basting a pig, roasting slowly on a steel grate positioned over oak logs burned down to coals, while women were putting covered dishes on one of three long wooden tables. Noreen was putting plates and eating utensils on the other two tables as one of Toby's helpers drove up on a tractor pulling a wagon with four washtubs, each containing blocks of ice. The washtubs contained holes

FLORIDA GOLD

so the ice water could drain out. Around the ice were Coca-Colas and large glass jars of tea. He got off the tractor and began busting up a block of ice with an ax.

"You gonna shoot that fancy new shotgun today, Jeb?" his friend Jim asked, as he and Jack walked toward a group of men talking, comparing shotguns and sipping iced tea.

"That's why I gave it to him," George said as he walked up. "Hello, Son."

"Hey, Dad."

"I hear Jack's going to be shooting your .410, Jeb." Ron Burns said.

"Yeah."

"If I remember, you were about Jack's age when I gave it to you for your birthday," George remembered.

"That's right. It was for my sixth birthday, and I went to my first dove shoot with it in this same cornfield."

"Jack will probably outshoot all of us," Ron Burns added.

"Even Ben with that fancy automatic," Peter Helms said as Ben Blalock walked up carrying a new semi-automatic shotgun, the action open so everyone could see that the gun was unloaded and safe.

"Does that thing really shoot six times, as fast as you can pull the trigger?" Peter asked.

"Yep. I figure I need all the fire power I can get."

"You just want folks to see that new shotgun in action so they'll buy them from your store," Ed Butler offered and everyone laughed.

Margaret headed to where the women were putting covered dishes on a table, carrying her covered dish of butter beans slow cooked with smoked hog jowls.

"Did you hear about Louise?" asked Irene, a friend of Margaret's from church.

"No, what, is she OK?"

"She caught Jerry with his secretary."

119

"You mean that little blonde tramp. She's young enough to be his daughter," Gladys replied.

"I told her that she should do something about that girl. That kind is always trouble," said Gloria. Where'd she catch them?"

"Jerry said he had to work late, so Louise decided to surprise him with her fried pork chops and biscuits at the office," Irene explained. "She caught them on Jerry's couch."

"Why, that's terrible."

Two of Toby's helpers lifted the pig off the steel barbecue grate, carried it over to the end of the table with the covered dishes, and began slicing it up, putting the slices on a large platter. "Massa Walker, the meat ready," Toby said as he walked up to the group.

"Great, Toby."

The group assembled at the two set tables and stood behind their benches. George walked to the end of one of the tables and said, "Everyone, thank you for coming today. Toby tells me there have been a lot of birds coming into this field in the late afternoons, so I think we may have another good shoot. Let us pray.

"Dear father in heaven, thank you for this day and that we are able to come together as friends and family and enjoy the bounty you have blessed us with. And Lord, please watch over us and keep us safe as we enjoy today's hunt. Amen."

"George, I believe the birds are starting to come in," Ben told him about an hour after everyone had finished stuffing themselves on the succulent, tender roasted pig and the dishes and desserts prepared by the women, each their own specialty. Jeb and Jack were putting shotgun shells in their brown shooting vests while George took three folding camp stools out of the trunk of his car.

"Jack going to sit with you?" George asked.

"Yeah."

FLORIDA GOLD

"Tell you what. Let him sit with you awhile, then come sit with me awhile. I'll be on the next stand down from you. That OK with you, Jack?"

"Yes, sir."

The hunters loaded onto the flat bed wagon pulled by the tractor, each with their gun, action open to show it was unloaded, and a folding camp stool to sit on. The women sat at the tables, some talking while others played gin rummy. After dropping off Ben, then Peter, the tractor went about seventy-five yards and stopped in front of a small pine tree on the edge of the corn-field. About fifty yards behind the pine was a pond surrounded by cypress trees and palmettos.

"Let's go, Jack," Jeb told him.

"Good luck!" the others said.

Jeb and Jack together said, "Good luck to you too."

Jeb was setting up their stools and leaning their unloaded guns against the pine tree when Jack asked, "Are those doves?"

Jeb looked up as five doves dipped down to only about 20 feet above them, then shot upward, dodging back and forth as they flew back toward the pecan hammock where everyone had eaten.

"Those are doves."

Seconds later there was a *boom-boom-boom* and a loud "Damn!"

"Ben must have missed," Jeb observed, grinning. "Jack, we'll take turns and you can go first. Here, put a shell in your gun." Jeb also loaded his. Three ash-colored specks appeared in the distance, heading toward Jeb and Jack. As the trio of birds got closer, diving and zigzagging, still heading their way, Jeb whispered, "Sit still until I tell you, then stand, point, and shoot." The three birds continued their erratic journey, then Jeb said, "Now."

Jack stood, cocked the hammer, aimed at the one in front, and fired. At the shot, the bird veered widely as the trio

121

turned to their right. Jeb fired twice and one bird crumpled and fell.

"Good shooting, Jeb," a disappointed Jack said as Jeb went to pick up the dove.

"Hey, don't feel bad. Most people miss way more than they hit. Let me give you some pointers."

"OK. This sure isn't like shooting rabbits, is it?"

"Nope. When the bird is coming toward you like these were, point the gun underneath him, then swing the barrel through him. When the barrel is in front of his head, shoot. If the bird comes over you from behind, point the barrel above him, then swing the barrel under him and shoot when the barrel is just below him. And if the bird is flying across in front of you, point the barrel behind the bird. Then swing through the bird. When the barrel is about a foot in front of him, shoot.

"So you have to shoot ahead of them?"

"That's right. It's called leading. You have to shoot where the bird's going to be, not where he is."

"Like you showed me for passing a football?"

"Yeah, like that. Get ready. Here comes one from our right."

Jack sat very still. When the bird was about fifteen feet to his right and about twenty-five yards in front of them, he stood, swung the gun as Jeb had instructed and fired. The dove crumpled to the ground.

"Good shooting, Jack!" Jeb congratulated him. Whistles sounded from the field as other hunters, recognizing the "pop" of Jack's small gauge gun, congratulated him with the dove hunters' signaling whistle, usually used to announce birds coming into the field. Jack was shaking with excitement as he went to retrieve his first dove.

"How many did you and Jack end up with, Dad?" Jeb asked as they were unloading back where the tables were about an hour before dark.

FLORIDA GOLD

"I need to count, but I think I got twenty-six and Jack got sixteen, nine of those when he was with you. What about you?"

"Thirty-two, I think," Jeb replied as they walked over to where Toby and his helpers were dressing doves, mainly removing the breast where most of the meat was.

"Did I hear that Jack got sixteen?" Ron Burns asked, walking up.

"Yeah," a proud Jack replied.

"That's pretty good for a first hunt, especially with a single-barrel .410."

"What about you, Ron?"

"Forty-one."

"That be high o' the day," Toby said.

"What's that, three years in a row now?" George asked.

"You know that L. C. Smith fits me like I was born with it," Ron replied modestly. "What about you, Ben? How'd you do with the automatic?"

"Fifteen," Ben said in a low tone.

"FIFTEEN?" Jeb shouted. "You mean Jack beat you with a single-barrel .410?" he announced in a comical tone as other hunters walked up.

"I just need to get used to the gun. I've never fired it before today. Plus, my shoulder is bothering me. I must have slept wrong last night."

"Excuses, excuses," Ron kidded.

Ben and Margaret became engaged the day Jeb and Irma Sue left Savannah for their European cruise. Ben sold his business investments to George for the $9 million he had offered, including his two department stores, and he and Margaret were married on December 29, 1921. They left the next day on a honeymoon and extended travels abroad and weren't scheduled to return until mid-March.

In mid-February, Amanda and Irma Sue, who was four months pregnant, were having lunch. "Have you heard from Margaret and Ben recently?" Amanda asked.

"Yeah, just a few days ago I got a letter from Milano. They're bicycling across Italy, and it sounded like they were having the time of their lives."

"That's great. Irma Sue, I wanted us to plan Jack's birthday."

"Yeah, I was also thinking about it. It's Wednesday of next week."

"Jeb is going to give him a new 20 gauge double-barrel shotgun. Then he and George are taking him quail hunting in Albany, and he'll get to shoot his new shotgun."

"Yeah, Jeb told me. That's great. I know Jack will have a wonderful time."

"The other thing he's been talking about is going to Carnival. His classmates have been talking about it, so I think we should plan to take him. We have only been a few times, because it's so crowded and noisy, but everyone needs to experience the Mobile Carnival at least once."

"I hear it's the oldest carnival celebration in the United States."

"Yes, that's true. It was actually how Mardi Gras started."

"Why don't we plan to take Jack next Wednesday, on his birthday? Then we can have a birthday dinner at our house afterward."

"That sounds good to me."

Digger Sims, fifty-one years old, stood about five foot eight inches, had a round pot belly, and was partially bald. His dark, beady eyes seemed to always dart back and forth and would never make contact with whomever he was talking to. He always seemed nervous, as if he were about to get caught doing something wrong. If there was a scam, Digger had been involved in it - peddling "miracle medicines" that were really

FLORIDA GOLD

just concoctions laced with morphine, cheating at cards, pick pocketing, selling Florida swampland to unsuspecting buyers, smuggling illegal whiskey across the Mexican border. Digger was always only a few steps ahead of the law. His latest venture was the worst, however, because unlike the others, people were hurt, both emotionally and physically. It was also his most profitable venture.

State child-labor laws enacted between 1909 and 1918 in Florida, Georgia, Alabama, and various other states made it unlawful for children under the age of fifteen to work except in agriculture. Then, it was required that they be the natural children of the farmer who owned the farm they were working on. Prior to this, orphanages had been a good source of child labor for unethical farmers, who worked them mercilessly. In fact it was some of the horror stories from these "child work camps" that contributed to the awareness that child agricultural labor laws were needed.

Digger's new scheme was kidnapping young boys and selling them to unscrupulous farmers as child labor. At $200 to $300 each, depending on the boy's age, the pay was the best he'd ever made. The economics for the crooked farmer made sense. An adult male farm worker in 1921 earned $3 a day as pay, for a six-day work week. The price of the kidnapped boys between the ages of seven and twelve, the oldest most farmers would accept them (older boys just captured were too difficult to control), was one-third the annual cost of an adult worker. Even allowing for food, clothing, and shelter, such as it was, and the fact that the boy worker was, on average, only about half as productive as a man would have been, it meant that the boy's price was paid back in about a year from the savings over hiring men. The farmers kept the boys until they were fifteen or sixteen, when they became too big of an escape risk. They were then simply tied and blindfolded, taken miles into the woods, untied, and left. The farmers was able to avoid getting caught because the boys never really knew where they were, and they were warned if they escaped alive and brought the law, all the boys in the camp would be killed. This concern also kept law enforcement from aggressively pursuing the boy slaves.

Nobody really knew the boys' ages. They were just judged by size. But the captured boys usually told them how old they were. The child labor farms would probably not have worked with independent farmers, because people in town would have ultimately figured out that something about the farm wasn't right, particularly if they visited. So the successful child labor camps were owned and operated by timber companies, on their tens of thousands of acres of private property, with no trespassing signs and locked gates at all entry ways. The landowners' incentive was that farming crops like cotton, tobacco, and peanuts with cheap child labor was much more profitable per acre than turpentine or logging, but unfortunately the market would not support nearly the acreage. The labor camp operators were legally lessees who sharecropped the land from the timber company. That way, if they were caught, the timber company thought it was not liable.

Digger usually scouted a new place for likely boys to capture, and preferred those from poor families that were young, about seven to nine. That way, the parents couldn't afford to pursue him as aggressively, and the younger boys were easier to control. But this time, he'd gone on a three-day drunk, lying up with various prostitutes, and had run out of time. He drove to the carnival in Mobile, parked his car, stuffed a rag and small bottle of ether into his pocket, grabbed some matches and a couple of firecrackers, and began to stalk through the large crowd.

Amanda, Irma Sue, and Jack got to the carnival at three thirty on February 22, the afternoon of his birthday. George and Jeb weren't coming. They would meet them at seven for

FLORIDA GOLD

dinner at George and Amanda's house. "What do you want to do first?" Irma Sue shouted over the loud crowd.

"I wanna ride the Ferris wheel."

"I think it's this way," Amanda shouted.

She led the way through the crowd, with Jack following and Irma Sue behind. Suddenly there was a loud bang. Everyone looked in its direction, and a woman screamed, thinking it had been gunfire. In the confusion Digger grabbed Jack, put the ether-soaked rag to his nose and mouth, and carried the limp boy away as if he were simply a sleeping child. No one paid any attention.

"Where's Jack?" Irma Sue shouted anxiously.

"I don't see him!" Amanda yelled excitedly. "We just need to calm down. I'm sure he got lost in the crowd in the confusion when the firecracker exploded."

"OK, OK."

They continued to search for about half an hour, starting with the Ferris wheel, repeatedly calling Jack's name, but he was nowhere to be found.

"Let's call George on this pay phone," Amanda suggested.

"First Community Bank," a female voice answered.

"Hey, Joan, it's Amanda."

"I'll connect you with George right away, ma'am."

"Hey, Amanda, is Jack enjoying the carnival?"

"George, we can't find him, he's disappeared."

"What?" Amanda told him what had happened.

"I'll get Jeb and we'll come right over. Jeb will bring the birthday party picture of Jack he has on his desk. Meet us at the carnival entrance."

In about twenty minutes George and Jeb walked to the entrance and met Irma Sue and Amanda. "Mister, where are the people in charge of the carnival?" George asked a ticket clerk. He gave them directions and they were soon knocking on the door of an office in a trailer.

127

"Yes?" a man replied as he answered the door.

"I'm George Walker, he said extending his hand.

"Ken Sanders," the man said in response as they shook hands.

"This is my family," George said, and then he explained the situation and Jeb gave him the picture of Jack.

"I'll have my people thoroughly search the park. Don't worry, we'll find him. It would probably be best if you wait in here," he suggested as he motioned toward a couch and chairs.

"I'm not waiting, I want to go with them," Irma Sue said.

"I understand, ma'am, but you'll just slow us down."

"Let's let them do their job, Irma Sue," Jeb suggested.

"OK."

About an hour later, Ken came back in with a worried look on his face. "I'm sorry but I don't think he's here anywhere. We also asked people if they'd seen anything that might look like a boy being taken by force, but none had."

"What do you think happened?" Jeb asked.

"A child labor dealer probably took him. We had that happen last year in New Orleans," Ken explained.

"OH MY GOD, NO!" Amanda shrieked.

"Now dear, calm down. We don't know for sure that's what happened," George offered.

"What's a child labor dealer?" Irma Sue asked.

Jeb explained it to her, and she burst into tears.

"Now let's not jump to conclusions," George told them. "I'm going to call Police Chief Burns and get him right on this."

The police chief agreed with Ken, that it was probably a labor dealer. He sent his police all over town checking with people to see if they'd seen anything, and he put up roadblocks on all the roads leading out of the city and at the port.

FLORIDA GOLD

It didn't matter. By the time the roadblocks were up, Digger was over fifty miles out of town, headed to a large farm in the woods north of Blountstown, Florida, about two hundred miles away. They had been traveling for about two hours when Jack began to wake up.

"Where am I?" he asked groggily. "And why are my hands tied? And who are you?"

"We're takin' a little trip."

"Where?"

"To a nice boy's camp out in the woods. You'll get lots of fresh air, sunshine, and exercise."

"Why are my hands tied?"

"'Cause, I don't want you to try and escape from this wonderful adventure."

"Where're my sister and Mrs. Amanda?"

"OK, enough questions. Sit still and SHUT UP or I'll give you a whipping!" he said as he showed Jack a heavy razor strap. The backseat had bars over the windows and doors and between it and the front, effectively making it into a cage. It was the same setup sometimes used to transport prisoners, and so drew no attention. When Digger was transporting a boy, he was usually asleep from the ether or it was after dark. When it wasn't he had black curtains he put over the bars between the back and front seats and between the side windows and the bars.

They stopped in the woods about a hundred miles from Blountstown and Digger relieved himself. "Need to go?" he asked.

"Yeah," Jack replied.

"Put on that harness in the seat next to you."

"Why?"

"So you don't run off. Now, if you want to go, PUT IT ON!"

Jack obeyed, and Digger opened the rear door and let Jack out, grabbing the strap on the harness and then untying

129

Jack's hands. When Jack was through, he loaded him back into the car. Then he went behind a bush where he had hidden a five-gallon can of gasoline, which he filled up the tank with. He didn't want to take the risk of Jack being seen at a gasoline station. When he got back to the car, he took two ham sandwiches out of a sack along with two Coca-Colas. "Hungry?" he asked. He liked the boys fed before they got to the farms, because they were in a better mood than they would be on an empty stomach.

"Yeah." Not knowing what was going to happen to him, Jack decided to eat while he had the chance.

When they were on their way again, Digger asked, "What's your name?"

"What's yours?"

"They call me Digger."

"I'm Jack."

"How old are you, Jack?"

"Today's my seventh birthday."

"Well, happy birthday."

He's one of the smart ones, Digger thought. *Not struggling to escape because he knows he cain't, eating because he's not sure when his next meal will be.*

About thirty miles west of Blountstown, Digger pulled off the road and put the black curtains in place. "Cain't have you knowin' where you're a goin'," Digger explained. On the way he took a couple of detours to further confuse Jack about what direction they were taking. It was after eleven when they arrived at the entrance to the twenty-six-thousand-acre acre turpentine and timber operation where the farm was located. At the entrance were a locked gate and a sign that said "Amalgamated Land Company. No Trespassing. Trespassers Will Be Shot." Digger used his key to open the gate and enter. He had notified the farmer, Zeke Judd, that he would be coming with a boy tonight and Zeke was waiting.

FLORIDA GOLD

"We're here, boy," Digger said as he got out of the car and let Jack out. About a hundred feet to their left, several mongrel dogs were barking loudly and rearing up against the pen that held them.

"Not that again," Jack said in a desperate tone as Digger got the harness out of the car.

"Just a precaution," he said as he was putting the harness on Jack. "If you try to escape, the dogs will get you afore you git far, and if not, there's the gators an' bears. But you don't know that yet, and if you git kilt, I don't git paid, so this here will protect both our interests."

As they walked across the area toward the house, Jack shivered in the cold night, the silver light of the half-moon casting eerie shadows as the cold breeze swayed the limbs on nearby pine trees. *Will those dogs ever stop barking?* Jack thought.

The white paint was peeling off the modest wooden house, and when they stepped onto the front porch the unpainted wooden floor creaked with their every step. A kerosene lamp on the wall next to the door added to the meager light from the moon.

"Digger, you're late," Zeke growled as he opened the door before they had a chance to knock. Zeke, fifty-five years old, was of medium height, partially bald, and about thirty-five pounds overweight with an excitable demeanor about him, resulting in a quick temper. A "type A personality" by today's definitions.

"Findin quality takes time."

"Come on in and let's get a look at this boy. Digger, he's only a squirt." Zeke always did this to try to get the price down.

"He's bigger than the average seven-year-old." At four foot three and sixty-three pounds, Jack was about the size of an eight-year-old boy.

"He's not worth $200. I'll give you $175."

131

"Yeah he is, I told you he's big for his age, and probably strong."

"OK, let's see. Jack, I bet you can't lift that fifty pound sack of flour over there five times."

"Not with this harness on."

"OK, take it off."

Jack did, then darted for the door. But a black employee who was positioned in the shadows just outside the door grabbed him. Zeke back handed him across the face, making his nose bleed slightly. "Don't try anything like that again, boy," he threatened.

"At least he's got spunk," Digger observed.

"That's OK, we'll break that. As long as he's got a strong back we don't care about anything else. What did he have in his pockets, anything valuable?"

"Nah."

"He took my cross!"

"Your cross? OK, Digger, hand it over."

"HERE," Digger said, reaching in his pocket.

"Hmm, probably a family keepsake. Here, boy, you can keep it."

"Thanks, Mr. Judd."

"It might be worth something. We could sell it and split what we get," said Digger.

"Don't you know nothing about working people? Yeah, we might be able to sell it for a few dollars. Then I'd have a boy that was so upset it'd be a week or so before I could get anything out of him. I let the boys keep little things like this that they have from home. It keeps them in better spirits, so they work better."

"What about my $200?" Digger asked.

"OK, OK, $200," Zeke finally agreed as he gave Digger four $50 bills.

132

FLORIDA GOLD

"It was a pleasure doin' bidness with you, Zeke," Digger said. "Oh, I need my harness." Zeke handed it to him and he left.

In the days following Jack's abduction, a major search was launched, but they found nothing. For boys taken by child labor dealers they usually didn't. They saw to it that every major newspaper in the Southeast got a picture of Jack and the story of his abduction, and announced that George Walker had put up a $3,000 reward for anyone bringing Jack back alive or providing information leading to his safe return, but other than attracting a lot of false leads from opportunists and crack pots, it did no good.

Although it took a couple of weeks to track them down, they contacted Ben and Margaret, who promptly returned to Mobile. The whole family was distraught, particularly Irma Sue and Margaret.

Willis, the black man who had grabbed Jack, was one of the boys' two black guard/supervisors. Zeke preferred black supervisors because in the 1920s South, it was an insult and belittling for white boys to be supervised by black men. What it mostly did was engender sympathy for the boys from the black workers, who understood all too well about slavery from the stories told by their grandparents. Willis led Jack to a gray two-story wood frame barracks and into its dimly-lit interior. "This where you gon' live, boy."

The first floor consisted of a mess hall with two long tables and benches that each sat twelve, and a kitchen with a pitcher pump and sink for water, kerosene stoves and ovens, an icebox, and a food preparation table. The second floor was a dormitory for sleeping twenty boys, with a narrow bed, linens, a pillow, and a blanket for each. The large windows and high ceiling ensured air circulation. Limited light came from kerosene lamps hanging from hooks on the overhead rafters. The bathroom had twelve toilets, and there were

133

twelve shower heads in a large open shower room. There was a small separate room at each end of the barracks where the two guards lived. In separate isolated rooms were two cells for boys who misbehaved or broke the rules. The cells' conditions were basic and sparse – a blanket on the hard floor, a towel, and a tin pan to wash in. Out back was a large wood-fired iron wash pot for boiling clothes, wash-tubs and wash-boards for cleaning them, and clothes lines for hanging them on. The boys were expected to clean the barracks, bathroom, and shower and do their own laundry on Sundays.

Willis led Jack upstairs and showed him to his tiny bed. The other boys were asleep, exhausted from a day plowing in the fields. "Ain't no reason to try an escape. You fifteen mile from a hard road, thirty from town, an' they's swamps, gators, bears, and panthers in them woods. We also gots hounds to track you down, an' when you foun', thangs git real nasty. Now git to bed."

Jack climbed into bed, and stared at the ceiling. When everything was dark and quiet, just-turned-seven-year-old Jack began to cry softly. *I wonder if I will ever see Mama, Irma Sue, Mr. Jeb, or any of my family again, he thought. What's going to happen to me?* Then Jack remembered the ivory cross. He held it to his heart and prayed, "Dear God. Please help me to not be afraid and be alright. And God, try to keep Mama, Irma Sue, Mr. Jeb, and Mr. and Mrs. Walker from worrying too much about this 'cause I know you're gonna protect me. And help Mr. Burns find me. In Jesus' name I pray, Amen."

At five a.m., the other black guard/supervisor, Fuller, began beating a tin pan and repeatedly shouted, "TIME TO GET UP!" The kerosene lamps were all lit as the boys scrambled out of bed. We gots a new boy. What yo name, boy?"

"Jack Thomas."

FLORIDA GOLD

"Call me sir when you's talkin' to me."

"Yes, sir."

"Well, Jack you gots forty-five minutes to use the toilet, dress, an' eat. Then you go to de barn behind de barracks."

Jack went to the bathroom, but all the toilets were being used. He had no clothes but the ones he was wearing, so he went downstairs to eat.

"What you doin' in here now?" the fat black cook yelled. "The food ain't gon' be ready fo about twenty minutes. You must be dat new boy."

"Jack Thomas."

"Call me ma'am when you's talkin' to me!" she shouted.

"Yes, ma'am."

Jack went back upstairs and found an available toilet. Afterward, he washed his hands and face and went back to his bed. There were four pair of blue denim overalls, seven cotton shirts, and some underwear and socks, including one pair of long johns on the bed. A pair of work boots was on the floor next to the bed. "Them's yo new clothes," Willis told him.

Jack dressed and went downstairs to the mess hall. The boys were getting their breakfast - fried bacon, corn-meal mush, milk, and two biscuits - from a serving line and finding places at the tables.

"Jack Thomas, huh?" asked a skinny, red-haired, freckle-faced boy who looked about ten.

"Yeah. You?"

"Harry Osborne. Where you from?"

"Mobile. You?"

"Jacksonville."

"How long have you been here?"

"About a year. Caught when I was nine. It's hard to keep track because there are no calendars."

"What about our schooling?"

"Ain't none. We work sun up to sun down, six days a week, then clean this place and wash clothes on Sundays."

"Is there a church?"

"Nope. There are four rules you need to obey to survive here: never complain, don't try to escape, do what you're told, and address all adults - Negro or white - by sir, ma'am, Mr., or Mrs."

"Thanks. I'm not going to the field. They told me to go out to the barn."

"Me too. The work in the fields now is plowing and disking to get the fields ready to plant the crops in April. They don't use boys under eleven for that. Our main work in the field will be planting the crops, hoeing weeds, picking cotton and tobacco, digging peanuts, and pulling corn for horse and mule feed. We'll also bail hay, grind cane, and make syrup in the fall. The other times, the three of us that are under eleven are used for chores around here such as cleaning out stalls, planting and tending the vegetable garden, washing dishes, gathering eggs, milking the cows, that sort of thing. Today, I think we're going to help with a hog killing. It will be the second one this year, and probably the last one until next year."

There was a large fire in front of the barn with a large three-legged iron wash pot about three feet wide and thirty inches deep over it. Jack and Harry walked up to the fire and another boy was already there. It was cold, about thirty-five degrees, and Jack was shivering without a jacket as he warmed his hands over the fire.

"You look cold," the boy observed.

"Yeah. Hey, I'm Jack Thomas."

"Teddy Parker."

"Ever been to a hog killin', Jack?" Teddy asked.

"Yeah, when I was five and we operated a turpentine camp, but I don't remember much."

FLORIDA GOLD

"Well, you'll learn soon enough," Teddy explained. "They like to have them on cold days, because the meat keeps better."

Just as it was getting daylight a number of men came up in two pick-up trucks and Zeke came out of the farm house with a teenage boy that looked to be his son.

Everyone gathered around the fire, and Zeke said, "Most of y'all know my sixteen-year-old boy, Blaine. Well, he's going to be in charge of the hog killin' today."

"Let's git the .22 loaded an git to it, then," Blaine said, obviously cocky with what he viewed as this important responsibility. "Arnold, you shoot 'em, and Jethro, you stick 'em. Phil, you, Ed, and Joe scald 'em and scrape 'em. Mack, you and Dub gut 'em. The men had butchered hogs many times and each had their own specialty, although everyone scraped carcasses and trimmed meat for sausage and lard. The butchering needed no supervision and Zeke knew it, but Blaine was too stupid to. Zeke felt that he was giving his son valuable management experience.

"You must be Jack, the new squirt," Blaine teased.

"Yeah."

"'Yes, sir' to you!"

"Yes, sir."

"That's better. Harry is squirt one and Teddy is squirt two, so I reckon that makes you squirt three. That OK with you?"

"Yes, sir."

"The three squirts," Blaine taunted while Jack suppressed his anger at this buffoon.

Arnold positioned himself on top of the rail fence around the hog pen with the .22 rifle while Jethro sat on the left side of him. When they were in place, someone herded a group of hogs toward them and Arnold fired a small .22 caliber bullet into the head of a 230-pound hog, which dropped immediately. Jethro jumped off the fence with his sharp knife

137

and, turning the hog onto its back, inserted the blade at the base of its throat, plunging the knife downward toward the breast bone. Blood immediately spurted out of the jugular vein. Sticking, or bleeding the hog was important so the meat wouldn't be saturated with blood. "Jack, why don't you learn to be a shooter?" Blaine suggested. "Get on the fence next to Arnold so he can show you where to shoot the hog."

"OK, sir," Jack replied as he climbed onto the rail fence.

"I try to hit 'em between the eyes, just above the eye line," Arnold was explaining when Blaine sharply shoved Jack off the fence and face-down into the hog pen below. Then Blaine began to laugh tauntingly. No one else thought it was funny as Jack got up, covered in wet muck on the cold morning, and tried to brush off the mud and hog feces.

"Well, didn't anyone else think that was funny?" Blaine yelled. At that a couple of the workers laughed half-heartedly. Most just glared at Blaine. After all, Jack was only a little boy and it was a cold morning. "You stink, hog squirt three," Blaine teased, and laughed again.

"Yes, sir," Jack replied respectfully, struggling to control his rage. At that, Arnold and Phil grabbed Blaine and dragged him, struggling and shouting profanities, to the edge of the hog pen, lifted him over the fence, and threw him in. On seeing this, one of the men had run into the house to get Zeke. He got there just as Blaine was getting out, and he saw Jack, already covered in muck.

"I want them all horsewhipped!" Blaine yelled. "Jack tried to make it look like I shoved him into the pen to get the men riled up so they'd throw me in."

"Is that true, Jack?" Zeke asked.

"No, sir. Blaine asked Arnold to teach me how to shoot the hogs, and when I was on the fence, Blaine pushed me into the pen."

"That's how it happen, Mr. Judd," one of the workers said.

FLORIDA GOLD

"Does everyone agree with Jack and Ed?" All nodded silently. Zeke knew nobody would be dumb enough to jump into the hog pen muck without being shoved. So he said, "OK, let's get back to butchering. Blaine, you come with me."

"But Daddy, I..."

"NOW!"

"Can I go clean up, Mr. Judd?" Jack asked.

"Yeah, yeah, go ahead," Zeke replied. What the incident did was reinforce to the men what a mean idiot Blaine was, and what strong character Jack had, even as a little boy, for not losing his temper or crying.

When they were inside, Zeke shouted, "SIT DOWN." Blaine silently obeyed. "Do you actually think I'm stupid enough to believe anyone would willingly jump into that hog muck?"

"But Daddy, I was just trying to show the men that I was tough and in charge."

"By picking on a seven-year-old boy? What you showed the men was that you're mean and stupid. Now you may never be able to supervise them. Well, this was the last time," Zeke said, remembering all the other dumb mistakes Blaine had made with the men. "Maybe if you go back to school and get an education you can get an office job somewhere. You're just not cut out to manage men."

"But Daddy...!"

"That's it. But this time you're going to boarding school so you're not around those idiot friends of yours. They're a bad influence. I think a military school might teach you some discipline. My uncle went to Carlisle in Bamberg, South Carolina. I think that may be the place for you. Since we have family that is alumni, maybe your low grades won't keep you out."

"I ain't goin'!"

"Don't talk back to me, boy," Zeke said, backhanding him across the face. "You're goin' and that's final!"

139

ROBERT ALLEN MORRIS

Two men pulled the hog out and over to the wash pot of hot water and doused him several times in the pot. Then men came forward with bell-shaped tools and began to scrape the hair off the hog, which, after scalding, released the hair readily. This process was repeated until ten hogs were killed, stuck, and scalded. Then slits were cut in the Achilles tendons in their back legs and the hogs were hung up by inserting hooks underneath the Achilles tendons, their heads down.

After taking a shower and changing clothes, Jack came out of the barracks and walked up to Arnold, who was shaving a hog carcass. "Here," Arnold said as he handed Jack a straight razor. "Ever shave a hog?"

"No, sir."

"It's easy. Just tilt the razor slightly and shave off the little remains of hair." The hog carcasses, already stripped of most of their hair, were being shaved to get the last of it off.

Mack, Dub, and Ed went to the shaved hogs and made a cut from between the hind legs to the breast bone. They then began to peel out the hogs' lungs, heart, liver, stomach, and intestines, using a knife to cut these lose from the backbone as they expertly peeled downward. Four of the fresh livers were taken inside where black cooks were frying them as a treat. They were soon brought out and Jack got to taste the first fried fresh pork liver he could remember. *It's excellent*, he thought as he gobbled chunks of the succulent, pungent organ.

Next, the carcasses were laid out on tables, and the hind quarters were cut and trimmed into hams. The back strap, or loin, was removed next to each side of the backbone, and one shoulder from each hog was removed. The other would be cut up for sausage. Then the ribs were cut away from the carcass, leaving the middle for bacon. The hams, shoulders, loins, and slabs of bacon would first go into a heavy salt solution for several days to preserve them, then into the smokehouse. All the rest would be cut into chunks, ground

FLORIDA GOLD

and seasoned for sausage after the fat under the skin had been cut off and cut into cubes for cooking into lard. The cubes of meat for sausage would be stuffed into a casing, made by running water through a length of small intestine to clean it out. This fresh sausage would then be put into the smokehouse with the other meat. The lungs, called lights, were hung on a clothesline and water poured down the esophagus to fill the lungs. The water-filled lungs were then trimmed along the edges, releasing the water in small streams, cleaning out the lungs. These would be stewed and fed to the boys in the barracks, as would the pork hearts. Jack, Harry, and Teddy were all busy cutting the meat into cubes for lard and sausage as were most of the rest of the crew when the other butchering was done.

Lunch was fried pork, corn bread, and mustard greens. The fresh fried pork was very good. One of the helpers took the same lunch to the workers in the field. Once the butchering was done, around five thirty, the wash pot used to scald the hogs was cleaned out, another fire was built under it, and the cubes of pork fat were dumped into it to cook down into lard and cracklings, the fried remnants of the pork fat and skin.

By dark, everyone was sitting around the fire. Cracklings were skimmed off and taken into the house where they were put into crackling cornbread, which was then served for dinner out by the fire, along with buttermilk, fried fresh pork sausages, and butter beans. Zeke was not a nice or generous man, but even he knew the value of well-fed workers.

Blaine never showed up at Carlisle. Zeke got a telegram from the school that he hadn't been on the train when it arrived. *He must have jumped off somewhere along the route and run away*, Zeke thought. *That boy never was right*.

As the days grew into weeks, Jack thought almost constantly about his family in Mobile. He missed his mother and Irma Sue, and his new family, Jeb and the Walkers.

Remembering the many good times he enjoyed in the brief period that he was in Mobile was his only happy thoughts. Horseback riding and fishing at Spring Creek Ranch, that first Christmas at the Walker's ranch house, his first dove shoot and quail hunt. He was terribly homesick. The ivory cross was comforting. But it was something Mr. Walker had told him that enabled him to cope with his situation the best. *Jack, life isn't fair. Some folks have it a lot worse than others. But it's how you deal with it that counts. It's how you deal with the pain, dangers, risks, challenges, and most important, the choices that you face, that really counts. That's what determines the man you will grow up to be.*

Jack soon settled into his new life. It really wasn't unbearable. The days were long and the work exhausting, but they had good food to eat, clothes to wear, and a roof over their heads. Things could have been much worse. If only he'd known just how bad they would get.

Things were not going well with the Walkers and Blalocks back in Mobile. Irma Sue and Margaret were devastated, and horror stories about the child farm labor camps told by well-meaning friends made things much worse. Irma Sue was in such a state of worry and grief that she hadn't gained the amount of weight she was supposed to, and she didn't sleep very well either. Her doctor kept warning her that she could lose the baby if she didn't get more rest and sleep, but she just couldn't. In June, when she was eight months pregnant, Irma Sue began bleeding and went into labor. They rushed her to Providence Hospital.

"Everything's going to be fine, Irma Sue," Jeb said, trying to calm her down.

"But Jeb, the baby's a month early!"

"Doctor Richardson is the best, he'll take care of you and our baby," Jed replied, very worried.

142

FLORIDA GOLD

Two men rolled a gurney out to their car, lifted her onto it, and began pushing her inside the hospital, Jeb walking alongside, holding her hand. Jeb's parents and Margaret and Ben arrived shortly and were directed to a waiting room. Everyone was worried, because Jeb's call had sounded alarming. Bleeding and going into labor a month early was serious in 1922.

"Mr. Walker, your family is here, but the doctor doesn't want her to have visitors."

"OK, can you give them an update on her condition?"

"Certainly, when we know more."

The doctor gave her a mild pain medication and she was able to relax. Then, as he was preparing for the delivery, she screamed, blood began spewing from under her gown, and she went into convulsions. "It's a ruptured uterus! Nurse, bring me a scalpel and sponges!"

"She passed out!" Jeb exclaimed.

The doctor listened for a heartbeat and could find none.

"I'm sorry, son. We've lost her."

"NO! NO...!"

"Maybe I can save the baby! Scalpel."

"Yes, Doctor," the nurse replied as she handed him the scalpel.

"And take him out of here."

"Come on, Mr. Walker, I'll take you to your family," another nurse said soothingly to Jeb, who was sobbing.

"What's going on, Jeb?" George asked.

He was unable to speak, so the nurse explained the situation to everyone. Margaret fainted, and Ben caught her as she was falling. George and Amanda begin consoling Jeb. A few minutes later, the solemn doctor walked into the waiting room.

"I'm sorry folks, I couldn't save him."

"It was a boy?" George asked.

"Yeah, your first grandson, George," Doctor Richardson answered.

"I NEED TO GET OUT OF HERE!" Jeb shouted anxiously.

"You don't need to drive in your state of mind, Son, I'll go with you," George offered.

"NO, I just need to be alone," Jeb replied as he hurried out of the hospital, tears streaming down his cheeks. The two families went to George and Amanda's house to grieve together, hoping Jeb would return and join them soon. About half an hour after they got home, there was a knock on the door.

"Yes?" George said as he opened the door. It was Police Chief Ron Burns.

"George, can you come out side?"

"What's up?"

"I hate to tell you this, but we just found Jeb's car crashed into an oak tree where Government Street makes that sharp left and turns into Fulton Road. It was still burning when we got there, and the body inside is almost unrecognizable. But we think its Jeb because of the Crimson Tide ring on his finger. Can you come and identify that it's him?"

George began to hyperventilate and Ron grabbed him as he staggered. "George, are you OK?" Ben asked as he came out to see what was going on. George was crying.

"Ben, I'm afraid it's Jeb. He's been in an accident," Ron explained.

"Was he hurt?"

"He was killed, Ben!" George screeched. "In less than two hours I've lost my daughter-in-law, my grandson, and my son!"

"Irma Sue and the baby?" Ron asked incredulously. By this time, Amanda and Margaret had come outside and Ron told them the awful news. Then he called for an ambulance. Luckily, Ben was able to take charge of the situation. George,

FLORIDA GOLD

Amanda, and Margaret were taken to the hospital, given sedatives and put into rooms to sleep. When they were asleep, Ben went and identified the body.

CHAPTER NINE

April 6, 1925. Three years later.

"Mr. Judd, I think I've come up with a way to increase your profits and give us boys Saturday afternoons off," ten-year-old Jack said.

"Now why in hell would I want to give you boys Saturday afternoons off?"

"Because it's part of what will increase your profits."

"I don't have time for bullshit, now git on that wagon and git to the field."

"Yes, sir."

Zeke kept thinking about what Jack had tried to tell him. What if he had a good idea? He was definitely the smartest boy in the camp. And 25 percent of the increased profits would be Zeke's. A combination of greed and curiosity led him to ride out at lunch time to the field where Jack was planting corn.

"Massa Judd want to talk wif you," Willis told Jack.

Jack went over to Zeke's truck. "Yes, sir?"

"Explain the idea you got that'll make me more money."

"It's called positive incentives."

"What?"

"You make people want to work harder because they personally benefit from it."

147

ROBERT ALLEN MORRIS

"How?"

"With us boys, set weekly goals that result in more work getting done than now. Then for those that achieve them, give them Saturday afternoon off and a dollar."

"If y'all could do more, why not just threaten to beat you if you don't?"

"Because that's negative incentive, and it actually results in less work because the workers fear and hate you."

"Boy, you been out in the sun too long. That's the stupidest thing I ever heard."

"It worked when my father, Pete Thomas, used it in turpentine camps he managed for the Amalgamated Land Company."

"Your daddy was Pete Thomas?"

"Yes, sir, he was."

"You're not old enough to remember that."

"My mother and sister told me about it."

Zeke had heard about how much more profitable Pete's operation was than the others, and he wondered how he did it. Zeke wasn't about to tell Jack that Amalgamated owned this labor camp. Maybe this idea would work.

"Come see me after supper and let's discuss it some more."

"Yes, sir." Jack's heart raced with excitement as he went to gobble down his lunch.

Zeke agreed to give Jack's idea a try. They would start the next Monday. On Saturday after work, Zeke would announce the changes to all the boys after telling the supervisor/guards. It would be told as Jack's idea, because he would take the blame and get the beating if it failed. Jack would answer questions if asked.

"Harry, we need to get everyone together," Jack said in a low tone at dinner. "I want to tell them about something."

"Tomorrow night while Willis and Fuller are taking their showers."

FLORIDA GOLD

"OK. Let's spread the word."

The next night the boys hurriedly assembled in the barracks bedroom. "We don't have much time, so I'll be quick," Jack began. "I've convinced Zeke to give us Saturday afternoons off and a dollar a week each if we work harder."

"What? No way," Martin, a twelve-year-old, replied.

"No, this is for real. We've got to show that the time off and the dollar make us get more done than we do now," Jack explained.

"You mean I'm finally going to have to work my ass off?" Gary, an eleven-year-old, asked.

"Only if you want Saturday afternoons off and a dollar a week. Those that aren't interested don't have to participate. But if enough of us don't do this, he'll stop the program. Because for it to work, he's got to make more money, which means being able to farm more acreage with the same amount of labor."

"What we gonna do with money in this place?" Edwin, an eleven-year-old asked.

"You'll have it when you get out. A dollar a week is fifty-two dollars a year. And I know we'd all like Saturday afternoons off."

"Yeah, shit-for-brains!" Harry added

"Ever think when we get out of this hellhole, money for a bus ticket or train ticket and a few meals might be helpful?" Harry added.

"How'd you get him to try this?" Danny, a thirteen-year-old, asked.

"My father used to do things like this in turpentine camps and he had the most profitable camps in his company. Zeke remembers that. He wants to do it to put more money in his pockets." The boys debated it for a few minutes, then agreed it was worth a try.

"Remember guys, you haven't heard about this yet," Jack warned.

149

On Saturday after everyone had returned from the fields and taken showers, Zeke explained the new incentive-based work plan. "We're going to give it a month as a test," he explained. "Willis and Fuller will have work goals for you starting Monday. If you don't meet them, the test is over and Jack gets a lashing with the whip."

"Can we skip our lesson tonight?" Harry asked. "I'm kind of tired."

"Sure," Jack replied. For the past year, Harry had been teaching Jack how to read, write, and do arithmetic three nights a week. Harry had been nine and in the fourth grade when he was abducted, and his mother had been a school teacher. When he'd gone to Zeke about Harry giving him lessons, Zeke had said fine, as long as it didn't affect their work. They'd gotten some school books from Zeke's wife, Helen, who at one time had also been a school teacher. Jack was a fast learner, and they'd about covered all that Harry could teach him. In the process, Jack and Harry had become close friends.

The boys exceeded the work goals set by Willis and Fuller, and Zeke grudgingly admitted that Jack's idea had worked. Since they finished the planting several weeks early, Zeke had the boys clearing land for additional acreages of crops to be planted the following year.

Jack also convinced Zeke to let his wife teach school to the boys that wanted schooling, which was about half of them. Blaine had been killed in a failed bank robbery. Apparently he'd tried to shoot one of the bank guards and the revolver misfired, whereupon Blaine looked down the barrel to see what was wrong and pulled the trigger, blowing a hole in his head. Upon hearing the news, Helen had become depressed, and Jack pointed out that teaching might cheer her up, which it did. However, Zeke had insisted that the boys each give back twenty-five cents per week for the lessons.

FLORIDA GOLD

They'd agreed, and so met with Helen for school on Saturday afternoons and Saturday nights after supper.

About three years later, Zeke suffered a heart attack, but survived. "Mr. Judd," the doctor had said, "it's time to slow down and retire, or you might have another heart attack and not survive that one." Zeke had enough to retire on, especially with the additional money he'd made over the past three years using Jack's employee incentive ideas.

Amalgamated found a new lessee for the expanded farm, Harlan Kirkland, who moved there with his wife, Theresa, a month before Zeke was to leave, to learn his way around. Harlan was forty-four, over six feet tall, and muscular, with red hair that was usually dirty, and a deceptive, sleazy look about him.

On a Saturday morning in late October of 1928, Zeke and his wife left for Lake City, where they were going to live in retirement. That morning the boys and supervisors assembled to bid farewell, although most were glad to see him go. Harlan seemed like he would be a much more agreeable and easygoing boss than Zeke had been. Zeke had told Harlan that Jack was the smartest boy on the farm, was trustworthy and honest, and would be capable of running the farm in Harlan's absence. Harlan had acted happy to learn this, but actually he was afraid. Smart boys, in his opinion, were dangerous because they could see through lies and get support from the other boys. They were the biggest threat of a group's escape, and of being caught running an illegal labor camp.

Unknown to Amalgamated, Harlan had bought a twenty-acre farm about twelve miles farther into the woods than this one, which he planned to secretly farm with camp labor, equipment, and materials, pocketing most of the sales revenue as profit. It was surrounded by impenetrable swamp filled with alligators and water moccasins and had only one road, an old logging trail, that led to it. He could effectively

151

block escape on the logging trail with a huge gate and fence placed across the road and extended into the edge of the swamp. Any boys going to work there could stay several days in the run-down cabin without supervision and not be able to escape, avoiding the long trip to and from the farm each day. Harlan decided to take Jack to operate this farm. That way he was removed as a threat of organizing a group escape.

"Boys, things are gonna be different around here from now on," Harlan bellowed to the group after Zeke and Helen had left. "Zeke Judd was a bad manager, and sloppy. I'm surprised he was as profitable as he was, giving you Saturday afternoons off and paying you to do the work you should do anyway. If you don't do as much work for me as you were doin' for him, it'll be five lashes with the whip! And the money he wasted on food! Well, it's no more pork chops and fried chicken. From now on its chitlins, hog jowls, pig's feet, and chicken stew. And there will be no more fresh milk. I'm sellin' all the milk cows but one I'll keep for my family, and you'll have powdered milk. You'll have powdered eggs too. NOW LET'S GIT TO THE FIELD!"

Great, we've got a stupid tyrant for a boss, Jack thought.

On Sunday afternoon, Harlan came to talk to Willis. "Get me three boys. I want to build a gate and about 200 steps of fence across the road in the woods. I want Jack Thomas to be one of the boys." *So he'll realize it's impossible to escape through*, he thought.

"Yassah, Massa Harlan."

The boys, supervised personally by Harlan, spent three days in the woods with cross cut saws and axes selecting and cutting down huge old cypress trees that had rotted away to just the heart. Heart cypress would not rot. These were about twenty to twenty-five inches in diameter and about fifteen to twenty feet long. The heart cypress was split in half with axes and wedges, and was to be the materials for the gate and fence, which took eight days for them to build. Both were

FLORIDA GOLD

twelve feet tall, with half logs that were spaced only an inch apart and covered on the inside with strands of barbed wire spaced six inches apart. The fence extended about fifty yards into the swamp on each side of the gate. They built ladders that they positioned and stood on in the swamp, and nailed half logs and strands of barbed wire to trees until the quicksand-like muck, which was too thick to swim in, got about seven feet deep - too deep to wade in and more than covering the head. Other than that, the road out, with dense swamp on each side, led right through the camp, and anyone traveling on it would alert the dogs, who would bark and howl, alerting Harlan that someone was trying to escape. The Sunday after they'd finished building the gate and fence, Harlan asked Fuller to send Jack to his house.

"Jack, Zeke told me you were the smartest boy in camp."

"I think that's what he thought, but like you said, he was a bad manager."

Harlan wasn't sure if this was an insult or not, so he ignored it. "I've decided I want you to operate my twenty acre farm up in the swamp. Meet me outside the house at seven tomorrow morning and bring your clothes."

"Yes, sir."

They arrived at the farm just after nine o'clock. As Harlan drove away in the truck, he left a small parcel of fat back, hog jowls, and cornbread for Jack, and some musty, stale corn for the hogs. It was to be the last food the thirteen-year-old would receive from Harlan in the three years he tilled the man's land.

Walking into the sparsely furnished, rickety old farm shack, he noticed a large gaping hole where a fireplace should have been. Decrepit wooden shutters on the windows hung loosely and the cold November wind easily blew in. There was a lone slim cot in the dark corner of the room, and he inspected the dingy mattress, stuffed with Spanish moss filling and held together with feed-sack ticking. A thin, dank

153

blanket lay across the cot, intended to be his cover against the winter chill. There was no pillow to lay his head on. And his humble dwelling had no back door, exposing him to intruding wild animals. That night and many to follow were sleepless.

Huge rats crawled on the rafters above him. He couldn't help but wonder what would happen if one fell on him. And he almost froze to death. There was a cow that tried to push against the hole in the wall where feed sacks hung to cut the wind out, and the noise she made would scare him throughout the night. The china berries that fell from the tree and hit the house's tin roof as he was drifting off to sleep were almost as frightening.

Within two weeks, he had pneumonia. His chest pounded with pain. The winter wind raged and the cold air circulated throughout the house. Sick as he was, he took some lard, put it in a saucer, tied a rag around a chip of wood, and made a light until it burned out. Needing to relieve himself, he managed to get to the edge of the porch. He fell off. He could see beneath the house to the other side. Clearly visible were the strong legs of a bull, and he was scared. Jack pulled out the ivory cross and began to pray. "Dear heavenly father, please give me the courage and fortitude to survive this ordeal and go on to live a productive life, furthering your purposes in whatever ways you have planned for me. Help me not to hate my captors, but to pity them, oh Lord, for their short-sightedness, their greed, and their evil. Thanks, Lord. In Jesus' name I pray, amen."

He knew he had seen the bull, but suddenly the bull ran, and then he saw a pair of human legs. That is the last Jack remembered for a while. When he became conscious, he realized someone had put him on the porch. His head lay on a burlap bag that wasn't there before. The sun was coming up in the east and it warmed his body. He fell asleep, and when he awoke again the sun was setting down in the west. He was

FLORIDA GOLD

able to get up and hand-grind some corn and cook some grits on the wood-burning stove. He ate heartily. From that day on he was never scared again. He never felt alone again. After that experience, Jack would lie in bed at night, and even the rats roaming the rafters looked beautiful. The cows would be bellowing outside, and his body freezing cold, but he'd feel safe, as if someone was with him.

He would never figure out who picked him up and put him on the porch, but he always considered this to be the first memorable encounter he had with the Lord.

Six weeks later, Harlan visited the farm. This time he brought some chickens for Jack to tend along with the cows and hogs. They were put in an existing coop. In a few days, Jack discovered dead chickens all over the place. He buried them. When Harlan returned, to Jack's horror, he was forced to lie on a large mound of dirt while Harlan beat him with a heavy flat shovel. Harlan, seriously into witchcraft, accused Jack of casting a spell on his chickens so he wouldn't have to feed them.

Jack never knew why he said that when the hogs and cows survived, but his wife was into voodoo too, and even if they got a headache, or stumped their toe, Jack was accused of casting a spell or causing their problems. When they beat him they called it "beating the evil spirits" out of him.

Many years later, Jack researched it and discovered the chickens had had coccidiosis, an existing condition in the old coop.

The beating put Jack in bed unable to move. In a few days, Theresa went out to the farm and found the undernourished eight-five-pound, thirteen-year-old boy in terrible condition. She managed to load him into the truck and take him back to the main farmhouse. She applied a salve to his wounds, and for three weeks, Jack was barely able to get out of bed. However, once he was up and around, Harlan

155

returned him immediately to the twenty-acre farm, where he lived a recluse life for the next 2 ½ years.

Once a week, Jack walked the four miles to the giant gate where he would "tote" back two pails of slop left by Willis or Fuller for the hogs. Barefooted, the spindly, undernourished youth made his way in summer's heat or winter's cold. With no food, he quickly learned to fend for himself. He added salt to the hog's corn to keep weevils out. He would use a hand grinder to make grits, and use the salt off the corn husks to season his grits. He used a bent straight pin with an attached string to catch catfish and bream from a nearby creek. He found berries and roots from the surrounding woods to eat. He drew water from a muggy well that filled his bucket with wiggle-tails from mosquito larvae. He found that if he quickly hit the bucket, they'd go to the bottom so he could drink from the top.

Summer months meant fighting mosquitoes that swarmed through the palmetto fronds and feed sacks he'd placed over the windowless and door-less shack. He burned cow dung to smoke them out. To fight the red bugs, that would also suck his blood out, he put the four corners of his bed in saucers of kerosene.

Every night he'd try to pick the bugs off the moss mattress, where they'd be visibly crawling all over. In the morning the bed would always be covered with his own fresh blood where he'd rolled over and squashed them. He soon learned to boil the moss before stuffing it into the mattress, and that took care of the red bugs."

Equipped with a hoe, Jack was expected to keep prickly briers from growing on the farm. He had twenty acres to clear, and the brier bushes could grow as tall as seven feet. He cleared land and planted corn and peanuts for the hogs kept on the farm. Two and a half years passed while Harland's cruel punishments continued. Survival was a daily task along with the long hard hours of work it took to run the farm

FLORIDA GOLD

alone. But Jack would soon meet the one man who would save his life.

One day, about a year and a half after Jack had been brought to manage the farm, he was fishing in the creek that bordered the swamp. He looked up and thought he saw someone standing off at a distance, but then they vanished. I must be seeing things, he thought. But this encounter dominated his thoughts for the next few days. It happened again when he was digging palmetto roots to eat. Only this time he yelled, "I see you! Who are you?"

A tall man, straight as a young pine and dressed in buckskins quietly answered from behind him, "I Hal Pate-Chobee."

Jack jumped, startled that someone was behind him. "He son, Kauna," the man explained, pointing to a boy about nine years old standing off in the woods, who was the person Jack had seen.

"My name's Jack, Jack Thomas," he said, offering his hand.

"You come," Hal Pate-Chobee requested. Then he turned and started off into the woods.

What have I got to lose? Jack thought. *If they'd wanted to kill me, I'd be dead.* They went about three miles, and then off in the distance in an oak hammock, Jack saw several tipis and wood smoke. He followed Hal Pate-Chobee into one of the tipis and an Indian woman got up.

"Alaqua, my squaw," Hal Pate-Chobee, said, pointing to the woman who looked to be in her mid-thirties. "Sit." Jack sat on the dirt floor. The boy, Kauna soon came in with a wooden bowl filled with a type of stew. "Sofkee. Good. Jack eat." It was made of venison, sweet potatoes, onions, and rice, and was very good to the ravenous Jack, who wolfed it down. "More?" Hal Pate-Chobee asked.

"Yes, please," Jack replied. Alaqua looked pleased that Jack liked her stew so well, and she brought him another bowl. Alaqua then brought him little fried cakes made of coontie root and mashed sweet potatoes, and a drinking gourd filled with fresh water. It was the best food Jack had eaten in years.

When Jack had finished, Hal Pate-Chobee said, "We talk." At his remark, Alaqua and Kauna quietly left the tipi.

Jack learned that Hal Pate-Chobee meant "big alligator," Kauna meant "leaping bullfrog," and Alaqua, "sweet gum tree." They had been part of the Apalachee tribe. Most had been put on a reservation in Alabama, but this small band, called the Chine, had not, instead moving into the large swamps and woods north of Blountstown when Hal Pate-Chobee was a small boy. They were self-sufficient - hunting, trapping, fishing, and growing vegetable gardens - and didn't bother anyone, so the people in town left them alone, pretty much ignoring them. They traded alligator, deer, and otter hides for food staples such as salt, sugar, and rice. Obviously they knew the way out of the swamp without going past the labor camp, but Jack decided not to pursue this point in their initial meeting.

"You're my friend," Jack said as he grasped Hal Pate-Chobee's hand and forearm.

"Friend," Hal Pate-Chobee replied.

"It is time that I go."

"You come again?"

"Yes."

It was late in the afternoon when Jack left for his shack. But for the first time in years, he was excited. The Indians would be able to show him how to escape!

About two days later, Jack returned to the Indian camp in the late morning. He went to Hal Pate-Chobee's tipi and Alaqua came out. "Hal Pate-Chobee and Kauna hunt. You eat?"

"Not now," Jack replied, resisting the temptation. He didn't want them to think he only came to eat. Jack went back

FLORIDA GOLD

outside and Alaqua introduced him to some of the other members of their small band. He went over to where some children were playing with a venison-skin ball and played with them. Soon several Indian males came into view. They were carrying two deer suspended from poles and Kauna had a large turkey. Apparently the animals had been shot with bows and arrows. The women busied themselves dressing the game while the men fixed bowls of the Sofkee. When he saw Jack, Hal Pate-Chobee's face lit up.

"My friend," he said as he greeted Jack. Kauna fixed him a bowl of the stew, and Jack sat with the men around the large cook pot, eating hungrily. When they'd finished, Hal Pate-Chobee introduced Jack to the other men from the hunting party as they stuffed pipes with tobacco and smoked.

Jack began, "You know the way to town, Hal Pate-Chobee?"

"Hal Pate-Chobee know."

"Will you show me?"

"Long journey. You not ready." At that, Jack's spirits sank.

"I teach. Make you ready."

"What do I need to learn?"

"How stay alive. Not get lost in swamp. I teach."

The women soon finished dressing the game and joined them. Hal Pate-Chobee gestured toward their tipi, and Jack followed Hal Pate-Chobee, Kauna, and Alaqua inside. As Alaqua was eating, Jack took the gifts he'd brought out of the worn canvas bag. "For my friends," Jack said as he handed Alaqua a mirror, Kauna a hatchet, and Hal Pate-Chobee a bone-handled hunting knife. By their expressions, he knew they liked the gifts. Hal Pate-Chobee gestured at Kauna, who disappeared, but quickly came back with a wooden bow and six stone-tipped arrows. "Thank you, my friend," Jack replied when Hal Pate-Chobee presented him with the bow and arrows.

"Jack shoot?" Hal Pate-Chobee asked.

159

"Not very well, but I'll try.

"Shoot," Hal Pate-Chobee said as he stood up and went out of the tipi. Kauna took a deerskin hide, put a black spot on it with a piece of burnt wood, and hung it on a pine tree about thirty feet away.

Jack strung an arrow, drew the bow and released. It didn't even hit the tree. Kauna was struggling not to laugh.

"I show," Hal Pate-Chobee said, taking the bow and an arrow. "Look at target. See it hit in mind." He drew and released, and the arrow hit dead center.

"Now you," he suggested, handing Jack the bow and another arrow. Jack drew and released again, and this time he hit the edge of the target. "Keep shoot. Get better."

Jack decided to leave the bow and arrows with Hal Pate-Chobee because he didn't want Harlan to find it and give him a beating. He explained, and Hal Pate-Chobee, who had seen Harlan beating Jack, understood. Over the next weeks and months, Jack practiced with the bow and arrows, and became a proficient shot. Hal Pate-Chobee also taught him to track and quietly stalk game, how to tell directions by reading the stars, how to find and identify wild plants that were edible, how to tell if water was polluted, how to make and set snares - for animals and people, and how to take the advantage when someone was chasing you by maneuvering them into trouble. Hal Pate-Chobee also taught Jack self-defense, and how to silently kill anyone who was a threat to him or his loved ones. Jack would not need these skills for his escape, but they would help save his life and the lives of others years from now in the war.

Jack grew strong and tall with the nutritious food and exercise, and became an expert woodsman. Harlan could tell Jack must be eating well, but he couldn't understand how.

FLORIDA GOLD

It had been almost a year since Jack and Hal Pate-Chobee had first met when the Indian said one night at dinner, "Jack ready to go from here."

"Yes, my friend. It is time. Will you show me the way?"

"Hal Pate-Chobee show. Jack need come next sun. Leave next sun. Man come kill Jack. Hal Pate-Chobee hear."

"Why?"

"Jack older now. He think Jack escape. Bring law. Lock man up. He mean."

Jack went back to the shack and prepared his escape. He'd bring extra clothes to throw in the swamp to make Harlan think he'd drowned trying to get away.

The next morning as Jack was preparing to go to the Indian camp, Hal Pate-Chobee came into the shack. "Jack leave now, man come. I see."

Jack quickly gathered up his things and checked his pocket to be sure he had the seventy-one dollars[5] he'd saved from his incentive pay under Zeke. They went about a mile to the edge of the swamp and Jack made tracks off into it, wading out about waist deep, then threw the shirt, overalls and work boots out there. He wore buckskin moccasins. Jack and Hal Pate-Chobee left, staying inside the tree line and covering their trail as they heard Harlan's truck coming.

Jack and Hal Pate-Chobee went about a mile south of the Indian camp, and Hal Pate-Chobee took Jack into the woods and to the edge of the swamp.

"Up," Hal Pate-Chobee said. Jack looked up, and about thirty feet off the ground, suspended in a large cypress tree, was the beginning of a rope bridge. Hal Pate-Chobee handed Jack a map drawn on buckskin with charcoal. Apparently the rope bridge went about a hundred yards from tree to tree through the tree tops, then ended on the other side of this narrow strip of mucky swamp. From there was a trail Jack could follow that would lead out to a road, and to

---

[5] The same as $1,088 in 2013.

Blountstown. Hal Pate-Chobee handed Jack a small deerskin bag with pinole (parched ground corn) and venison jerky. When mixed with water, the pinole made a high-energy mush. "Hal Pate-Chobee put along trail," he explained. "Your journey take four suns." Hal Pate-Chobee handed Jack his bow and arrows. "May the great spirit guide and protect you, Jack Thomas, Hal Pate-Chobee's friend."

"I will miss you, Hal Pate-Chobee, my friend," Jack replied. Then he slung his bow and quiver of arrows over his shoulder and climbed the rungs made from cypress branches to the rope bridge. Hal Pate-Chobee faded silently into the woods.

George and Amanda took the loss of their son, grandson, and daughter-in-law hard. Margaret did too. Finally, Margaret could no longer bear the memories in Mobile, and she and Ben sold the house and left for Europe, where they intended to retire and live the rest of their lives. "We're going to live in a small village we liked in Italy, just outside of Milano. Contact us at this address if Jack is found," Ben told George.

George's health began to fail from depression, and his business began to decline. Amanda stayed in her room most of the time, oblivious to most of what was going on. The stock market crash in 1929 was hardly noticed by George, who was still very depressed. But his businesses noticed it, particularly without his close attention. George lost most of his net worth. Jeremy Johns, George's friend and trusted business colleague, was the executive vice president of Citizens and Southern Bank in Savannah when George contacted him and ultimately sold him his bank for a very reasonable price. Jeremy helped George sell his other businesses and assets.

"Well, George, with the sale of Spring Creek Ranch and your interest in Fields' department stores and Southern Atlantic Railroad, that about wraps it up. If the sale of the house here in Mobile goes through next month as planned,

FLORIDA GOLD

once all the debt is paid off, you should have ownership of the house in West Palm Beach and a little over $800,000 in cash."

"Jeremy, with my state of mind and health, I could never have done this without your help. Thanks. At least I got out with enough for Amanda and me to retire on. And thanks for agreeing to be executor of my estate. With my health, I feel better knowing Amanda's financial affairs will be effectively taken care of if something happens to me."

"George, you paid for my senior year of college, then hired me and trained me when my own father wouldn't speak to me. You're like a second father to me. You know there's nothing Denise and I wouldn't do for you and Amanda. But don't look so glum. I could think of a lot worse fate than being retired in West Palm. When you and Amanda get settled, Denise and I will come down and we'll all go fishing."

The combined strain of George's depression and failed businesses had taken their toll. When they were getting packed to move to West Palm Beach, he had a severe heart attack, and was pronounced dead on arrival at Providence hospital in March of 1931.

After losing her only son, her grandson and her daughter-in-law, her husband's death was the final blow for Amanda. She withdrew inside herself and seldom talked, mostly unaware of what was happening around her. Jeremy got Amanda's financial affairs in order, settled George's estate, and set up a trust fund with the $530,000[6] remaining from George's retirement fund. His wife, Denise, moved Amanda to her home in West Palm Beach, and hired a twenty-four- hour nurse to live with and take care of her.

---

[6] The same as $8.1 million in 2013.

CHAPTER TEN

Willis drove the truck up to the shack and Harlan went inside. "He ain't in there," Harlan said as he came out. "Maybe he's in the field." They went to the field but no Jack. "Maybe he's fishin'," Harlan suggested. "You go look at that fishin' hole up there while I check down here."

"I cain't finds him nowhere, Massa Harlan."

"When I find the son of a bitch, he'll git fifteen lashes with the whip."

"What that?"

"Where?"

"Off there in the swamp."

"It's clothes. Willis, let's cut a pole and try to get them out."

"Yassah." Willis cut down a thin cypress sapling and knocked the small branches off of it with his hatchet. Then he waded out toward the clothes and pulled them in with the sapling.

"That's Jack's clothes," Harlan said.

"Even his boots. A gator must a got him."

"Probably. Just saved me the trouble. Let's go."

Jack's escape had gone as smoothly as any could have. Harlan never suspected a thing.

ROBERT ALLEN MORRIS

Jack made good time along the narrow trail, with its twists and turns to avoid the ever-present swamp. His excellent physical conditioning helped. He found the bags of pinole and jerky, and even shot a rabbit with his bow. On his trip, he thought about what he was going to do, and made a plan. He thought he had enough money for train fare, new clothes, and meals, so he would catch the train in town, go back to Mobile, and find his family. Then he would tell his family and the sheriff in Mobile about his ordeal, and get them to go and arrest Harlan and the rest of the adults in the work camp, close it down, and return the boys to their homes.

It was four days later when he emerged onto a dirt road. The map said go left, which was south. He stayed off the road and inside the tree line, not wanting to leave tracks. About a mile down the road, he came to a fence, gate, and sign that said "Amalgamated Land Company. No trespassing. Trespassers will be shot on sight." *So the work camp is owned by the same company my grandpa worked for that cheated him out of promotions,* Jack thought.

He made it into town the next day, and checked into Hotel Annie, the only lodgings in town. Then he went to the general store and bought some clothes and shoes. Afterward, he took a bath, dressed in his new clothes, and went to the train station. "I'd like a ticket for the next train to Mobile," he told the clerk.

"You look happy enough to have found a pot of gold," the clerk said.

"I am."

"What happened?"

"It's a long story."

"Train leaves at seven tomorrow mornin'."

"Any good places to eat around here?"

"Hotel has the best food in town."

FLORIDA GOLD

"Thanks." Jack was ecstatic at finally being free, being able to take his first hot bath in over three years, and having a comfortable bed to sleep in.

He arrived in Mobile at three fifteen and hailed a taxi at the train station. "Do you know where George Walker lives?" "I know where he used to live, but he died last spring." "Would you take me to his house?" "Sure thing."

Jack recognized the large house as they pulled into its circular driveway. "That'll be a dollar," the driver said.

"Here, and please wait on me." Jack was nervous as he walked toward the door. He rang the doorbell, but a strange woman answered. "I'm Jack Thomas. Is Amanda Walker here?"

"She doesn't live here anymore," the woman replied, shocked.

"What about Jeb and Irma Sue Walker?"

"Do you know Police Chief Burns?"

"Yes, ma'am."

"Just tell the cab driver to take you to the Mobile police station. Ron Burns can give you the details."

When Jack had left, the woman made a call to the station. "Chief Burns, please."

"Who's calling?"

"Faye Morton."

"Faye, how are you today?" a booming voice answered.

"Ron, guess who was just here?"

"Who?"

"Jack Thomas."

"Are you sure?"

"He resembled Jack as a boy, and knew specifics about the Walker family. I'd recognize those crystal-blue eyes anywhere. That's Jack Thomas."

"Son of a gun. I guess they finally let him go."

167

"Or he escaped. Anyway, I didn't tell him anything. He's on his way to see you."

"Thanks, Faye."

Jack entered the police station and told a man at the desk, "I'm Jack Thomas, here to see Police Chief Burns."

"I'll ring his office."

A few minutes later a tall, barrel-chested man with hairy forearms who looked to be in his mid-fifties came out. Jack recognized him in spite of the years since he had seen the man.

"Jack Thomas," said Jack, extending his hand.

"Ron Burns. So it really is you!" Ron said. He recognized Jack, remembering him from the dove shoot hosted by the Walkers at Spring Creek Ranch in 1921, plus all the pictures he'd used in their search for him.

"Can you tell me how to find my family?"

"Come into my office and we can talk in private."

When both were seated, Ron told Jack the shocking, sad story. Jack was visibly shaken.

"So only my mother and Mrs. Walker are still alive? And my mother lives in Italy?"

"That's right. I'm sorry, Jack."

"Do you know how to contact my mother?"

"I'm afraid not. Her husband, Ben, left an address with George, but when he died so suddenly nobody could find it to wire them about George's death and the funeral. Before I forget, there's the reward money."

"Reward money?"

"Right after you was kidnapped and we couldn't find you, George put up a $3,000 reward to be paid to anyone bringing you back alive or providing information leading to your safe return. Jeremy Johns, a friend of George's who bought his bank and was executor of his estate, told me at the funeral that he never reclaimed the reward money. As far as

FLORIDA GOLD

I'm concerned, you rescued yourself and should get that money. I'll give Jeremy a call after our meeting."

"Thanks, Mr. Burns."

"That's Ron. Now I want to hear what happened to you and how you got free."

Jack told the entire story. How Digger Sims used an ether-soaked rag so Jack would not be noticed in a crowd. The work farm, their barracks, the crops they farmed, his idea that improved productivity and got the boys paid for it. About Harlan Kirkland and his treachery, the twenty-acre farm Harlan secretly owned that Jack had tended for the last three years, and about his Indian friends and how Hal Pate-Chobee had helped him to escape.

"That's an amazing story," Ron observed. "It's a wonder you're still alive, what with such a run-down shack to live in and having to live on whatever fish, roots, and berries you could get, and the beatings."

"The Indians definitely saved me," Jack replied. "I know how to show you and your officers where this place is. I would like to go arrest the adults there and free the boys. Maybe even fine the company. Amalgamated owns the land and the camp, and probably others like it."

"Oh, with what you know, we'll be able to do a lot more than that. Stay at my house tonight and we'll make a plan. I'll also invite Jeremy and his wife, Denise, to join us for dinner. I'm sure they'd like to meet you and hear your story, as will my wife, Betty. Maybe Jeremy can bring the reward money. I'll bet you'd like a good home-cooked meal, huh?"

"I sure would, thanks," Jack replied.

"You wouldn't believe how good simple things are like Coca-Colas, a hot bath, a radio to listen to," Jack explained, still somewhat overwhelmed at being free, as he and Ron were sitting in the living room sipping the sodas and listening to the news.

"And soon some of the best pot roast and mashed potatoes in Mobile," Ron added.

"Hon, would you get the door?" Betty called out from the kitchen.

"Sure, dear," said Ron.

"Denise, Jeremy, it's good to see you again, do come in," Ron said as he answered the door, hugging Denise and shaking Jeremy's hand. "I'd like both of you to meet Jack Thomas."

"Jack, it's a pleasure," Jeremy said as he shook Jack's hand.

"Were you really in one of those dreadful child labor camps?" Denise asked in her Savannah drawl.

"Yes ma'am, I was."

"Why, it's a wonder you're here," she replied.

"Ron, can we go in your study? asked Jeremy. "I'd like to discuss some things with Jack."

"Sure. Denise, Betty…"

"I'll go and see if Betty needs help finishing dinner," said Denise, walking off.

"Jack, please don't be offended, but I need proof of who you are before I can release the reward money to you," Jeremy explained as they sat down in leather chairs in front of Ron's large walnut desk.

"Isn't my and Betty's opinion that he's Jack Thomas good enough?"

"Ron, how old was Jack the last time you saw him?"

"Six, it was at a dove shoot that George had."

"And now he's sixteen. How can you be sure it's Jack? That's a lot of reward money. Information about Jack's kidnapping was in the news after it happened, and information about the Walker family was always in the news, often with their pictures. So it would be easy for someone to…"

FLORIDA GOLD

"Mr. Johns, I understand, and I agree with you," Jack interrupted. "Your job is to protect the Walker family's interests. George Walker was an honest and fair man, and I believe you must be as well, otherwise he wouldn't have trusted you with his financial affairs. Nor would he have bailed you out of jail, paid for your senior year at Alabama Tech after your father disowned you, and given you a job in one of his banks. Did you and your father ever make amends with each other?"

"How did you know about that?"

"Jeb Walker told me about it when he was telling me about the importance of recognizing character and giving worthy people a second chance."

"Proof enough, Jeremy?" Ron asked.

"More than enough. Can you excuse me a minute?"

"Sure."

As Ron and Jack walked back into the living room, Betty came through the dining room door and announced, "Dinner's ready."

"We'll be in as soon as Jeremy gets back," Ron replied.

"Where'd he go?"

"To his car to get Jack's reward money, I think."

About that time, Jeremy came in carrying a wide leather belt and a leather case that Jack recognized. *It's the Fox,* Jack thought. He fondly remembered the quail hunt where Jeb had first shot the fine hand-crafted shotgun that had been a Christmas present from his father.

"Dinner's ready," Betty repeated.

As they were finishing the wonderful meal she'd prepared, Jack said, "Mrs. Burns, that was the best pot roast I've ever had."

"Thank you, Jack. There's more to come. We have homemade pear pie for dessert."

171

"Betty, let's wait a bit for that. I'm just dying to hear Jack's story," said Denise.

Jack told his story again.

"Why, you poor thing," Denise said. "Betty, we've got to fatten him up. You must come have dinner with us tomorrow night. I'll fix my fried chicken, and we'll have butter beans and stewed tomatoes from our garden last summer, and biscuits, and for dessert I'll fix..."

"Denise, Jack may have plans of his own," Jeremy interrupted.

"Mr. and Mrs. Johns, I'd love to come."

"Wonderful. Betty, why don't you and Ron join us? It'll be a feast."

"Why, we'd love to, if Ron will be free."

"I'm good for some of Denise's fried chicken any time."

"Enough talk about food. I have something for Jack," Jeremy said as he walked over and got the belt and leather case from the table in the foyer.

"Here is your $4,485,"[7] Jeremy said as he handed Jack the leather money belt.

"I thought it was $3,000," Jack said.

"It was in 1921, but it's been earning interest at an average of 4.1 percent a year, and that's been compounded back into the original amount."

"I remember Mr. Walker telling someone about interest, but I didn't hear everything he said. I guess there's a lot I need to learn," Jack observed.

"Jack, do you know what's in the leather case?" Jeremy asked.

"The Fox sixteen-gauge Jeb got for Christmas?"

"That's right," Jeremy said as he handed the case to Jack.

"Why, what a beautiful gun," Denise observed as Jack removed the double-barrel shotgun from its case.

---

[7] The same as $68,755 in 2013

FLORIDA GOLD

"It's yours, Jack," Jeremy told him. "It was the only thing out of George's personal items that Amanda didn't want sold. She asked me to keep it and give it to you if you were ever found, or if not, sell it and donate the money to the University of Alabama in Jeb's name.

"I - I don't know what to say." Jack was visibly moved by Amanda's gift as his thoughts returned to the wonderful times he and Jeb had at his first dove shoot, and later roaming the woods and fields on Spring Creek Ranch together hunting rabbits and quail - Jack with the .410 Jeb had let him use, and Jeb with the Fox. Jeb had even let him shoot it several times.

After Jeremy and Denise left, Ron and Jack began to make their plan.

"Jack, because Amalgamated owns land in several states and because this involves kidnapping and slavery, this is a federal offense. We will have to get the feds involved."

"OK."

"What would be our best way for a surprise capture? We don't want them to kill the boys because we're coming after them, like they all threaten to do."

"Mr. Kirkland stays up drinking on Saturday nights until past midnight. Then he sleeps late on Sunday mornings. I think we should sneak into the camp about an hour before daylight and surprise him in his bedroom. They have dogs that will detect us coming and start to bark, and it will be two Negro foremen that will go to wake Mr. Kirkland - Willis and Fuller. We need to stop them from doing that."

"What about his wife?"

"Theresa gets drunk too, so she'll also be passed out."

"OK, I'll call my contacts at the Bureau of Investigation tomorrow, and we'll schedule a meeting to discuss our plan."

The next day, Jack used $600 of the reward money to buy a Model A Ford.

173

Two agents from the Bureau of Investigation, Alexander Cook and Bill Clayton arrived four days later. When they heard Jack's story, they were shocked. "Mr. Glover will want to hear this himself," they said.

So Jack and Ron took the train to Washington. Jim Glover, director of the BOI, was a round-faced man with piercing eyes who stood about five foot ten and weighed about 175 pounds. His hair was slicked back and he had on a gray pin-striped suit with a pink tie. After Jack told his story, Mr. Glover said, "Our agents believe there could be as many as six companies, mostly engaged in turpentine and logging, that are operating these illegal labor camps. We just don't have proof that will stand up in court. Are you prepared to help us get them all?"

"Yes, sir."

"Son, you're doing a great service to your country by helping us catch these criminals."

"Thank you, sir."

"Mr. Burns, I'd like to appoint you as a temporary special agent to lead this mission. Is there someone that can handle the day-to-day activities of your office?"

"Yes, sir. Bob Seabrook can handle it."

"Good. I will select your team and they will be at your office in one week to begin."

A week later, there were six agents at Mobile police headquarters. Ron and Jack led them to a conference room. Agent Alexander James was in charge of the other agents. Agent James stood about six feet tall with broad shoulders, dark-brown hair and inquisitive brown eyes. His mild-mannered personality hid the fact that he probably knew a dozen ways to quickly kill an adversary. Jack and Ron laid out their plan for a surprise capture. "The thing I don't like are those dogs," agent Cook added. "Other than Willis, Fuller, and Harlan, are there any other employees other than the boys who might be there?"

FLORIDA GOLD

"Sometimes Arnold, Jethro, Ed and Phil come in from the turpentine camp if extra manpower is needed, like at a hog killing or stringing tobacco."

"Is there any chance they could be there?"

"Not much, although they did come and play cards sometimes on Saturday nights with Mr. Judd. I wasn't around the camp enough to know if they ever play cards with Mr. Kirkland."

"That's just not worth the risk," agent Cook said. "Barking dogs could ruin the whole thing and get those boys killed. We've got to find a way to deal with those dogs."

"We need someone on the inside," agent Cook suggested.

"Maybe we could get one of our men to replace Willis or Fuller," Agent Clifford suggested. "Jack, how do they pick the adults who supervise the boys?"

"Mr. Judd said he liked ex-convicts because they didn't have many other choices and would work cheap. He also liked Negroes, because being supervised by them helped break the white boys' spirit. I don't know about Mr. Kirkland."

"That's probably a company policy," Agent Paxton offered. "Our intelligence says the employees of these work farms are chosen by the company, not the farm manager. Do we have any Negro agents?"

"No, but we do have two Negroes who sometimes do contract work for us?" Agent Cook replied

"Are they any good?" agent Clifford asked

"Yeah, as good as most of our agents, in my opinion," Agent Cook replied

"Why don't we use one of them? Give them a phony prison term and release. Abduct Willis or Fuller and try to get our man to replace him. Then he can drug the dogs so they won't be a problem," Agent Clifford suggested. "He can also give us regular reports on the situation inside the work camp."

175

"It will take some extra time, but I'd rather be safe than sorry," said Agent James. "Jack, what would be the best way to capture Willis or Fuller without being noticed?"

"They come to town to buy supplies, such as flour, sugar, salt coffee, but also farm supplies like wire, nails, lumber, and other things. Sometimes Mr. Judd or Mr. Kirkland comes with them, but usually they are alone. They could be captured on one of those visits to town."

"Did both come, or just one of them?"

"Both, usually on Saturdays, once a month. But also other times if they need something and can't wait for it until a scheduled trip. "

"Who supervised the boys while they were gone?"

"Mr. Judd and later Mr. Kirkland. Mr. Judd and Mr. Kirkland both felt like this helped them better keep in touch with what was going on in the field. I think the farm manager felt better trusting Willis and Fuller to get supplies on a charge account than to run the camp if they weren't there."

It was time to execute their plan. Jack remembered that it was usually the first Saturday of the month when Willis and Fuller came to buy supplies. Agents Clifford and Cook took Jack with him and they got rooms at Hotel Annie in Blountstown on Friday, October 2. The next morning at about ten, Jack saw Willis enter the general store. Fuller went to the blacksmith shop. Jack headed to the store, with agents Clifford and Cook behind him. Jack entered and shouted, "Hey Willis!"

He looked up, saw Jack, and Jack ran out of the store and down an alley.

Willis followed, shouting, "You bettah stop, Jack!"

When Willis rounded the corner and headed into the alley, Agent Cook grabbed him and held a pistol to his throat. Agent Clifford came up from behind and knocked him unconscious. They put him in their car and handcuffed him, then everyone got in, and they sped away. They were headed

FLORIDA GOLD

to Tallahassee, fifty-five miles away. About twenty minutes into their trip, Willis regained consciousness. A look of terror came over him as he realized what was happening. Mr. Kirkland had always said Jack would get them caught. But he thought Jack was dead. Everyone rode in silence. Finally, Willis asked," What gon' happen to me?"

"That's not up to us," Agent Clifford replied. "Maybe you'll find out more when they question you." It was about noon when they arrived at the federal law enforcement offices and went inside. Agent James was waiting on them and he led Willis into a small room with a table and six chairs. Jack joined them.

"State your name," agent James requested.

"Willis Green."

"Jack, is that who he is?"

"Yes, sir."

"Is he the man who was your guard and supervisor at the Amalgamated Land Company labor camp?"

"Yes."

"OK, Willis, here's how I see things. We have two choices. Either you can testify in federal court about what happened at the labor camp, identify the people in charge, and the company that owned it, or we can release you."

"Sets me free?"

"Yeah. But first, we'd get a newspaper reporter to get Jack's story, and identify you as one of his captors, with your picture, maybe even get it on the radio. Then we'd let it leak that you escaped and where we thought you were. I'll bet the fathers of some of those boys in the work camp would somehow find you."

"Please, Massa, don' do dat."

"You'll testify, then?"

"Yassah, yassah."

Agent James got in touch with Albert Martin, one of the black contractors who sometimes worked for the agency. He was a plain clothes police officer in Chicago, mainly policing black neighborhoods. He also did extra work on the side to supplement his meager salary. He had an understanding boss who realized that this extra work improved his skills and experience as a police officer.

"Where's Willis?" Harlan demanded when Fuller returned.

"I don' know, Massa Harlan. He jus' disappear."

"Probably ran off with some whore. He'll probably be back in a few days, and then I'll give him a whippin' he won't forget."

"Yassah."

It was about a month later when Harlan got a letter from the Amalgamated office in Atlanta.

We have a replacement for Willis. His name is Floyd Harkins. He was released from Raiford Penitentiary in Raiford, Florida on parole two months ago. He will arrive on the train in Blountstown on Monday, November 16 at 10 a.m. Meet him there.

"Good, they finally got me somebody to replace that piece o' shit, Willis. Maybe he's better," Harlan told his wife.

"Floyd," who was actually Albert Martin, arrived on schedule and Harlan was there to pick him up. In a scheduled telegram to Agent James, sent when he was in town getting roofing tin, Albert wrote,

Conditions in this camp are bad. The boys are undernourished and skinny. Several of them are sick. I'm ready to act on this whenever you are.

178

FLORIDA GOLD

Agent James replied,

*We will be there at about five-thirty this Sunday morning.
Drug the dogs and Fuller as planned.*

It was about four thirty a.m. on Sunday, November 29, and Jack plus six federal agents led by Agent James and Chief Burns arrived at the Amalgamated gate. A bus followed the group. Albert had managed to get them a key. They opened the gate and drove to a spot about a mile from the camp where Jack told them to park off in the woods. Armed with pump shotguns, pistols, and tommy guns, the agents, followed by Jack, crept silently toward the camp.

They arrived at the farmhouse. The door was unlocked, and they entered in the darkness, only moonlight providing any visibility. Jack silently pointed toward the bedroom. Suddenly a dog in the bedroom began to yap sharply. Harlan and Theresa jumped up, just in time for Agent James to shine a flashlight and point his shotgun at Harlan's head. Six other guns were pointed at the couple. Jack lit a kerosene lantern.

"Hey, Harlan," Jack said, smiling.

"YOU! I knew you were trouble!"

"Shut up!" Chief Burns shouted.

"Jack, take Agent Clifford to the boys' barracks," Agent James told him.

"Yes, sir."

They went inside and upstairs. Albert was beginning to light the lanterns and the boys were waking up. Only four remembered Jack, who hadn't been to the barracks in over three years. Agent Clifford told them what was happening and several started to cry, overjoyed at being released. Agent Clifford went into the still-unconscious Fuller's room and handcuffed him. Agent Clayton went to get the bus and driver. By noon the boys were checked into a Tallahassee hotel and enjoying a large, hearty lunch.

A doctor was called to give the boys checkups. All were OK, just malnourished and exhausted. Most had bruises and marks indicative of beatings.

At the federal law enforcement offices, Harlan was being questioned by agents James and Clifford. "If you'll give me immunity, I'll tell you where all the other camps are," Harlan said.

"Oh, I think we can find that out on our own," Agent James replied. "We already know most of the companies doing this. We just needed proof. And now we have it."

"I won't testify unless I get immunity. It'll be Jack's word against mine."

"What about the boys?"

"They're just boys. I think they were on a Boy Scout trip, got lost, and we were letting them stay with us until we could contact their parents. They made the rest up," he replied, desperately and unbelievably.

"And their parents?"

"They want to get a big payoff from a lawsuit. They're biased."

"Well, none of that really matters. We have Willis, who has agreed to testify, and I'll bet Fuller agrees to testify too."

"You arrested Willis?"

"Yep." At that, Harlan seemed to sink down, and a depressed look came over his face.

On Monday, agents James and Clifford went to Atlanta and arrested the officers of the Amalgamated Land Company. Chief Burns, Agent James, and Jim Glover posed with Jack for a newspaper photo. The headline of the accompanying story would read "Bureau of Investigation Raids Amalgamated Land Company Child Labor Camp, Arrests Manager and Supervisors." In the story it said that they had plans to arrest the managers and supervisors of the other camps. However, the day before the story was to be released, federal agents

FLORIDA GOLD

were already stationed at the entries to all five turpentine and timber company properties suspected of operating labor camps. As the farm managers fled, they were all caught and arrested, and the camps liberated. The officers of all the companies with child labor camps were also arrested.

The press reported Jack's entire story in several continuing parts. Jack became a hero, and numerous grateful parents sent thank-you letters and some sent money. Jack answered all the letters and returned the money. Mr. Glover asked him to be available to testify at the trials, which were expected to take over two years.

Ron and Betty Burns invited Jack to have Christmas dinner with them, their son, Jake, daughter-in-law, Karen, and two grandchildren, Ronnie and Kim. "Jack, as our guest you have first choice on the turkey. What part do you want?" Ron asked as he began to carve the golden brown turkey.

"This is a real treat for me. The last time I had turkey was at the Walker's ranch for Christmas in 1921, ten years ago. I believe I would like a drumstick."

"It's yours," Ron replied. After he finished carving the turkey, Ron said, "Let us bow our heads and pray. Dear heavenly Father, thank you for this opportunity to celebrate the birthday of Jesus Christ with our good friend, Jack Thomas. Bless the boys and their families that Jack helped to free. And thank you for the bounty that you have bestowed upon us this special day. In Jesus' name I pray, Amen."

"Amen," everyone said.

"Jack, your ordeal was one of the most fascinating stories I've ever heard," Karen said as she passed the platter with the carved turkey around the table.

"I'm just glad they were able to free those poor boys," Betty added as she ladled giblet gravy over the stuffing on her plate.

181

"Yeah, and arrest the crooks who were behind all of it," Jake replied as he took the bowl of green beans from his mother and heaped a generous portion on his plate.

"Without Jack, we wouldn't have been able to do anything," Ron added as he buttered a hot, flaky roll.

"It was a well-executed team effort with the BOI, local authorities, and the press. I'm just glad the boys are back with their families and the camps are shut down," Jack said as he spooned stuffing onto his plate from the platter Karen passed him.

"Is Mr. Thomas a hero, grandpa?" Kim asked.

"Yes, I believe he is," Ron replied as he refilled his glass with iced tea from the large pitcher.

Later, after apple pie and ice cream, followed by coffee, when everyone was leaving Ron asked, "Jack, what are your plans? When you get older, I could certainly use you on my police force."

"Thanks, but I think I'll head back to Florida, then maybe go south to citrus country. I read that there's a good future in the citrus business."

"Well, good luck. And don't hesitate to call me if I can ever be of any help."

"Thanks, Mr. Burns."

Harlan was detained at Raiford Penitentiary to await his federal trial. He got in a fight - his arm was cut and he needed stitches. The prison doctor was away, so he was taken to a local doctor. On the way, a group of angry men stopped the prison car and took Harlan - a vigilante group of angry fathers whose sons had been in labor camps.

"Where you takin' me?" a horrified Harlan asked.

"We're gonna have a nice little picnic out in the woods."

They took him about twenty miles out of town, and drove down a narrow rutted road to the edge of a swamp. More angry men were there waiting, swigging moonshine,

FLORIDA GOLD

and there was a hanging noose suspended from a tree. "Here, tie his feet together with this rope," one of the men said as he handed a three foot long piece of rope to the man who had tied Harlan's hands behind his back earlier.

"Now let's pull him up in this tree by his feet so he'll be hanging upside down," another man told the group after Harlan's feet had been tied, taking a swig of moonshine.

"Yeah, but strip off his shirt first so he'll really feel the lashes from this whip," another man suggested as he unfurled a long cow whip.

"Please, please, I'll do anything," Harlan begged.

The men looked solemnly on as he was given thirty lashes, his screams echoing through the swamp. Afterward, he was hanged. Two men took a small skiff and rowed about fifty yards out into the pond on the edge of the large swamp and dumped his body. Before they even got to the bank, large gators were fighting over it. His body was never found, and none of the vigilantes were ever caught.

CHAPTER ELEVEN

It was just after eight a.m. in Winter Haven, Florida on Monday, January 4, 1932, when Jack drove through the open gate next to a sign that said "Sun Sweet Citrus." There was a number of flatbed trucks parked in a large mustering yard, and an equipment shed and shop with a tin roof to his left. To his right was a one-story white cinder block office building with about a dozen parking spaces in front. Jack entered into a small foyer, where a secretary was seated at a metal desk busily typing. "I'm Jack Thomas, and I came to inquire about the job for a harvesting supervisor."

"Just a minute," she replied, and disappeared into the building.

A few minutes later a man who looked to be in his late fifties walked up. He had a bulldog chest and jowly face, and brown wavy hair now partially gray and thinning. "Bill Brantley," he said as he extended his hand.

"Jack Thomas."

"Come on back to my office, Jack." As they entered the large cluttered office, Bill said, "Can I offer you anything, coffee, orange juice, water?"

"Thanks, I'm fine. I hear you're looking for a harvesting supervisor."

"You know anything about harvesting citrus?"

"No, but I can learn. I've managed a small farm."

185

ROBERT ALLEN MORRIS

"Wait a minute, aren't you the Jack Thomas that helped break up those child labor camps?"

"Yes, sir."

"What you did was great!"

"Thanks. Will you hire me?"

"I'm afraid not. I need someone that knows citrus harvesting, plus I remember from that article that you're only sixteen."

"That's legal working age, and I'm a hard worker. I tell you what, I'll work for the rest of the season for free, and learn from whoever you hire, then you can start paying me or I'll find work somewhere else."

"Fair enough, Jack. Since you will be helping, I'll get one of our grove managers to fill this job until we see if you work out."

"Fine. Could you tell me a little about your operation?"

"Sure. My brother Bud and I started it with about 200 acres of citrus groves our father left us in 1910. We planted 350 more acres of groves, and expanded into custom harvesting and hauling. We're also the largest member and the manager of a grower cooperative fresh citrus packinghouse with a juice canning plant, Lakeside Citrus. In addition to the fruit from our own 550 acres of groves, we also harvest fruit from roughly 4,100 acres of groves owned by other growers."

"Impressive. When do you want me to start?"

"Be here at 6:30 in the morning."

"Thanks, you won't be sorry."

Jack arrived promptly the next morning. He walked over to the shop, where a trailer was being loaded with wooden ladders.

"Mornin', Bill," said Jack.

"Mornin'," Bill Brantley said, shaking his hand. "Jack, this is Charlie Knabb."

186

FLORIDA GOLD

"Good to meet you, Jack," Charlie said as he shook Jack's hand, then spit tobacco juice into the dirt. "You ready to go?"

"Yep." Charlie was a red-faced man over six feet tall, with short wavy black hair just beginning to turn gray, wearing black-rimmed eyeglasses. The door of the Ford pickup made a creaking sound as Jack opened it and climbed in, pushing clipboards with papers attached, a red-and-white pack of beechnut chewing tobacco, and several shotgun shells out of his way. There was a single barrel shotgun on the seat, its muzzle in the floor.

"For snakes," Charlie replied as he moved the shotgun over to give Jack more room. "Also get rabbits sometimes. My wife makes the best rabbit stew in Polk County."

They rode out to a grove several miles away and pickers were just getting out of an old bus. Each got a long canvas sack with a strap and slung it over their shoulder. Then they took wooden ladders off the back of a truck. Other men were unloading wooden boxes.

"They pick the fruit into the bags, then unload them into a wooden box. Each box holds about ninety pounds of fruit," Charlie explained. "Bill will give you your picking and delivery schedule each morning. Right now, we're delivering to three packinghouses. We harvest grapefruit, tangerines, and temple, Hamlin, Pineapple, and Valencia oranges. The grapefruit starts first in September, then the tangerines. All the oranges but the Valencias and Pineapples start in October or November. The Pineapples start in January, and the Valencias in March. We finish up with Valencias in June. Just before the start of each variety's harvest, before you can begin, you will need to test the fruit to determine when the sugar - called the Brix - and the Brix-to-acid ratio meets US Department of Agriculture standards. You'll also need to learn to estimate the number of boxes of fruit in a grove, so you'll know how much labor will be needed to pick it and how long it will take. Also, check the ladders regularly to be sure they're safe."

Jack was an eager learner who mastered the job quickly. In only two months, Charlie told Bill that Jack was ready to be a harvesting supervisor. "I'm learning from him now," Charlie explained.

"What are you learning?"

"For one, how to better estimate a crop of fruit. I always rode through the grove, looked at the crop, looked at what it picked last year, and made my estimate. Jack does that too, but he groups the trees by age category (under 4 years old, 4-5, 6-8, 9-13, etc.) and variety. His estimate was closer than mine on the last three groves we did. And the labor! He's designed an incentive system that pays them more than the standard rate for every box they pick above a certain quota. Their increased productivity is actually reducing our harvesting costs. You don't want to lose him to another company."

Jack was made a harvesting supervisor, and began receiving a paycheck. By the next season, he was made manager of harvesting, with five supervisors reporting to him. "Charlie, I'd like to learn how you manage a grove," Jack said one day when they were harvesting.

"Sure, where do you want me to start?"

"Start with planting the trees."

Over the next few days, Charlie told Jack about all aspects of grove management - rootstock selection, grafting, planting, fertilizing, spraying to control pests, hoeing and disking to control weeds, irrigation, etc. Jack absorbed it all.

In the two years to come, Jack would wind up working in all parts of the business, managing harvesting, managing groves, working in the packinghouse and going with Bill to discuss fruit pricing and delivery with the packinghouses.

But while he was learning all about the citrus business, Jack also knew he needed to continue his schooling. So on

FLORIDA GOLD

Monday, September 19, 1932, he went to the principal of Winter Haven High School and told him that he'd pay for a private teacher. "I think Mrs. Martha Leslie would be ideal. She teaches tenth grade and is real smart. Her husband, Don, is an accountant. Here is her telephone number."

"Ma'am, I'm looking for Mrs. Martha Leslie," Jack said as he walked up to the receptionist in the principal's office of Winter Haven High a few minutes before his three thirty appointment.

"Room 104, four doors down that hallway on the right," she replied, gesturing.

As Jack walked down the tall-ceilinged hallway, he wondered what it felt like to be a high school student, to participate in sports, hang out with friends, and go on dates – to just be a normal teenager. Well, he'd never get to experience that. But if the tutoring arrangement he wanted to make with Mrs. Leslie worked as he hoped it would, at least he'd get a version of the education he'd missed.

Jack knocked lightly on the door to room 104. A tall, slim attractive woman in her mid-thirties with black hair in a finger wave and wearing a green floral dress opened the door. "Mrs. Leslie, Jack Thomas, here for our meeting about you tutoring me."

"Yes, Jack, please come in."

They worked out an arrangement where she taught him on Tuesday, Wednesday, and Thursday nights, and Saturday afternoons, starting the following Saturday.

"Don, I've agreed to that tutoring arrangement with Jack Thomas that we discussed," Martha told her husband that night.

"Was he OK with the $8 a week?"

"Yeah, he was fine with it."

"Great, the extra money will certainly help out."

189

"Because of his work schedule, I've agreed to teach him here rather than at the school if that's OK."

"Sure, that's fine."

"Is he the Jack Thomas who helped to rescue all those boys in the labor camps last year?" asked Carolyn, their twelve-year-old daughter.

"Yes, it's him," Martha replied.

Carolyn's heart skipped a beat. Her teacher had read the newspaper articles about Jack's story to the class when it had come out, and Carolyn had been fascinated. She'd even cut the three-part story out of the newspapers and kept it, the first of which had a picture of him standing with police Chief Burns and Bureau Director Jim Glover. She'd heard he was working for a citrus company in Winter Haven, but some of her friends said that was just a rumor.

"From what I read in the paper, he sounds like a fine young man," Don observed.

"It must have been horrible, growing up like that, worked like a slave, no family," Martha added.

"Well, we'll get to meet him Saturday afternoon."

So Jack Thomas is coming here this Saturday? Carolyn thought. *Maybe I'll get to see if he lives up to those stories or if they were just exaggerations to sell more newspapers,* she told herself, trying to ignore how exciting the prospect of meeting Jack was to her.

"Actually, Gus and I are going bass fishing on Saturday afternoon," Don remembered, "so if it's OK, I'll meet him another time."

"Sure, that's fine."

At two p.m. on Saturday, Jack parked on the side of the road next to the white two-story wooden house. It had 311 in black numbers above the door on the large screened porch. *This must be it,* Jack thought.

Carolyn heard Jack's car door close and looked out of her upstairs window as the tall, lean, broad-shouldered young

FLORIDA GOLD

man walked across the front yard toward their house. His gait was assured, like he was master of his domain. The ringing doorbell made Carolyn jump as it interrupted her thoughts.

"Come on in, Jack," Martha said as she welcomed him.

"Thank you, Mrs. Leslie," Jack replied as he walked into the foyer.

"I've set up the dining table for us to begin your lessons."

Jack Thomas is in our dining room and I'm sitting in my room? Carolyn thought. *How dumb is that? What should I do? GO AND MEET HIM! But I can't meet him dressed like this! What was I thinking? OK, OK, calm down. What do I have to wear?* She hurriedly rummaged through her closet and finally selected a red plaid skirt and white shirt. She put them on, slipped into her flat shoes, ran a brush through her shoulder-length black curly hair and thought, *Now what? I know. I'll see if he wants a Coke.* She descended the stairs on shaky legs as she kept reminding herself to calm down.

"I'm sorry to bother you, but would you like a Coke, Mr. Thomas?" Carolyn asked as she boldly strode into the dining room.

"I take it this lovely young lady is Carolyn?" Jack asked as he politely stood.

"I'm sorry. Yes, this is our daughter, Carolyn."

"I'm Jack Thomas, your mother's newest student," Jack offered as he gently pressed her hand.

"It's a pleasure to meet you, Mr. Thomas," Carolyn replied, her emotions raging like a small boat being tossed at sea. She blushed and looked down at the floor, then away, not sure where to set her gaze, afraid he might see how he affected her.

"That's Jack. And I would very much like a Coke."

"I'll have one too," Martha told her.

What a cute girl, Jack thought. *I'll bet she's who my mother looked like when she was twelve.*

191

Carolyn went into the kitchen and leaned on the counter to steady herself. *Oh, heaven!* She thought.

Carolyn had always thought most girls were foolish - giggling at dumb things, afraid of lizards and spiders, dreaming of a Prince Charming. As an only child and not a son as her father had hoped, Carolyn was raised as a tom boy. She preferred going fishing or bird hunting with her dad to playing with dolls or going to her friends' tea parties. She was close to her dad and very intelligent. She listened and learned from him when he explained men and their romantic (sexual) motivations to her. She'd decided that when she was old enough, her dating would be with friends only, and platonic until she'd finished college and was emotionally ready to decide about marriage and her partner for life. But now that she'd just met seventeen-year-old Jack Thomas, she was no longer sure about anything. He was not like any other boy or man or person she'd ever met, and she didn't know what to make of what she'd experienced on this September afternoon in 1932. But there were several things of which she was sure. He was the most exciting man she'd ever encountered, and he left her feeling like she had never before. And he was the man she wanted to marry when she grew up - the one she intended to spend her life with. But that was years away. He was a very attractive man, the kind beautiful women threw themselves at. What would she do if he fell in love with someone else and married before she was old enough to go to him?

The Amalgamated Land Company had gone to trial first, in March of 1932. It lasted over a year, but in June of 1933, the federal government won, and was awarded $500,000 from the company in damages. Amalgamated was also required to pay $2,500 to each of the boys - or if they were minors, to their families - in restitution, and the company's officers were sentenced to life in prison. In honor of Jack's

FLORIDA GOLD

request, Amalgamated was also required to give the Chine Indian tribe and their descendants the legal right, in perpetuity, to live on their twenty-six thousand acres of land north of Blountstown and hunt, trap, and fish on it without payment. Any subsequent owners of this land would be required by law to honor this right of the Chine tribe.

Jack asked that the perpetual property rights provided to the Chine tribe be awarded in a ceremony at their village. He'd contacted the congressman from his district, Richard Fraser, who agreed to perform the ceremony, and Jack went with him to the Amalgamated Land Company's property. The new CEO of Amalgamated, Bob English, was also coming to sign the agreement.

As they rode past where the barracks Jack had lived in had stood, he stopped the car.

"Is this where the camp was, Jack?" asked Congressman Fraser.

"Yeah, it was my home for five years, before I moved to the shack."

"I can't imagine what a nightmare all of that must have been."

"I wouldn't have made it out alive if Hal Pate-Chobee and the Indian tribe we are headed to see hadn't helped me."

The large gate across the road had been removed, and the shack where Jack had lived for three years had been torn down. They soon arrived at the Indian village. Bob English was already there and talking with Hal Pate-Chobee, who was dressed in ceremonial clothing and wearing a colorful headdress, as were other members of the tribe who were there. When Hal Pate-Chobee saw Jack he smiled broadly and strode over to greet him. "Jack Thomas, my friend," the Indian greeted him warmly.

"Hal Pate-Chobee, my friend," Jack replied. "Hal Pate-Chobee, this is Congressman Richard Fraser. He will perform the ceremony."

ROBERT ALLEN MORRIS

"Congressman Fraser, welcome to our village."

"Thank you, Hal Pate-Chobee."

"Come, Jack. We go inside. Talk. Smoke." Jack followed him into the tipi.

"Jack brave warrior. Get evil men arrested. Free boys," Hal Pate-Chobee said as he lit a pipe, puffed on it, and handed it to Jack.

"None of that could have happened without your help, Hal Pate-Chobee," Jack replied, puffing on the pipe.

"Gift you had them give, right to live on land, will it be taken away like many treaties?"

"No, Hal Pate-Chobee. This isn't a treaty. It is a real estate entitlement that's now part of Florida law. Not only does it grant the right for you and the Chine tribe and all of your descendants to live, hunt, trap, and fish here forever, it prevents the government from ever being able to make you and your descendants live on a reservation."

"Jack special friend to Hal Pate-Chobee and tribe."

"It's the least I could do, Hal Pate-Chobee."

The ceremony went smoothly, and Hal Pate-Chobee graciously accepted the signed document on behalf of his tribe.

Jim Glover agreed with public sentiment that the $500,000 plus whatever was awarded from the other five companies should go to Jack after court costs were deducted. Without Jack's help they wouldn't have liberated the labor camps or even had a winnable case, plus Jack had suffered the loss of his family because he was held captive. Once the Amalgamated case was won, the other companies each settled out of court for a $250,000 fine, $2,500 paid to each of the boys who were in the camps, or their families, and ten years in prison for their company officers.

194

FLORIDA GOLD

In July of 1934, Jack received 1.4^8 million from the settlements. The $2,500 settlements from each of the six companies to the boys that were in the camps came to $15,000^9 per boy, or per family if the boys were still minors. The press picked up the story and Jack was mobbed by people with get-rich-quick investment opportunities. The Bureau of Investigation arranged for Jack to tell his story to leading magazines as a way to give the public an example of the good the BOI was doing (and to get a bigger budget).

In August, *Esquire Magazine* featured nineteen-year-old Jack on the cover as the wealthiest teenager in America. Then, in October, *The Cosmopolitan* (later named *Cosmopolitan Magazine*) featured Jack on its cover with the caption "Jack Thomas, America's Dashingly Handsome Teenage Millionaire." Jack quickly became a national teenage hero and a heartthrob. Young women were going nuts trying to meet the attractive, young, heroic millionaire. Jack was polite, but refused their advances. He wanted to focus on his career and felt he was too young for marriage or the diversion of a relationship. Jack used $18,000 to build a four bedroom house on Lake Eloise in Winter Haven.

It was lunchtime at Winter Haven High, and a group of fourteen-year-old girls were huddled around the Cosmopolitan with Jack's picture as they ate their sandwiches.

"He's so dreamy," Janet said, a faraway look in her eyes.

"Hey! Carolyn!" one of the girls shouted as Carolyn was leaving the lunchroom.

"Does Jack Thomas still take lessons from your mother?" Fay asked as Carolyn walked up to the table where the group was sitting.

"No, he finished them last June."

---

[8] The same as $24.3 million in 2013.
[9] The same as $260,700 in 2013.

195

ROBERT ALLEN MORRIS

"Found someone who's not married and he can take on a date to take lessons from, huh," Phyllis suggested.

"No, he finished. He did a lot of studying on his own, and Mom says he's real smart."

"He looks real strong too. I bet hunting with those Indians and working that farm built a lot of muscles," Ann observed.

"He's handsomer than Tarzan," said Phyllis.

"There is no Tarzan, it's only a story. Johnny Weissmuller plays Tarzan," Fay added.

"I bet he's as brave and strong as Tarzan," Janet added. "What was he like, Carolyn?"

"He was polite, charming, you know, a lot like the articles say."

"Yeah, and he's also rich," Fay replied.

"There's a lot more to a good husband than money," Janet said.

"I think he's more charming than Clark Gable..."

"Carolyn, are you OK?" Phyllis asked as Carolyn got up and ran out of the lunchroom. She went into the girls' bathroom, into a stall and began to cry. *With practically every girl in America crazy about him, I don't stand a chance,* she thought as she sobbed.

"Bill, you ever think of selling Sun Sweet Citrus?" Jack asked in late August as the season was getting ready to start.

"I thought you'd be retiring with all that money, Jack."

"I'm too young to retire."

"Well, my brother, Bud and I are both pushing sixty, and none of our sons are interested in the business, so yeah, I think we'd consider it, if the offer is high enough."

"How about $950,000 for everything - groves, trucks, office, shop, harvesting equipment, plus your controlling interest in the packinghouse and Lakeside Citrus, the canning plant?"

FLORIDA GOLD

"I'll discuss it with Bud tonight."

The next morning, Bill called Jack into his office. "You've bought yourself a citrus business, Jack."

"Great!"

"Jack, is that you?" asked Harry Osborne, Jack's old friend from the labor camp. It was January 2, 1936, and they were both at the grand opening of Cypress Gardens in Winter Haven.

"Harry, how've you been?"

"Great, you?"

"Can't complain."

Harry Osborne was as red headed as when he'd been in the labor camp, and now also had a red mustache. A solidly built five foot eleven inches tall with eyes that were dull green but shrewd looking, dressed in corduroy pants and a short-sleeved flowery shirt, he was standing in a line to see the water ski show.

"I didn't know where you were living. The newspapers didn't say, I guess to protect your privacy after that settlement. What are you up to? I assume you're retired."

"No. I bought a company - Sun Sweet Citrus. What about you?"

"I'm an accountant for a timber company based in Jacksonville. When I got out of the camp at fifteen, my mother tutored me through the equivalent of high school, then I used part of my $15,000 to fund going to college to get a degree in business from the University of Florida. I graduated in 1934."

"Married?"

"No. Got a steady girl, though. You?"

"No, not even a steady girl. I've been on a few dates. Where are you staying?"

"At the Polk Hotel in Haines City."

"Well, cancel your room. You're staying with me."

197

"Great."

Jack and Harry got reacquainted, and caught up with what had been going on in each other's lives. One morning at breakfast, Jack said, "Harry, come to work for me. I need a good accountant and a number two in my business. I plan to grow, and I can use all the management help I can get. Whatever they're paying you at the timber company, I'll pay you fifty percent more and pay your costs to move down here."

"Really? Jack, you've got a deal! There's just one thing - my girl, Jean. I'm going to tell her about the new job and ask her to marry me. Will you be my best man?"

"I'd be honored."

Harry was married a month later, and by September, he and his new wife, Jean, had moved into a house in Haines City, and he'd started his new job as vice president of finance and operations for the Sun Sweet Citrus company.

Jack's annual profits, after his salary and allowing for equipment replacements, averaged about $85,000[10] a year, although they were volatile, mostly due to production and price volatility created by unpredictable weather. He saved most of it, and added it to the $400,000 he had left from the law suit settlements.

On December 7, 1941, Japan bombed Pearl Harbor, and the US entered World War II. On a Monday the following June, Jack said, "Harry, I want to defend my country. I'm going to join the Marines."

"What? Jack, you don't have to do that. You own a large company. I'm sure you could get a draft deferment."

"I don't want one. I want to fight for my country."

"But what about the business?"

---

[10] The same as $1.4 million in 2013.

FLORIDA GOLD

"You're capable of running it. I'll give you a promotion and a salary adjustment."

"I'm more worried about you than the business."

"If I'm killed in the war, I'll set it up so the business goes to you." Although Harry tried, he couldn't talk Jack out of enlisting.

On July 11, twenty-seven-year-old Jack Thomas left for basic training at Paris Island, South Carolina. Thirteen weeks later he headed home on thirty days leave.

"Guess who's back in town?" asked Sandra, Carolyn's closest friend.

"Who?"

"Everyone's dream boat – Jack Thomas."

"He's finished basic training?"

"I guess."

Its time, she thought. After eight years, it was time, it was finally time to meet him again, but this time as an adult. To see if he would be as attracted to her as she was to him.

Jack was having lunch in a diner with Harry and they were discussing the business. "Mr. Thomas?" a female voice said.

"Yes?" Jack looked up and almost fell out of his chair. She was gorgeous, taller than average, probably about five seven or five eight, and slender, with an incredibly sexy body. Her rich brunette hair flowed over her shoulders, and her face was radiant. Her eyes were wide-set, large and deep blue, and seemed to dance with excitement. Her face was narrow, its features distinct, with a creamy smooth complexion and the angles and shadows of a model. Her mouth was full and generous. As Jack looked at her, he realized that she was the most beautiful woman he'd ever seen.

"It's me, Carolyn Leslie, Martha's daughter."

"Sure, I recognize you now."

"Guess I'm all grown up."

"I'll say," Harry replied, glad that he could finally speak.

199

"Why don't you come to dinner tonight at my parents' house and we can catch up. I know they'd like to see you."

"OK, thanks for inviting me."

"Carolyn started her senior year at Florida State College for Women in September," Martha said.

"That's great. What are you studying?"

"I'm majoring in education. I plan to teach high school English after I graduate next June."

"And she'll make a wonderful teacher," her father added.

"I'm sure she will, Don," Jack agreed. Dinner was interesting and Jack felt himself increasingly drawn to Carolyn. It was more than her beauty. Something about her was powerfully attractive. Carolyn went back to school on Sunday and Jack immersed in his business for the remainder of his leave.

December 4, 1942

Carolyn,

Just a quick note to say how much I enjoyed seeing you again after all these years. I'm fully enmeshed in advanced infantry training here at Quantico. Our group is pretty diverse geographically, ranging from Tom Peters from New York City to Jim Yarborough from Chicago, to Jimmy Taylor from Dothan, Alabama. But these are a great bunch of guys, all committed to helping us win this war.

Jack

December 10, 1942

Jack,

I was pleasantly surprised to hear from you! It sounds as if you are really enjoying what you are doing and are with a great group of guys, which I'm sure makes things a

little easier. It's hard to believe that this is my last year at FSU. A couple of my classmates are going on for their master's degree, but I'm ready to start teaching. I can't wait until graduation.

I was just wondering... if you get any leave for Christmas?

Carolyn

December 18, 1942

Carolyn,

I only get Christmas Day off, and Jerry Barnes has invited me to spend it with his family in Charlottesville, about two hours from here. Thanks for sending the picture. You're a very beautiful young woman, and smart too. All my friends are envious. They think you are my girlfriend, but I told them I wasn't that lucky, that we're just friends. I might be able to get some leave after I complete my training in January. If so, would you go out with me?

Jack

December 26, 1942

Jack,

I got the picture you sent and you look so handsome in your dress blues. I think about you a lot - all the time actually. I really hope that you will get that leave and that I will be able to see you soon! I would really like to go out with you. And I'd LOVE to be your girl and have you call me your girlfriend.

Carolyn

January 9, 1943

Carolyn,
Boy, am I lucky. You're my girlfriend and I'm getting a combat assignment! I have one week's leave before I ship out, and should get into Winter Haven Friday night, January 22. Can you get away from school that weekend? I'll call your mother's house that Saturday morning after I get home.
Jack

It was late morning on January 23, 1943, and the day was pleasant and sunny, about seventy-four degrees. Martha and Don had invited Jack to have lunch with them. Carolyn had on a white linen dress and was wearing a big straw hat, wandering through her mother's flower garden in the back yard.

"Carolyn, Jack's here," she heard her mother call from the back door. She watched the broad shoulders, trim hips, and long legs as he walked easily across the yard toward the garden. He was an extraordinary-looking man, particularly in his Marine uniform. She found herself blushing and embarrassed when he smiled at her.

"Hello, Carolyn," he said as he walked up. His eyes ran over her like sprinkles of warm summer rain.

"Hi, Jack." She felt so foolish. *Is that all you can think to say?* she thought. Her stomach tightened and felt like it was filled with butterflies. His bright-blue eyes were too much for her, the way he searched her face, the way he smiled. She looked away.

"It sure is good to see you," he said, taking her hand gently. Lightning strikes went up her arm.

"Oh, Jack, I've wanted to see you so much. I'm so glad you have this leave."

"I am too."

"Lunch is ready," Martha called from the back door.

FLORIDA GOLD

That Saturday, Jack, in his Marine dress blues, rang the doorbell at the Leslies' house promptly at six thirty p.m. "Come on in, Jack," Don greeted him warmly when he answered the door. "Carolyn should be right down."

"Hey again, Jack," Martha said as she came into the living room. "Would you like something to drink?"

"Hi, Jack," a melodic voice said from the stairs. Jack's knees grew weak, and he almost stumbled as he realized again how incredibly beautiful she was. Carolyn was wearing a navy-blue skirt, white bodice, and red trim with a bow at the neckline. The fitted dress also had delicately placed pleats that accentuated her figure. Her beautiful black curly hair, spilling from beneath the dark-blue felt suit beret, was done in a top reverse roll, and she had on white gloves and wore blue, low-heeled pumps.

"Carolyn, you look stunning," Jack replied when he found his voice. "Mr. and Mrs. Leslie, I'll have her home by midnight."

"We certainly won't worry about Carolyn when she's out with you. You just have a good time, Jack," Don offered.

"We're going to the Lake Region Country Club?" Carolyn asked excitedly as Jack turned onto the winding road lined with oak trees that led to it.

"Yeah, Harry got us a company membership and he keeps reminding me I should use it more. What better occasion than this?"

I keep forgetting that Jack's a very wealthy man, Carolyn thought. *I guess it's because he doesn't act like it.*

They pulled up to an entryway covered by a green canvas awning, and as uniformed attendants opened the car doors for each of them, one said, "Good evening, Mr. Thomas, welcome back to Lake Region. How does it feel to be a Marine?"

203

"It feels great, Craig. I'm looking forward to fighting for this great country of ours."

The entry foyer led into a large ballroom with varnished oak walls, tall beamed ceilings, and chandeliers. There were tables for four and six throughout the room, each with white linen tablecloths, and china, silver, and crystal place settings. At the front of the room was an area for dancing, with seats and band instruments off to one side. A grand piano was playing softly.

"Mr. Thomas, it's good to see you again, sir," the hostess said. "And who is your friend?"

"Miss Carolyn Leslie."

"Welcome to the Lake Region Country Club, Miss Leslie. Mr. Thomas, your table is ready."

"Mr. Thomas, my name is Malcolm, and I'll be your waiter this evening, sir."

"Thank you, Malcolm."

"May I bring you something to drink?"

"I'll have white wine," Carolyn replied.

"And I'll have Jack Daniel's on the rocks."

Malcolm came back carrying their drinks, followed by another waiter carrying the roses Jack had ordered that morning, and said, "I believe these are for the lady."

"Oh, Jack! They're so beautiful! You're so sweet and thoughtful, thank you."

"A beautiful lady needs beautiful flowers," Jack said to a beaming Carolyn.

"We would like this 1934 bottle of Chateau L'Eglise," he said as he ordered their wine.

"A very good selection, sir. It comes from the Pomerol region of Bordeaux, I believe."

Once the waiter left, Jack said, "I really enjoyed your letters. They were the only ones I got, other than a few about the business from Harry."

FLORIDA GOLD

"I forgot, you don't have any family, do you?"

"Not any longer. But I've got friends like you and your parents, and Harry, and Jerry from my unit. I feel lucky. So what are your plans after graduation? Do you know where you're going to teach?"

Soon, the waiter brought their wine and opened it to breathe before decanting it. Then he took their order.

"I'll have the crabmeat-stuffed grouper," Carolyn said.

"And I'll have the fourteen-ounce strip, medium rare."

As they were finishing their dessert and coffee, the band started up again, playing "I'm in the Mood for Love," with a talented female vocalist singing. "Would you like to dance?" Jack asked

"Yes, very much."

They began a slow dance, and Jack held her at a respectable distance, in spite of the fact that every fiber in him wanted to hold her close. This was, in fact, their first date and he kept reminding himself that he had to be respectful of that. She pulled him closer and said teasingly, "I like this much better." She felt her bones melting, her body pliant when she slipped into his arms.

The feel of her incredible body against his and the innocent loveliness of her angelic face were all he could think about. He wanted to kiss her more than he'd ever wanted anything, but somehow he resisted, reminding himself that it wasn't proper to act on his desire on their first date.

Every movement of his powerful body swept through her, making her tremble. She felt the heat raging through her and wondered if he could feel it too. She reassured herself that this wasn't a dream, that she was awake, that she was in his arms, and wholly alive for the first time in her life. She wanted him to kiss her, wanted it with a sudden staggering force that wiped every other thought out of her head.

After they'd danced to "I'm Stepping Out with a Memory Tonight," and several other songs, Jack said, "It's warm for

January and the moon is almost full. Would you like to go out by the lake?"

"Yes, that would be nice," she replied, her mind on a roller coaster in dreamland.

He settled up the check, took her hand, and they walked outside. They strolled along a path beside the lake in silence, holding hands and enjoying the view with the moon's reflection cast across the lake, her beautiful hair moving slightly in the breeze. In the distance, an owl sounded it's *who, who, who-whooo*. Jack knew then that he had to hold her, that he had to kiss her, and if he was being too forward, then he was prepared to pay the price. "Jack," she began, her voice barely more than a whisper. "It's so good to see you again, and dinner was wonderful, and the roses, I..."

And then he took her in his arms, and she made a soft gasp as his lips met hers ever so tenderly, like a gentle experiment. One of his hands moved to cradle the back of her head, nudging it to the side so his lips could roam her jawline and inch back to capture her lips again, massaging her mouth into pleasant submission.

Their lips parted and Jack said, "I've wanted to do that all night."

"Oh, Jack, I've wanted you to, I've wanted you to so much." She attempted to speak clearly with a voice that had lost its strength while her emotions raged like a summer storm. Then his lips found hers again, her mouth seeking his in return, spinning the world into nothing. There was no hesitation or shyness now, but demand, their kiss growing harder, more insistent as her body seemed to melt to his. She explored the strength of his arms and felt the hard rippling muscles of his back as she plunged deeper into sensations she could no longer measure. She became filled with an all-consuming need to be his. Their lips drew apart and they held each other and looked deeply into each other's eyes. She

FLORIDA GOLD

struggled to climb back to reality, dazed and limp with a myriad of newly discovered desires.

Jack's mind filled with new and glorious thoughts. *Who is this wonderful and beautiful angel that has captured my heart so quickly, so completely? Will I wake up and find that this has all been a dream? Does this special, wonderful new feeling I have when I am with her mean I'm falling in love truly for the first time in my life?* And then he realized that he didn't know how long he'd been holding her and gazing into her eyes. With great reluctance, bordering on sadness, Jack saw that it was almost midnight, and knew he should be getting Carolyn home so her parents wouldn't be worried. That he needed to control his desires to go far beyond kissing. "It's late. I'd better be getting you home," he said.

"OK," she replied, a touch of regret in her sweet voice.

When they arrived at her house the front light was on. He walked with her to the door and asked, "Will you go to church with me tomorrow?"

"I'd like to, but I have to catch the train for school at ten thirty tomorrow morning."

"I'll give you a ride if you'd like?"

"Yes, I would."

"Great. What time do we need to leave from here?"

"Nine forty-five should be fine."

"I'll see you just before, then." He pulled her to him and she moaned as his lips found hers.

"I guess I'd better let you go inside," he said reluctantly. "I'll see you in the morning."

"I'll be ready."

Everyone was asleep, and it was dark except for one small light on in the hallway. Carolyn managed to maintain her composure until the door to her room was closed and she was inside. And then her knees buckled under her as she fell upon the bed, shaking with emotion. *Oh my God! I had no idea it would be like this!* she thought as she sat on the edge of her bed in a daze, taking in the events of the night, and especially how it felt when Jack had held her and kissed her.

"Well, how was the date last night?" Martha asked as Carolyn walked into the kitchen where her mother was scrambling eggs. A coffee pot was percolating, the rich aroma mixing with that of recently fried bacon, and biscuits baking in the oven. Don was sitting at the kitchen table sipping coffee, lost in the Sunday newspaper.

"It was...It was wonderful, Mom," Carolyn replied, her voice trembling slightly as she took the lightly browned biscuits out of the oven.

"Where'd you go?" Don asked, looking up from his newspaper as he crushed his cigarette out in the ashtray next to him.

"We went to the Lake Reg..." she started, and then burst into tears, hurrying back to her bedroom.

"What's the matter?" Don asked, standing up with a concerned look.

"I think I know what it is. I'll go talk to her," Martha said.

"It's that bad, huh?" Martha said as she lovingly stroked her daughter's hair. Carolyn was dabbing her tear-streaked face with a tissue.

"Oh, Mama. What I felt for him before was just a crush. But THIS! This is...I've never felt like this. I never even dreamed I could feel like this." She told her mother about their date, choking with emotion as she described their walk along the lake. "He's so wonderful, so nice, so...and when he holds me, I think I'm going to MELT."

"You know how your father and I feel about Jack."

"I know. But I'm so worried. I hate that war. What if something happens to him? Oh, Mama. I couldn't live if I lost him," she said, her voice trembling as the tears started to come again.

FLORIDA GOLD

"Is everything OK in here?" Don asked as he stuck his head in the doorway.

"Everything's fine. Our little girl's just seriously in love."

"I could've told you that. Let's eat before the food's gets any colder."

"Will you relax?" Martha told a fidgety Carolyn. "He's not supposed to be here for another fifteen minutes."

"Do I look OK? I'm not wearing too much makeup, am I? Maybe I should change this dress and put on the blue one."

"Carolyn, for the tenth time - YOU LOOK FINE. Now stop worrying."

The ringing doorbell interrupted Carolyn's thoughts.

"Good morning, Jack," Martha greeted him.

"Mornin' Mrs. Leslie." Jack was out of his uniform, dressed in tan slacks and a light-blue long-sleeved shirt.

"Come on in. Carolyn's ready, she's..."

"Good morning, Jack," a cheerful and composed Carolyn said as she walked up.

"My, you look lovely this morning, Carolyn," Jack told her.

There go those butterflies again, she thought.

"Hey, Jack. Carolyn said you went to Lake Region last night," Don said as he walked up and they shook hands.

"Yes, sir, we did."

"You ever play golf there? I hear it's a great course."

"No, I never learned to play. But if you'd like, I'll ask Harry to invite you. He plays there sometimes."

"That would be great."

"Call us when you get to your sorority house," Martha requested as she and Don hugged Carolyn while Jack loaded her bag into the trunk of his car.

On the ride to the train station, Carolyn sat next to Jack with her head on his shoulder. Neither spoke, preferring instead to ride in silence with their thoughts. They soon arrived, and Jack handled her luggage while Carolyn checked

209

the train schedule. "Train leaves in seven minutes," the clerk told her.

"Oh, Jack. I'm going to miss you so much. And I'm worried, I don't know what I'd do if something happened to you." She began to cry softly, and Jack pulled her to him.

"Shhhh, I'm going to be fine."

Her whole body ached from the terrible emptiness she felt inside. She was more conscious of Jack at this moment than she'd ever been of anyone or anything. When his lips brushed across hers, she held on to him desperately, as if she would fall. Their mouths pressed together, Jack's free hand tangling in her hair. Through his shirt she could feel the muscles of his shoulders, hard, smooth, rippling with his movements.

"Train 101 to Tampa, Gainesville, Lake City, Tallahassee, leaving in two minutes," a voice shouted.

"I'm in love with you, Jack." There. She'd said it. She'd told him.

"I'm in love with you too, Carolyn."

Her breath caught as his words spilled over her and through her. She was barely able to believe that at this moment he was telling her what she had wanted so much to hear him say for all those years. Her mind was filled with the most wonderful thoughts, and a glorious, happy glow began to engulf her, all the while his words echoing in her head. She tried to say something but couldn't. He filled in the silence.

"I know now that I never really knew what love was until I met you."

She knew that at this moment she was the happiest she'd ever been in her life. "Oh, Jack," she finally managed to say in a trembling voice.

"ALL ABOARD."

"Here, it's my Marine ring."

"I'll never take it off," she said, fastening the necklace it was on around her neck, the tears starting again.

FLORIDA GOLD

"You'd better go," Jack said as the train started moving slowly.

"Bye, darling, I love you," she told him through her tears.

I love you too, Carolyn," Jack shouted over the noise. "When I know it, I'll send you my address so we can write."

Carolyn's train got into Tallahassee at 4:50. She caught the five o'clock bus and was at the Chi Omega house by five thirty. As she walked into the great room, her friend Georgia said, "Hey everyone, Carolyn's back." The ballroom-size great room with its tall beamed ceiling, chandeliers, extended ceiling fans, and hardwood floor was spacious yet inviting. The dual stone fireplaces on opposite ends of the room and overstuffed sofas and chairs accompanied by cherry wood tables atop Persian rugs provided ample spaces for girls and their guests to visit and socialize. A group of her friends were listening to the radio, while other girls were talking, no doubt about their dates over the weekend that was ending.

"OK, we need to know how the date was," Ann requested. Most girls had forgotten about Jack Thomas in the years since his notoriety. However, Carolyn's bedroom was filled with memorabilia about Jack. The three-part newspaper article about the child labor camps, the issues of *Fortune* and *Cosmopolitan* with Jack on their cover, even a May, 1938 article in *The Saturday Evening Post* with Jack standing next to an attractive female Cypress Gardens skier that was his date for a charity event. The article quoted him saying he wasn't ready to get into a serious romantic relationship. Carolyn's memorabilia and talk about Jack had created a renewed interest about him among her friends, particularly about Carolyn's interest in dating him.

"Details, we need all the details," Carolyn's best friend Kim added in an amused tone.

"It was the most romantic, enchant..."

"She's wearing his ring!" Thelma shrieked.

"Is that really Jack Thomas's ring?" asked Ginny.

211

"Yes, it's his Marine ring."

"When did he give it to you?" Thelma asked.

"This morning, just after he told me he was in love with me."

"He told you he was in love with you?" Kim asked, a wishful, mellow tone in her voice.

"That must have been some date," Ann added enviously. "Did it end with breakfast?"

"It was the most incredible, romantic date of my life, if that's what you mean. If you mean did I sleep with him, the answer is no. And he didn't pressure me to. He was a real gentleman."

"Tell us all about it, Carolyn," said Kim. "Where did he take you, what did you do...?"

It was late - past midnight, and everyone was asleep but Carolyn. She sat in silence in the nearly dark great room, lost in her thoughts, the dying fire sending sparks up the chimney as its logs settled. Somewhere in the world a desperate battle was being fought - a challenge to the freedoms that Jack would soon help defend. Carolyn would fight her own brave battle. Hers would be the awful fear and constant worry that the man she so desperately loved would be killed defending those freedoms, and that their dreams, their future together would never be possible. But she supported him in his decision to go – because it meant so much. Because she knew deep down that as other couples faced the same challenges, that collectively having loving, supportive, and brave partners at home to return to would be important to winning the war.

CHAPTER TWELVE

PFC Jack Thomas
15th Infantry Regiment
3rd Infantry Division
PSC 812, Box 1000
Sigonella, Sicily – Italy

Chi Omega Sorority House
661 West Jefferson Street
Tallahassee, Florida
February 27, 1943

Carolyn,
I'm still trying to understand what has happened to me over the last month. My answer is that YOU happened to me. That cute girl who used to bring me coca-colas and snacks while her mother was giving me the education that I missed as a boy, grew up into an incredibly beautiful, smart, and interesting woman. Carolyn, you have captured my heart so totally, so completely that you constantly dominate my thoughts.

I didn't have to fight in this war. My citrus business was justification for a draft deferment because our government wants to keep its economy productive during the war. But I

213

joined the Marines because I wanted to help further the purposes of our great country in its fight against the dark movements of communism, socialism and fascism that threaten to engulf the world. I know that we will win this war, because America was formed as a country that is an instrument of God's purposes, to stand against tyranny, and to be a clear leader to the world able to restore peace and prosperity when it is threatened. And because American soldiers like me are committed to helping America carry out these purposes, to help it fulfill its destiny as a world leader.

But now I have another reason to help our country win this war – YOU. Carolyn, you are my shining star in this dark war, the light in my darkest hour, the doorway to my soul. I'm going to make you proud of me, and I'm coming home from this war as your hero. I'm coming home from this war so we can fulfill our love for each other.
I love you Carolyn,
Jack
P.S. You can write to me at the above address

FLORIDA GOLD

Chi Omega Sorority House
661 West Jefferson Street
Tallahassee, Florida

PFC Jack Thomas
15th Infantry Regiment
3rd Infantry Division
PSC 812, Box 1000
Sigonella, Sicily – Italy

March 20, 1943

Jack,

I secretly fell in love with you when I was a teenager and you were coming to our house for your lessons with my mother. I never acted on my feelings because I was so young, much too young for there to be anything romantic between us. But I grew up, and although it was hard for me to muster up the courage to be forward enough to invite you to our home for dinner with my parents, I now realize that it was the best decision I have ever made.

Although our romance is new, it has changed my world forever. You have entered my heart and my soul, and everything I felt for you as a young girl has magnified, has blossomed into the closest thing to heaven I can imagine. I thought I was in love with you before, when I was a teenage girl. But when we strolled along the banks of Lake Region on that enchanting night that I shall never forget, and you took me in your arms and kissed me, I discovered what real love is.

Passion, ecstasy, bliss, euphoria - all just words before. Now, because of you, feelings I have truly begun to experience for the first time. The morning after our date I woke up with a joy greater than I had ever felt as I realized that my dream was finally coming true. But my euphoria quickly turned to sadness, then to depression, because I knew what was coming. You were going to be leaving me. You would be going to a world of death and destruction, and your return home could not be guaranteed. That horrified me and will continue to horrify me until you are home from this war for good. My parents have recognized that their young girl has become a young woman desperately in love with a man who might be killed in this war, and although they are supportive and understanding, it doesn't stop the ache I have inside for you, to be with you.

I can't stop thinking about you, and I am finding it hard to focus in class because I day dream about you all the time. I dream about the first time you kissed me, about your touch, how your lips felt, how you held me, your fingers finding their way through my hair, about our future.

I'm crying. I HATE THIS WAR!

I'm OK now. I prayed for you to be safe, I prayed for us and our future together, and God is giving me strength. Jack, please be careful over there. I worry about you every minute of every day. If I lost you I would also die – of a broken heart. But our love is worth that chance. Although we are in different parts of the world, my thoughts are always with you. The distance only strengthens my love for you, deep within my lonely, almost broken heart.

FLORIDA GOLD

Please take care of yourself and write me as often as you can and I will do the same. I miss you terribly and love you so very, very much.
Carolyn

April 10, 1943

Carolyn,
I killed a man today, my first, and I feel awful about it. One of my friends, Lamar Burger, was lured into the open and wounded by a German soldier pretending to surrender. I ran to help Lamar, and the German began shooting at me. Because his shots were diverted away from Lamar toward me, two other men from our outfit got Lamar to safety and to the medics. I jumped behind a large tree and hesitated, realizing what I was going to try to do. Then I imagined that was you he had wounded, and I stepped from behind that tree and shot him in the head. The medics say that Lamar will be OK, he just may walk with a limp. My superior officers were impressed, but I keep telling myself that I took a life. I'll get over it. Because I know that killing is part of war.

I read your letter over and over. You have no idea how much it means to me. I thank God every day for bringing you into my life, for your love for me. Carolyn, knowing how you love me makes me brave. It gives me the will to go into battle and fight, because I know that I am fighting for our future together. I dream of holding you, touching you softly, intimately, kissing you passionately, and of much more that isn't proper for me to write to you about. That morning at the train station when I told you I never knew what love was until I met you, that was fact. But it's much more than that. Even though our relationship now is only through our letters, I know that we were meant for each other. I know that you are the only woman in the world for me.

217

Carolyn, I love you so much, so very much more than I can describe.
Yours always,
Jack

May 8, 1943

Jack,
I'm so sorry that you had to kill that man. But like you said, that's a part of war and it sounds like he was trying to kill you, so it was self-defense. I know that you would never let any harm come to me, that you will always be my protector. You are my knight in shining armor, and you have shown me the true meaning of what it is to love and be loved – completely, unselfishly.

Graduation is in less than a month – on June the 5th. The dean's office notified me that I will graduate with high honors. I sure wish you could be here to go to my graduation ceremony. My parents have planned a party at their house the Saturday after. But I fear that I will not be a good hostess as I will be in a melancholy mood as usual, missing you.

I got a job! I will be teaching 11th grade English at Winter Haven High beginning September 7th. Trisha Johnson, a friend who started teaching at WHH last year, has found a small two bedroom house that the two of us together can afford to rent. I'm all for that because I do not want to live with my parents, particularly since you are now part of my life. We need our privacy when you return from the war.

FLORIDA GOLD

Oh, Jack. I miss you so, and I do love you so very much. Please be careful. As I have said, I would not want to or be able to live if I lost you.

You are always and forever in my thoughts and I do love you so,
Carolyn

Jack's true combat initiation came when he took part in the invasion of Sicily on July 10, 1943. Shortly after arriving Jack was promoted to corporal after killing two Italian officers when they tried to escape on horseback. After Sicily was secured from Axis forces, his division invaded the Italian mainland, landing near Salerno in September, 1943. While leading night patrol, Jack and his men ran into German soldiers but fought their way out of an ambush, taking cover in a rock quarry. The German command sent a squad of soldiers in, but they were stopped by intense machine-gun and rifle fire. Three German soldiers were killed and several others captured. As a result of his actions at Salerno, Jack was promoted to sergeant.

January 8, 1944

Carolyn,
I have learned to use anger as my friend. Recently, another group of those damned Germans pretending to surrender killed three of our men. That did it for me! I killed all of their machine gun crew, then used their machine gun and their grenades to destroy their five other positions, which is all that I could find. Sorry, I needed to vent my anger to someone who understands me. Everyone is talking about what I did. I

219

thought that killing the enemy is what soldiers are supposed to do.

I am hoping to get some leave soon. It's been almost a year since I got here, and the Marines often give leave to soldiers that have been in battle for about a year. As always, I am thinking and dreaming about seeing you. I have held and kissed you a thousand times in my thoughts. I read your letters and look at the photos you sent me every day. You are so beautiful, so smart. I don't know what I did to deserve you. But I thank God that you are in love with me. I simply must see you. I'm going to make a request for that leave.

Yours always,
Jack

February 12, 1944

Jack,
The story of how you killed those German soldiers and then used their machine gun to destroy all of their enemy positions is all over the newspapers! It's even in news reels at the picture shows! They are saying that you are going to be awarded the Distinguished Service Cross, second only to the Congressional Medal of Honor!! You're a war hero!! I'm so proud of you, darling. And I miss you terribly.

I have been praying that you will get that leave – and very soon. I must see you, Jack. Will being a hero make it more likely for you to get that leave? I can't stand being away from you another day, not even another minute. Please, please, get that leave.

I love you very much and always will,
Carolyn

FLORIDA GOLD

February 22, 1944

Carolyn,
I'm getting forty-five days leave beginning March 16! Normal would be thirty days but I was able to get the extra fifteen because I own a business. My train gets into Winter Haven at 6:12 p.m. on March 16. Can't wait to see you, beautiful!
Jack

Jack arrived in Winter Haven on March 16, 1944. As the train pulled into the station he saw Carolyn through the window waving excitedly at him. He had forgotten how beautiful she was, and the sight of her in her black dress with spring-like floral, ribbon tie at the neckline, and pleated bodice, her beautiful brunette hair spilling over her shoulders, captured his thoughts like nothing else. He went down the steps and out of the train as she hurriedly weaved toward him through the crowd.

His face looked more mature, and impossibly handsome. Its features appeared carved from stone. "Oh, Jack, Jack, you're finally here!" They threw their arms around each other as their lips came together in a ravishing, then devouring kiss. The throng of people around them ceased to exist as each dominated the other's thoughts. He lifted his head, their lips parting, their breath warm and erratic on each other's faces. Her eyes fluttered open, dazed. She was trembling as he held her and looked into her eyes. His bright-blue eyes seemed to hold the mysteries of the depths of all the world's oceans. No words would come as she savored this moment she had dreamed of, had lived for agonizingly for what seemed like an eternity.

He got his bags, and with her arm tightly encircling his, as they walked to her car she exclaimed, "Jack, you're a war hero! The Distinguished Service Cross!"

"I had to make my girl proud of me, now didn't I?

"You'll always be my hero."

"As long as I'm your hero, that's all that counts for me. Over there, I'm just trying to do the job that needs doing."

Neither noticed the light traffic in the quickly darkening day as she quietly instructed him how to find her place, his arm around her, her head on his shoulder. "I've dreamed..." they both began, then chuckled as they realized that both were going to say the same thing.

They entered the dimly lit house, but before she could reach for the light Jack pulled her to him, tilted her chin up and found her lips as their arms encircled. She closed her eyes and allowed other senses to "see" for her, every sensation enhanced by the darkness - the feel of his soft, cotton shirt at her fingertips, the smoothness of his skin underneath, the intoxicating scent of his cologne, and her memory of his deep voice filled every inch of space in her mind. His lips skimmed over her jaw and touched her earlobe. She held onto him to keep from melting to the floor. As his lips met hers again, she wanted to smother him with affection, to let him know her heart was his, that she was his. It felt as if her heart would beat right out of her chest. His tongue plunged into her mouth as if she were new land and he an explorer. She gasped, her tongue meeting his, her breath growing ragged. And then his hands were roaming all over her, lighting fires, massaging, taking, the touch of him inciting her to a passion that made her body shudder with desire. Jack swept her into his arms and as he was carrying her to the bedroom, somehow she managed to gain control and said, "Jack, please stop! I want to save the first time for my wedding night."

FLORIDA GOLD

Jack gently lowered her to the floor as he again realized how special this angel God had sent him was. "I understand. I respect that, I just lost control. I won't let it happen again."

"Do you still love me?" Carolyn asked, her eyes welling up with tears.

"What? Of course! You're the love of my life, Carolyn. Come here," he said as he pulled her to him and they walked over to sit on the sofa. He gently pressed his lips to hers. "I didn't think it was possible to love someone as much as I love you, but what you just said makes me love you even more. I agree with your decision. I respect it, and I will not lose control that way again."

"Oh, darling, I'm so glad you understand," she said as she put her arms around him and their lips met in a gentle kiss. "Now tell me all about the war and what it's like over there. I read the stories about you in the newspaper, but I want to hear about it from you."

It was after midnight when they pulled into Jack's driveway. Harry had frequently checked on Jack's house and driven his car to keep it running. "Dinner tonight at Lake Region?" Jack asked as he opened the car door.

"Of course. What time?"

"I'll come by your place at six thirty."

The next morning Jack went to the office and met with Harry. "The Distinguished Service Cross! WOW! Congratulations, Jack!"

"Thanks, Harry, how's the business doing?"

"It's thriving in this improving economy. Labor costs are up but prices and profits are up even more."

"That's good. Harry, you're doing a wonderful job," Jack said as he was looking over the books.

"Jack, I've heard the federal government in a cooperative effort with the Florida Citrus Commission is trying to develop a new frozen concentrated orange juice that will taste as good as fresh squeezed, and be just as nutritious. The idea is to

223

send it to servicemen and expectant mothers among our allies in Europe. The research is being conducted at the University of Florida Agricultural Experiment Station in Lake Alfred, only fifteen miles from here. Have you heard anything about that?"

"No, but I'll see what I can find out when I'm back on duty. We can probably learn something about it from the experiment station in Lake Alfred, or from someone at the Florida Department of Citrus in Lakeland."

Jack spent time with Harry each day as they made decisions that would affect the business long-term that Harry had waited to get Jack's input about. The war had created a shortage of citrus harvesting labor and Jack wanted to explore the new Bracero agricultural labor program to bring in workers from Mexico as a way to obtain harvesting labor. As Jack researched the new frozen concentrated orange juice (FCOJ) from information he obtained at Lake Alfred, he thought it had huge potential. It would make good orange juice available year-round, not just from November into June when fruit was being harvested. It would taste much better than the canned juice available when citrus wasn't ripe. It would also make good orange juice much more convenient to make than squeezing fresh oranges.

Jack obtained a US Department of Agriculture publication entitled "Composition of Foods" that gave the nutritional values for raw and processed foods per 100 grams of edible portion. He learned that oranges had more vitamin C, vitamin A, thiamine, riboflavin, niacin, calcium, and potassium than apples, grapes, and pineapples, the other fruits that were made into the leading juices sold and consumed in the US market. Thus, he believed that the nutritional superiority of orange juice could be conveyed in advertising that would give it an immediate advantage in the competitive marketplace.

FLORIDA GOLD

With all that Jack had learned about orange juice from his research, he felt the market potential for it could be staggering, immeasurable. He thought the market could become large enough that fruit would be produced specifically for processing. Currently, fruit was produced only for the fresh market, and packinghouse eliminations - fruit culled from the fresh packing process for being too small or discolored - were the source of fruit for juice. It would be less expensive to grow fruit specifically for processing into juice since the appearance of the fruit would not be as important, and it would not have to bear the expense of being separated from fruit for the fresh market at the packinghouse. This would all result in improved economies from the grower to the final consumer.

"Jack, you really think this frozen concentrate could be big don't you?" Harry asked one day when Jack was sharing what he'd learned from his research.

"Yeah, I do. Big enough that I want you to plant five hundred acres of groves in the best varieties for juice - Hamlins and Valencias. And I also want you to buy Lakeside Citrus from our cooperative packinghouse."

"The canning plant? But we already own controlling interest."

"I want to own it outright. That's going to become a commercial orange juice concentrate plant, maybe the first one."

In the days and weeks after Jack's return on leave from the war, when Jack wasn't at work and Carolyn at school, or they were asleep, they were always together.

"Mr. Leslie, would you have lunch with me tomorrow?" Jack asked Carolyn's father a couple of weeks before he was to report for active duty.

"Sure, where?"

"How about the diner in Haines City?"

225

"OK, I'll see you there at noon tomorrow."

The next day, Jack looked carefully at the dozen or so cars, but he didn't recognize Don's in the parking lot. *I guess I got here first,* he thought nervously as he got out of his truck and headed toward the diner on this sunny, crisp Monday morning in April of 1944. He walked from the dirt lot past the neon sign that read "Haines City Family Diner." A blast of air and the sweet smell of hamburgers and French fries being cooked struck him as he opened the door and entered. He took a seat at an isolated table near the back.

"What will you have, Mister?" the waitress asked as she set a glass of water down on Jack's table.

"I'm waiting on someone to join me and we'll order then."

"Yes, sir." A few minutes later, Don arrived.

"Good to see you again, Jack. What's up?"

"Let's order first, then we can talk."

After they'd ordered, Jack said, "Mr. Leslie, Carolyn and I have grown very close over the past year, and I'm in love with her, and she says she's in love with me. I know proper courtships usually take longer, but with the war, that isn't possible. Sir, I'm asking your permission to ask Carolyn to marry me."

"Oh, that's great, Jack! You certainly have it. I've seen how close both of you have become, and I couldn't be happier for each of you. I can't think of anyone I'd rather have as a son-in-law. So welcome to the family!"

"Thank you, sir, now I just hope she accepts."

"Oh, she will. I don't know if you know this, and don't tell her I told you, but she's secretly been in love with you ever since you used to come to get lessons from Martha."

"She told me in one of her letters."

"That girl has always been able to make up her mind quickly about things that are important to her."

FLORIDA GOLD

Jack took a "business" trip to Jacksonville, purchased a three-carat diamond, and had it set in a white-gold band. On the Saturday before he was to leave for duty he asked Carolyn to have dinner with him.

"Of course," she replied. He planned to propose to her and give her the engagement ring at dinner that night at an elegant, romantic new restaurant north of Lake Wales, Chalet Suzanne. As they entered the 140-acre property at seven p.m., a miniature pink house with the words WELCOME TO CHALET SUZANNE greeted them. The winding brick-paved entry road was lined with palm and orange trees, and had an airplane landing strip on its north side. They pulled into the parking lot, which sat in front of the restaurant to the right, with twenty-six hotel rooms to the left. The restaurant and rooms had cedar-shingle roofs. A quiet fountain that sprayed water thirty feet in the air graced the entry to the restaurant.

"Oh, Jack, this is a really nice place!" Carolyn exclaimed.

"Yeah, Harry said Jean told him it was featured in the *Orlando Evening Reporter Star* a couple of weeks ago."

A fifty-foot covered brick-paved entryway bordered with ferns, peace lilies, and caladiums led through Spanish wrought iron-surrounded windows and double oak doors into the restaurant. The floor was wood parquet, with Persian rugs throughout. Early-twentieth-century furniture, oriental porcelain lamps, and silk upholstered love seats adorned the restaurant's entrance. Classical music was being played on a grand piano.

"Oh, Jack, this is the most elegant restaurant I've ever been in!" Carolyn gushed, thinking, *Is he going to propose to me here?*

The restaurant sat on the banks of a large lake, and Jack had a window-side table for them. "Jack Thomas, reservations for two," he told the hostess.

They were escorted to their table, which had a crocheted lace table cloth, crystal water and wine glasses, carefully

227

arranged silver on white linen napkins, and china plates, each with its own unique design. Their server soon came and lit the candle at their table. As he was filling their water glasses, he asked, "What will you have to drink this evening, sir?"

"Could we see a wine list?"

"Certainly, sir."

"I think we'll have the Veuve Clicquot Chardonnay. I had it in Paris recently and it was excellent."

The waiter's eyes grew large. "Are you Jack Thomas, the war hero?"

"Yes he is," Carolyn replied proudly.

"It's an honor to serve you, sir. And the wine is an excellent choice."

"Thank you," Jack replied.

"I'll have the duck confit *à l'orange*," Carolyn said, thinking again excitedly, *Is he going to propose to me in this elegant romantic restaurant?*

"And for you, sir?"

"The pan-seared rack of lamb."

They had key lime pie and coffee for dessert. Then Jack took the black velvet box that held the ring out of his pocket and put it on the table. He knelt before her and took her hand.

Oh my God, he's going to propose to me! She thought, a giddy excitement rushing through her.

"Carolyn, I love the way your eyes dance with excitement when I look at you, and the way you laugh at life's challenges. The way your hair seems to always be in your eyes, and how you can see the good in everyone. But most of all, I love you, more than I can express. Will you marry me?"

"Yes! Yes! Darling," she said as she threw her arms around him and they kissed tenderly, passionately.

Her voice was trembling - everything about her was. Then he carefully took the diamond ring out of its box and gently placed it on her finger. She was crying as they hugged

FLORIDA GOLD

and kissed. Later, they sat, holding hands in the candle light, gazing at each other, euphoric to know they would spend their lives together. She invited him to Sunday lunch the next day at her parents' house.

After they had said grace, her father said, "Jack, we couldn't be prouder that you're marrying our daughter and will be part of our family. You've done so much for so many - your daring escape from the work camp, helping the federal agents free all those boys and shut the camps down, running your own successful company, and now a war hero. You're the finest man we know, son."

"Thank you sir, it's an honor to be marrying Carolyn and joining your wonderful family." Carolyn just gazed at Jack, her eyes and heart filled with love and happiness.

The next day, Jack went to the office to see Harry. "Guess, what? I'm engaged!"

"You son of a gun! When?"

"At dinner Saturday night."

"Congratulations, Jack, she'll be a loving and devoted wife."

"I agree. Harry, now that I'm engaged, I'd like to make sure that if I'm killed in the war, Carolyn is taken care of. I'd like to give her a forty-eight percent interest in the company if I were to die. That way you'd still have controlling interest but she'd be taken care of financially."

"I think that's a good idea, Jack. I'll have the papers drawn up for you to sign right away."

As the time for Jack to leave again for the war approached, Carolyn grew increasingly sad and moody. "Jack's going to be fine. Look at all that he has survived in his life," said Trisha, Carolyn's roommate and friend.

"I know, and he's always met every challenge. But this is a world war! And he's so reckless. His bravery may end up getting him killed this time."

229

"With you to come home to? I doubt it. Let Jack go do what's important to him. If he's always worrying about how upset you are, that may just divert his attention enough to get him killed. Remember, you are engaged to Jack Thomas - a national hero as a teenager, and now a war hero. Show him the bravery and support that a man like that deserves from the woman he has chosen to marry and spend the rest of his life with."

"You're right, Trisha. I will pray for the strength to do that."

It was Sunday afternoon and Carolyn had driven Jack to the train station for his return to the war. They stood holding hands, waiting for Jack's train to arrive. As his lips met hers, tears filled her eyes. "Don't cry," he whispered as she hugged him desperately.

"Oh, darling, I'm so worried that you will be hurt or killed."

"Now, Carolyn, we've discussed this. It's important for me to fight for our country, to defend the freedoms our forefathers won for all of us. God will watch out over me – over us. We're soul mates. I have something for you," Jack told her. He took the ivory cross his grandmother had given him when he was a little boy out of his pocket, and handed it to her.

"It says, "𝕹o hardship is too great to bear as long as thou hast faith," Carolyn observed, the tears subsiding.

"My great-grandmother, Rebecca Porter, and my great-grandfather, Lieutenant Jack Henderson, a graduate of West Point from South Carolina, fell in love before he left to fight for the Confederacy in the Civil War as an artillery officer. When they were at the train station saying good-bye he gave this cross to her and told her to hold it to her heart and pray for strength when she needed it. She said it helped calm her fears and she believes her prayers helped bring him back alive and safe."

FLORIDA GOLD

Jack's train was coming in, and the clanging and whistle almost drowned out her words as she yelled, "Is that who you were named after?"

"Yes it is," Jack shouted above the noise. "General George Washington gave this cross to Jack Henderson's grandfather, John Henderson, just before they went into a major battle in the Revolutionary War. My mother gave it to me. That cross gave me the strength to survive the child labor camp, and it has frequently helped me to deal with adversity and challenges. Carolyn, the cross is now yours. Keep it with you at all times. Whenever you're real worried or scared, or it looks like there's no hope, hold it to your heart and pray to God and Jesus. They will give you the strength you need."

"But Jack, you need the cross in the war!"

"I want you to have it."

"Train 302 to Orlando, St. Augustine, and Jacksonville, leaving in three minutes," a voice shouted.

"Oh, Jack, I will treasure it always, and I know it will give me the courage and strength I need."

As they held each other, Jack said, "Carolyn, the time I've known you has been the most special and magical time I've ever had. You have redefined my life. I know now that you were the only woman I was ever intended to spend my life with. I love you more than any words can describe."

"Jack, with you I've found a joy and happiness that I never knew I could experience. I love you so much. You're the most important thing that's ever happened to me. I always imagined what it would be like for us, but I never imagined it would be anything as wonderful as this

"ALL ABOARD."

"Good-bye, Carolyn."

"Fight for our future together, darling. Help win this war!" she shouted as the tears began to come again.

"I love you, Carolyn," Jack shouted.

ROBERT ALLEN MORRIS

"Bye, darling...bye," she called after him, her voice breaking with emotion. Then she hurried out of the train station, tears flowing down her cheeks.

Jack reported for duty in Washington for nine weeks of training before being sent back to the war, and was promoted to second lieutenant. During that time he was able to find out more about the government's efforts into the development of FCOJ. The government was looking for supplemental funding from private sources, and was willing to grant a five-year period where the firm who provided the most funding would have exclusive rights to manufacture and market the new type of juice. As Jack already knew, the research was a joint effort between the US Department of Agriculture (USDA) and the Florida Citrus Commission (FCC), and was being conducted at the agricultural experiment station in Lake Alfred, Florida, whose main focus was citrus research.

Jack got in contact with Harry and told him to invest $200,000 in the USDA/FCC research in exchange for their five-year exclusivity contract. This would be around one-fifth of the approximately $1 million they had from money Jack hadn't spent from the labor camp settlements and savings from business profits. "And Harry, a third of the equity in any orange juice company we start from this will be yours."

"Jack! You're very generous, thanks!"

"It's not a favor. You've earned it and will continue to."

No other firm came close to Jack's offer, and on June 9, 1944, Jack and Harry were awarded the exclusivity contract, pending the successful completion of the FCOJ project and patenting of the process to make FCOJ.

On the morning of December 18, 1944, Jack led a squad against a courthouse held by enemy troops. While his men covered him, he dashed toward the building, surprised two guards at the door, and took them prisoner without firing a

FLORIDA GOLD

shot. He found other Germans in the cellar. These he threatened with hand grenades, forcing all twenty-six to emerge and surrender. His squad then occupied the building and prepared to defend it against powerful enemy action. The next day the enemy poured artillery and mortar barrages into the position, disrupting communications, which Jack repeatedly repaired under heavy small-arms fire as he crossed dangerous terrain to keep his company commander informed of the squad's situation. During the day, several prisoners were taken and other Germans killed when hostile forces were attracted to the courthouse by the sound of captured German weapons fired by the Americans.

At dawn the next day, the enemy prepared to assault the building. A German tank fired round after round into the structure, partially demolishing the upper stories. Despite this heavy fire, Jack climbed to the second floor and directed artillery fire that forced the hostile tank to withdraw. Then, exposing himself to enemy fire, he directed mortars to hit large forces of enemy foot soldiers attempting to reach the American position and, when this force broke and attempted to retreat, he directed deadly machine-gun and rifle fire into their disorganized ranks. Calling for armored support to blast out the German troops hidden behind a wall, he unhesitatingly exposed himself to heavy small-arms fire to stand beside a friendly tank and tell its occupants where to rip holes in the walls protecting approaches to the school building. He then trained machine guns on the gaps and mowed down all hostile troops attempting to cross the openings to get closer to the courthouse building.

With Jack's intrepidity and bold, aggressive leadership, his eight-man squad drove back approximately 140 of the enemy, killing at least 85 and capturing 61. Personally, he killed more than 30, and captured 44 prisoners. For this, he was promoted to first lieutenant, but that was only the beginning.

233

ROBERT ALLEN MORRIS

Jack wired plane fare for Carolyn and her parents and asked them to meet him at the airport in New York City. On June 6, 1945, he arrived in New York, and Carolyn and her parents were there to meet his plane. So were thousands of cheering fans. He was later given a hero's welcome where he was feted with parades, banquets, and speeches throughout New York City. Through it all, Carolyn and her parents were with him, sharing the glory. He introduced Carolyn in numerous press interviews as his fiancé, and that he planned to marry her after they returned to Winter Haven, Florida.

From New York, they went to Washington, DC. At a ceremony on the White House lawn, President Truman went to the podium and said, "Together on this day, we offer a prayer for peace and a tribute to those who defend it. Today, we say thank you to those who stepped forward to safeguard our security and our ideals. What better way to express our gratitude than by presenting this country's highest decoration for valor. For his conspicuous gallantry, bravery, and leadership at the risk of his life above and beyond the call of duty, Lieutenant Jack Thomas, US Marines, American hero, is hereby awarded the Congressional Medal of Honor. Your nation thanks you, and may God bless you. Our nation is blessed to have you as a citizen and as a US Marine." President Truman then placed the medal around Jack's neck, shook his hand, and embraced him. There was a thunderous standing ovation. Carolyn and her mother had tears in their eyes. *What did I do to deserve such a fine man as this?* Carolyn kept thinking.

Later, Jack was honored at a joint meeting of both houses of Congress, where he was given another standing ovation. He then met with the secretary of war, Henry Lewis Stimson. After that, Carolyn and her family returned to Winter Haven and Jack went to Fort Oglethorpe, Georgia where he was discharged. In addition to the Medal of Honor, in time he would receive the Legion of Merit and the French

234

FLORIDA GOLD

Legion of Honor. In all, Jack earned nine US medals, and three from Europe. He was an international hero.

When his plane arrived in Orlando, Carolyn was there to meet him. Over a thousand people were also there to shower him with praise. On Saturday night, to a packed football stadium in nearby Lakeland, Florida's governor, Millard Caldwell, gave a speech in Jack's honor. "Jack Thomas first gained national recognition in 1931 when he was only sixteen years old," the governor began. "A child labor camp survivor, Jack was instrumental in the success of federal agents who freed the enslaved boys, located and shut all the camps down, and punished the criminals who were responsible for these heinous crimes. Now his fame is international, for his leadership, bravery, and heroism that saved many lives and helped us win the war. When we are in the presence of Jack Thomas, we are in the presence of greatness." The standing ovation and cheering that followed were deafening, and lasted almost three minutes.

A celebratory banquet organized by Governor Caldwell's office for one hundred fans followed in a large banquet hall. After a speech by US Senator Charles Warren in Jack's honor, Jack was asked to come to the podium and say a few words. "I want to thank Governor Caldwell for having this lovely event, and each of you for attending. It was a pleasure and an honor to serve our great country in its time of need. And it's even more of a pleasure and an honor to be marrying Miss Carolyn Leslie. Carolyn, come up here with me." When a blushing Carolyn was standing at his side he said, "Everyone, Miss Carolyn Leslie, the love of my life." There was a standing ovation. Carolyn couldn't believe it. Here he was using his honored moment to tell everyone about them. But she could believe one thing - she knew Jack was the finest man alive, and she loved him so much she thought she would burst. Her parents felt the same way.

235

Next, Harry Osborne came to the podium and stood next to Jack and Carolyn. He said, "I first met Jack Thomas in an Amalgamated Land Company illegal labor camp. He was seven and I was ten. And we became friends. Even at that age, his strength of character and leadership was an inspiration and source of hope for me and the other enslaved boys. As one of many examples, at the age of ten, Jack came up with an incentive program to increase our productivity. The result was more profits for the farm and small weekly bonuses for us, giving us needed funds to cover our costs of returning to our families when we were allowed to leave the camp at fifteen. He was a life saver for me. Now we are business partners. Jack, you're the best friend I've ever had." They embraced to another standing ovation. Carolyn's mother was so emotionally affected by everything that she could no longer hold back her tears and had to briefly leave the room.

Carolyn had not heard about Jack's accomplishments in the labor camp. And she was moved when she learned of some of the things he'd done even as a young boy. Was there no end to the many impressive things about him? Then she had an idea. Why not assemble a scrapbook about Jack? She already had a number of newspaper and magazine articles about him. She could also gather newspaper articles and things he did as they moved forward. She would start tonight with the text of the governor's speeches.

Jack had tens of thousands of dollars in offers to advertise various products, but declined them all. The only advertising he did, which he funded, was several times on national radio. An announcer said, "Ladies and gentlemen, you may remember Jack Thomas, the Medal of Honor war hero. Well he's here to tell you about a new healthy juice product that will soon be available in stores."

Jack then said, "Many of you may not know how nutritious fresh-squeezed orange juice is. It has more vitamin C, vitamin A, thiamine, riboflavin, niacin, calcium, and

FLORIDA GOLD

potassium than apples, grapes, and pineapples, the other fruits that are made into the leading juices available in stores. But Florida oranges are only ripe from November until June. This product will be as tasty and nutritious as fresh-squeezed juice, but will be available year-round, and can be made in your kitchen in only about a minute. When it is available my partner and I will have exclusive production and marketing rights to it for five years. We think it will be available in less than a year. I will keep you updated on its progress so you'll know when to start looking for it in your grocery store."

His office was flooded with mail asking questions about the new type of tasty, nutritious orange juice that the Congressional Medal Honor winner was preparing to provide. There was so much mail that he and Harry had to build a new room onto the office and hire someone to open, read, and respond to all the cards and letters.

Jack and Carolyn set their wedding date for Saturday, August 18, 1945. She was twenty-five and he was thirty.

Carolyn's mother wanted them to have a big wedding at the navy chapel in Annapolis, which had been offered to Jack as a war hero. Thousands would want to attend, but Martha felt that with their senator's help they could get it reduced to about three hundred. Carolyn, being who she was, would have none of it. Instead she wanted a small wedding at the Methodist church in Winter Haven that she, Jack, her parents, and about thirty-five of their family and closest friends would attend. Carolyn prevailed, but her mother was disappointed.

On Tuesday night they met with Reverend Langford, the minister of the Methodist church they attended, who would be performing the ceremony. As was customary, they told him briefly about how they'd met, about their courtship, and their plans as husband and wife. His eyes reddened with emotion as they quietly tried to explain the depth of their love and affection for each other. He held both their hands, and in a

237

brief prayer he said, "God, our Father in heaven, these two wonderful people don't need me to bless their special union, for I know that a love like theirs must be heaven-sent. We thank you, oh Lord, for guiding Jack and Carolyn to each other, and for the special love they have for one another and for you, oh Lord. We pray to you in the name of Jesus Christ, our Savior, amen."

Harry had happily agreed to be Jack's best man, and Carolyn's friend Sandy was going to be Carolyn's maid of honor. There would be two ushers and two bridesmaids. They had their rehearsal on Friday night, August 17 at six p.m., and a dinner for the wedding party at Chalet Suzanne.

Jack rented a limo to take them from the church in Winter Haven to their reception at the Lake Region Country Club. After the reception, the limo would take them to the Don CeSar Hotel, a beautiful resort hotel on St. Petersburg Beach where they were spending their wedding night in a luxurious suite overlooking the ocean. Known as Florida's "Pink Palace," the Don CeSar, facing the powder-white sands of the Gulf of Mexico, was built in 1928 to resemble a Mediterranean-style castle. Born in the Great Gatsby era as a playground for the rich and famous, the iconic resort hotel's guests had included US Presidents, European royalty, and famous movie stars. Jack's car would be parked there.

It was Saturday afternoon, and Carolyn was standing at the back of the church with her father, waiting on the start of the wedding march. And then the music began, and they walked through the doors and began down the aisle. *This is it!* she thought excitedly. *The moment I dreamed of most for all those years. In a few minutes I'll be his wife!* As she continued down the aisle and saw Jack waiting on her, a joy, an aura came over her like she'd never experienced.

Jack was standing at the alter with Harry and the other two ushers when the pianist began to play the wedding

FLORIDA GOLD

march. Then Jack saw her and was moved by her breathtaking beauty. So was everyone. She was the most beautiful sight Jack had ever seen or imagined. Carolyn's floor-length dress was made of ivory taffeta and antique lace, with white satin arches and pleats and a train measuring five feet. The ivory satin bodice, which was narrowed at the waist and padded at the hips, drew on the Victorian tradition of corsetry. Her hair was arranged with a circlet of fresh orange blossoms, and she wore a pearl necklace.

As they said their vows to each other, Jack silently thanked God, as he had so many times before, for bringing this beautiful angel into his life. Then the minister said, "I now pronounce you husband and wife. Jack, you may kiss the bride." He gently lifted her veil, tilted her chin up to him, and put his arms around her as they kissed tenderly, sweetly, the realization that they were finally married filling each of them with an indescribably sweet joy.

Then Reverend Langford said, "Ladies and gentlemen, I present to you Mr. and Mrs. Jack and Carolyn Thomas." The room broke into applause and Jack noticed that Carolyn's mom was crying, obviously very happy for them. Jack felt like a king with Carolyn on his arm as they walked up the aisle and out of the church.

They opened their reception at the Lake Region Country Club with a waltz. Everyone seemed to have a great time and it was still going strong when, after changing their clothes, they left about two hours later. Their bags were already packed and loaded into the limo, so they headed straight to the Don CeSar Hotel.

Once they were inside their suite, Jack pressed his lips to the center of her palm. *Her hands are elegant,* he thought as he kissed her fingers one by one. *They might belong to a princess in a castle.* Their lips came together in a tender kiss as he trailed his fingers up and down her sides, sipping tenderly at her lips, then ravishing her mouth as their kiss went from tender to devouring - a deep drugging kiss that both soothed and enticed. Time spun out, drifted, stopped. Still, there was only his mouth against hers. He touched her hair, his fingers combing through, tangling in the luxurious length of it. When his lips left hers, it was to take a slow, lazy journey of her face until he felt her trembling fall away into pliancy.

Jack unzipped her dress and she slid out of it. Her beauty was beyond description, and her sexiness gripped him like a powerful drug that he craved.

"Now it's my turn," she said, her voice hoarse with desire. She was trembling as she unbuttoned Jack's shirt and removed it, unbuckled his belt, unfastened his pants, and slid them down. His heavily muscled chest and shoulders rippled when he moved, making her catch her breath. He aroused something in her she'd never felt, and she wanted him more than she'd ever imagined that she could want any man.

"Jack, I've dreamed of this night so many times."

"I have too," he said, his voice thick with passion. He kissed his way slowly down her cheek, her neck, and on down. Her skin was like cream, unbearably soft and fragrant. Her thoughts scattered, dimmed, reformed in a mixed maze, only to fly apart again. How could he know just how to touch, just how to caress to make her whole body shudder with pleasure and desire beyond anything she had ever imagined? But he did, and her breath sighed out in gasping moans as he showed her more.

"I want you now, Jack, now!" Her voice was ragged, like her breathing.

"I wake up shaking after I dream of you," he said, his voice thick with passion as he continued his sensuous massage, her body shivering with lust.

"I'm shaking, but I'm not dreaming now, please tell me I'm not dreaming," Carolyn said in an urgent voice hoarse with passion.

FLORIDA GOLD

Afterwards, Carolyn was overwhelmed. She had the look of a child that had just experienced something for the first time, an astonished look of pure joy. Never in her wildest imagination had she thought there could have been anything as wonderful, as overpowering and exciting, as this. As they held each other she was still shaking, and then she began to cry softly. "Carolyn, what's the matter, I didn't hurt you, did I?"

"No, no, darling, I'm fine. That was just such an incredibly intense emotional experience that it makes me cry, but these are tears of euphoric happiness." Jack held her while she cried, whispering softly into her ear how much he loved her, how beautiful and sensual he thought she was, and how gloriously happy she made him.

Finally, she stopped shivering, the tears subsided, and she gazed at him, the most beautiful look of love in her eyes that he'd ever seen. "Oh, darling," she said softly, her voice breaking with emotion. "Oh, darling..." But no more words would come, only a special glow about her that told him how intensely she must love him.

Holding her close, he spoke softly into her ear, "My beautiful, special lady, I love you. I love you so much more than I can express." She fell peacefully asleep in his arms. Jack silently thanked God again for bringing her into his life, and also fell asleep.

Carolyn woke up and at first couldn't remember where she was. Then she did, and looked over at Jack sleeping peacefully next to her. Making love with Jack had been the most incredible experience she'd ever had. How could any mortal experience be this overpowering, this exciting, this...She couldn't think of words to express how she felt. It was if she had been one person of one reality and life when she stood at the Alter, and had been transformed by an experience so phenomenal, so enchanting, that she was now

241

ROBERT ALLEN MORRIS

in another life. She felt like she was married to a man who couldn't be real. But he was real, and so was their intense, indescribable love for each other, and so now was a beautiful future more exciting, more fulfilling than anything she'd ever imagined.

What a special, giving man, she thought. She had dreamed about this night for years. *He'll never know how much I love him,* she thought as she gazed at him, *because there's no way to express such a deep love as I have for him.* Then she thought of the years she had waited for him. All the nights and weekends she had been alone, wanting to be with him. Her gut-wrenching worry when he was away in the war. But it had certainly been worth it. Then she carefully snuggled up to the man of her dreams and fell quietly back to sleep.

Al Bronson, a business associate of Jack and Harry's, had a luxurious vacation home on a relatively deserted island in the Abaco Islands of the Bahamas. Jack and Harry had been there several times on fishing trips with Al and some of Al's other business associates, and Jack was impressed with the remote tropical beauty. This was a rural area where the tourists didn't go. The largest of these islands was the site of a large sugarcane plantation that went bankrupt in the 1930s. Recently, a few individuals who liked privacy and a virtually unspoiled tropical paradise had built vacation homes there.

Norman Albury's sail shop was located on Man-O-War Cay, one of the Abaco Islands where the famous British sailing ships were built in the eighteenth century by Norman's ancestors. The next island over was Elbow Cay, where Hope Town was located, home of a picturesque lighthouse that helped guide ships through treacherous barrier reefs over a century earlier. Hope Town was so named because the ship captains hoped they could make it through the reefs and into the harbor. The best cracked-conch sandwiches found anywhere were served by a dockside restaurant in Hope

242

FLORIDA GOLD

Town. The water in the Abaco islands was crystal clear, and diving the reefs was a real experience.

Jack was able to use Al's vacation home for his honeymoon. It had no telephone, and could be reached only by boat or seaplane. There was a radio that could be used to get help in an emergency, and a diesel-powered generator that supplied electricity. Al's house sat on a cliff, with the Atlantic Ocean in front and a crystal-blue bay behind the house. The picture windows from Al's living room and master bedroom offered a spectacular view of the ocean, while the deck on the back of the house overlooked the beautiful bay. It sat above a mile-long deserted beach. The nearest house was three miles away, and its owners, who lived in England, were only there in June and July of each year.

The morning after their wedding, Jack planned for them to fly from Tampa to West Palm Beach, Florida where they would board a smaller private plane that Jack had chartered for the forty-five-minute flight to Marsh Harbor in the Abaco Islands. From Marsh Harbor, Jack had chartered a sailboat that would take them on the approximately one-hour trip to the island where Al's house was. When Carolyn asked about their honeymoon, all Jack would tell her was that they were going to the Bahamas. Since Jack wouldn't share more details, Carolyn suspected he had some kind of surprise in mind, but she couldn't guess what it was.

As they were boarding the plane at the airport in West Palm Beach, Carolyn asked, "Jack, a private plane? Where are we going?"

"To paradise, ma'am," the pilot answered.

And Jack said, "Carolyn, you heard the pilot."

As their plane was circling to land on *Marsh Harbor*, its tropical forest broken only by the narrow remote airstrip and the crystal-blue ocean below, the words Marsh Harbor crackled over the radio. "Jack, this place is beautiful, but where is Marsh Harbor and where are you taking me?"

243

"You'll just have to wait and see," he teased. A van met them at customs and took them to the relatively deserted marina where their sailboat was waiting. They stood on the quiet dock holding hands, the motion of the sea gently rocking the sailboat as their luggage was loaded aboard, a lone fishing skiff puttering across the bay.

"Jack, a sailboat now? Where are you taking me?" she asked again, excited and confused.

"A good friend of mine has a vacation home on a deserted tropical island that he's letting us have for the week, and in about an hour we'll be there."

"Really!"

"Yes, ma'am," replied Carlos, their sailboat captain.

"Oh, Jack, this is fabulous!" Carolyn exclaimed, thinking, *what an incredibly romantic way to spend our honeymoon. Will I ever stop discovering how rare and exciting this wonderful man is? Will I ever grow too old for just his look or his touch to make me feel giddy, like a young schoolgirl? Am I still a mortal, or will I soon find out that I'm really in heaven?*

"Mr. and Ms. Thomas, Mr. Bronson sent this for you," Carlos said as they climbed aboard. There was a bottle of Dom Pérignon champagne on ice and a basket of fruit, cheese, and bread, along with a note.

Jack and Carolyn, congratulations, and happy honeymoon! The house is stocked with groceries, so you won't need to leave until you want to. Also, the keys to my boat are in the drawer by the refrigerator. Use it as much as you want. Jack, you may remember that Conky Joe's in Hope Town on Elbow Cay is great for cracked-conch and grouper sandwiches, and it's only about a thirty-minute boat ride away. There's also a grocery store and drugstore on Man-O-War Cay. I hear the reef is just about perfect now for snorkeling. There's a nautical map of the area next to the boat keys. Have a wonderful time! Al.

FLORIDA GOLD

Carolyn laid her head on Jack's shoulder, and he put his arm around her as they sailed across the tropical waters toward their island, sipping champagne and enjoying the gentle breeze, the sounds of the sea lapping at the boat as it glided along. Carolyn said, "Oh, darling, every day is a new and wonderful experience with you. I'm so happy."

"I am too," Jack told her as he kissed her tenderly, thinking, *I'm getting ready to spend a glorious week in paradise with the woman of my dreams. Life can never be any better than this.*

They soon arrived at Al's dock, just below his house. While Carlos was bringing their luggage in, Jack and Carolyn were out on the deck overlooking the crystal-blue bay, lined with palm trees, banana trees, and lush tropical forest. "This is a paradise, Jack!" Carolyn gasped as she took in the exquisite beauty, a bonefish rippling the water as it was feeding.

"And it's all ours alone for the next week."

"Oh, darling, our dream will never end, will it?"

"Not if I can help it," Jack promised, and then he swept her into his arms and carried her across the threshold.

Jack and Carolyn spent a glorious week there swimming, snorkeling, catching their dinner and cooking it over a fire on the deserted beach, and making love as they watched the gorgeous red sun burn its way into the tropical sea each night. Jack had found his soul mate. And Carolyn had found hers too. They would be partners for life.

CHAPTER THIRTEEN

"Arlie, find out where Jack Thomas, the war hero, lives," Tommy Lee Dunaway requested to his banker.

"I'm not sure how."

"He's helping fund an orange juice research project being worked on by the Florida Citrus Commission. They're in Lakeland, Florida. They'll know."

Two days later, Arlie called and said, "He owns the Sun Sweet Citrus Company, and his office is in Winter Haven. The phone number is 2-8574."

"Good work. Now find a banker in Lakeland or Orlando that makes loans to citrus growers, packers, or canners and put them in touch with me."

"Tommy Lee Dunaway," he said as he answered his phone the next day.

"This is Ben Marvin with Citrus and Chemical Bank in Lakeland. Arlie Bennett said you wanted to talk to me."

"Are you familiar with the Sun Sweet Citrus Company?"

"Yes, they borrow operating capital from us."

"Have you been keeping up with the progress on developing a new type of orange juice the Citrus Commission and the USDA are working on?"

"Yes. We hold some of the grant money that's funding it."

247

"Good. I want to set up an account with your bank. I'm not sure how much, but over a million dollars. I'll be back in touch later this week to give you the details."

"Thanks for the business, Mr. Dunaway."

"Call me Tommy Lee."

"Florida Citrus Commission," a female voice said.

"Chairman's office, please."

"Mr. Jorgenson's office."

"This is Tommy Lee Dunaway. I'd like to talk to Mr. Jorgenson about the new type of orange concentrate being developed."

"Sure, I'll connect you, sir."

"Ed Jorgenson."

"Ed, this is Tommy Lee Dunaway. I'm thinking about investing some money in the development of a plant to make the new orange concentrate once it's perfected, and I wanted to know how much it would cost to build the facility."

"That could be a problem."

"Why?"

"Jack Thomas has provided grant money to assist the USDA in developing the concentrate, and in return, he will get five years' exclusive rights to produce the product. Nobody else will be able to make it for the next five years."

"Let me worry about that."

"OK. Our financial guy has worked on the numbers, so I'll connect you with him."

"Thanks."

"Finance and accounting, Bill Austin speaking."

"Bill, my name is Tommy Lee Dunaway and I'm interested in finding out how much it will take to build a processing plant to produce the orange concentrate the FCC is working on."

"That depends on a number of things. Assuming you have a citrus juice canning plant on the site, which is probably the most likely firms to build a concentrate processing and packaging facility, converting it to a plant to process six million

FLORIDA GOLD

boxes of oranges, the minimum size for an economically efficient plant, with a packaging line, we estimate would run $3-$5 million. We can't get closer because one has never been built before.

"How long would it take to build?"

"Probably twelve to eighteen months."

"Thanks, Bill."

Tommy Lee called Arlie. "Arlie, arrange for me to wire $5 million to the Citrus and Chemical Bank in Lakeland, Florida. Let me know when the funds are transferred."

Arlie told him two days later.

"Thanks."

"Citrus and Chemical Bank, Mr. Marvin's office."

"This is Tommy Lee, I need to speak to Ben."

"I'll put you right through, sir."

"Tommy Lee, we received your funds. What do you want us to do with them?"

"For now let them sit. But I want you to let me know when the project to make orange concentrate is completed."

"I'll be glad to, Tommy Lee."

Tommy Lee, now in his mid-seventies, had changed his ways about fifteen years ago. His oldest son, Jerry, Jack's birth father, had been killed in a raid on a moonshine still. Jerry had straightened up after getting Irma Sue pregnant, and become a responsible husband, father, and manager in Tommy Lee's organization. Tommy Lee's other two sons were not, and spent most of their time drinking and chasing women. Jerry had a different mother than Tommy Lee's other sons - a school teacher. But she'd been killed in a train wreck when Jerry was two, and Tommy Lee married his secretary about a year later. She was the mother of his other two sons.

After Jerry's untimely death, Tommy Lee had liquidated his moonshine empire and taken more of an interest in the church and charitable works, donating large sums of money to various charities. When he heard the radio news and read

249

the headlines with Jack's picture about him winning the Medal of Honor, he knew that was his grandson, and it made him very proud. He'd kept up with the Thomas family until after Pete's death when they moved to Mobile to live with Margaret's sister, but nothing since. The $303 Margaret had at the time of her move to Mobile had come from Tommy Lee. He'd also paid off a large amount of Pete's debts or she would have been in even more serious financial trouble. But he knew if he'd tried to help out more, as well as Margaret knew their books she'd get suspicious, potentially discover it was him, and reject all of it because she hated Tommy Lee for the business he was in and for what his son had done to Irma Sue.

He'd contacted Margaret's sister, Betty, who simply said, "Irma Sue married the son of a rich banker, Jeb Walker. That's all I know. We're not in touch anymore." When he contacted the bank, George's friend who'd bought the bank, Jeremy Johns, told him the tragic story of Jack's abduction and what happened to the Walker family, and about Margaret's marrying Ben and going to live an isolated life in Europe. Jeremy sent him some newspaper clippings about Jack's escape from the labor camp, his role in freeing the boys and shutting the camps down, and the reward for what he'd done. Tommy Lee had missed that because it happened the same year he lost his son, Jerry, but now he vaguely remembered reading something about it. *So Jack had been a hero even at sixteen,* he thought. At the time he learned that Jack won the Medal of Honor, since Jack didn't need any help financially, he'd decided it would be best if he stayed out of Jack's life. But when he found out that Jack was going to start a company that made and sold the new concentrate, he wanted to help him get his start.

He would initially be an anonymous source of capital. However, once Jack started to pay it back, he'd meet Jack, let him know who he was, and the true circumstances around his

FLORIDA GOLD

birth. Then he would let Jack keep the funds – a well-deserved gift from his grandfather, who wished he'd been able to help Jack more in his lifetime.

Jack and Carolyn returned from their honeymoon on August 26, and Jack went in his office the morning of August 27. Carolyn was going to continue to teach until she became pregnant and the baby was predicted to be a month away. "What do you hear about the FCOJ project?" Jack asked Harry.

"They're close. A breakthrough could happen any day now. We're going to need capital to convert Lakeside Citrus into an orange juice concentrate plant."

"Yeah, I've been thinking about that. Did they give you an estimate of what it might cost?"

"Their rough estimate is $4.6 million. We have about $700,000 in cash and can probably borrow about $800,000 against the value of Sun Sweet, but that still leaves $3.1 million that we need."

"We're going to need to find an investor or investors. Contact Ben over at Citrus and Chemical Bank and see if he has any suggestions."

"OK, that's a good idea."

"Jack, Ben has the perfect investor. He's anonymous, has up to $5 million to invest, and only wants quarterly financial reports. He's willing to provide the entire $5 million if we need that much, and only wants twenty-five percent of the business in return. We decide when to repay it."

"He sounds perfect. I do want to reserve the right to pay back his investment in full in exchange for his twenty-five percent equity whenever we choose."

"I'm sure that won't be a problem."

On September 7, the joint efforts of the USDA and the FCC paid off when Ed White, one of the scientists working on

251

the project, reported that the process of making FCOJ had been perfected, and the project was a success. However, Jack's exclusivity contract could not be granted until the patent had been given preliminary approval. Jack and Harry were in a poker game at their packinghouse the night they heard the news and were elated. They took their wives to Chalet Suzanne to celebrate. "Here's to what will hopefully be the start of a successful juice business," Jack said as he raised his wine glass in a toast.

"I second that," Harry added as they all raised their glasses.

In November, Carolyn discovered she was pregnant. She told Jack, who was elated. They decided to tell her parents the following Saturday night at dinner at their house. When everyone was seated, Jack said, "Carolyn and I have good news. Carolyn?"

"I'm pregnant."

"Oh, that's wonderful news!" Martha said.

"When's the baby due?" Don asked.

"Next June."

"Oh, a June baby. How sweet," her mother said. "Now you must quit that dreadful job and let Jack hire appropriate staff to help out."

"Mom, I plan to work as long as I can, and I can take care of Jack and me."

"What? No way. You don't know what you're in for. Your husband is wealthy, he adores you and will give you anything you want, and you want to work almost until you go into labor?"

"Yep."

"I don't understand you at all."

Jack and Don exchanged amused glances and decided to go into the living room and let the women figure this out on their own.

FLORIDA GOLD

"I'll hire as much help as Carolyn wants but now she doesn't want strangers in our house."

"I understand, Jack. But Martha is a headstrong woman."

"So is Carolyn. It will be interesting to see how this plays out."

"I agree."

On March 5, 1946, the patent was granted pending status. The next day, they were allowed to try the new product. It was, indeed, almost as good as fresh-squeezed, could be made in about a minute by a housewife, and could be stored frozen for months, always fresh tasting when reconstituted with three parts water. The package would be a six-ounce container, which would yield twenty-four ounces when reconstituted with water. It was made from fiberboard, with tin end caps. It would come in six-packs, with a case totaling twenty-four six-ounce servings. Jack knew they had a winner.

The process to make FCOJ entailed sending the freshly-squeezed juice to an evaporator where vacuum and heat were used to remove excess water in order to obtain a base concentrate of forty-five degrees Brix, which is about a four-and-a-half-to-one strength ratio to normal single-strength juice as it comes from an orange. The oil and water-phase essences that give orange juice its flavor were lost in steam during the evaporation process. FCOJ relied on fresh-squeezed juice that was pasteurized and added to the concentrate, when it was reduced from forty-five to forty-two degrees Brix, to restore its taste. This was called cut-back. The bulk FCOJ was then quickly frozen and stored at fifteen degrees or lower in fifty-five-gallon drums until it was to be packaged and sold. To make single-strength juice from the forty-two-degrees-Brix concentrate, three parts water was added and it was mixed.

ROBERT ALLEN MORRIS

Jack hired Ira Long as his plant manager. Ira had managed a canning plant in Dade City for the past nine years. Ira was a mild-mannered man of about average height with piercing gray eyes, who was always interested in the details of anything he managed. He believed in treating his labor fairly, and because of that the plant he managed had never become unionized. Ira went to the Citrus Experiment Station in Lake Alfred and was taught how to use an evaporator and the processing activities he would need to know. He was also told what needed to be built. Ed White, one of the scientists who developed FCOJ, provided oversight to the building of the new plant. Ira immediately got to work installing the evaporator and other equipment required to make and package FCOJ in their Winter Haven caning plant, Lakeside Citrus. By August of 1947 the equipment was installed and tested, and the plant was finished. They would be ready to start processing in the 1946/47 season, which would begin in November.

On June18, 1946, Carolyn went into labor. Her mother had been staying with them the past few weeks to help out. She got Carolyn's already-packed bag and called Jack at the office. "Jack, its time. We're headed to the hospital now."

"OK, I'll meet you there."

Jack sat in the waiting room, thinking about their baby that was soon to arrive, and about the parental pledge he planned to make. He also thought about his own childhood. The closest person to a father he'd ever known had been Jeb Walker, and that had only been for a little over a year. After that, his childhood had been a nightmare.

Carolyn was in labor for about three hours before the baby came. It was a seven-pound, eleven-ounce boy.

At 7:33 p.m. the doctor came in to show Jack and Martha the new baby boy. The doctor said, "You may hold him if you'd like." If the baby was a boy, they had agreed to name him Jeb, after Jeb Walker.

FLORIDA GOLD

As Jack gently took him he said softly and lovingly, "Hi there, Jeb. I'm your dad. Welcome to the world. And at this time of your entry into this physical world, I make this pledge to you and to God. Jeb, I will always love you and be there for you, for as long as I live. You can depend on me to always be on your side and in your corner in life, no matter what. I understand that being a parent is not about me and what I may want, but about you and what you need to help and guide your growth into a responsible adult. I understand the importance of being a good financial provider; the importance of spending time with you and experiencing things in life together; the importance of teaching you of virtues such as ethics, honesty, and compassion, not by what I say, but by the examples I set in how I live and how I treat others; and the importance of a secure home and loving family for you to grow up in; and I will always do my best to provide you with these. One of God's most special gifts and one of mankind's most important responsibilities is that of parenthood, and in making this pledge to you and to God, I acknowledge my acceptance of that responsibility. I love you, Jeb."

As Jack handed baby Jeb to his grandmother, she had tears in her eyes, and with emotion in her voice she said, "I think Jeb's one lucky boy."

"It's his mother and I that are the lucky ones," Jack replied.

After handing the baby back to the doctor, Jack and Martha went to Carolyn's room, but she was sleeping and the nurse said she would probably sleep for another hour or so. Martha called Don and told him that they had a new seven-pound, eleven-ounce grandson named Jeb.

Jack called Harry and gave him the news. "A son, huh? Congratulations!"

In December of 1947, Jack went on national radio with an advertisement. Someone who sounded like a newsman

255

said, "Ladies and Gentlemen, you may remember war hero Jack Thomas's promise to bring you a new, tasty, nutritious orange juice. Well, it's here, and it's called Premium Select, made by Tropical Juices Inc. We have the Congressional Medal of Honor winner who helped fund its development to tell you about it."

"Hello everybody, I'm Jack Thomas. Everyone, this is a great product. As tasty and nutritious as fresh-squeezed orange juice, which you may remember has more vitamins and minerals than other juices, it is less expensive than buying fresh oranges and juicing them and is available year-round. I loved this wonderful product enough that I invested $200,000 dollars in its development, and I will give five cents to orphanages to help our homeless children for every six-pack container sold."

"Remember, that's Premium Select made by Tropical Juices, available now in your grocery store," the announcer reminded the audience at the end. On the orange-colored container was Jack in his Marine dress blues, war medals proudly displayed, drinking a glass of the orange juice.

Grocery stores were a mob scene. Everyone wanted this new nutritious, convenient product, funded and provided by America's war hero. Jack and Harry were not able to initially meet all of the distribution demands. That first year they sold over three million cases, each with four six-packs of six-ounce cans of the juice. In its second year, sales of Premium Select orange juice almost tripled. It would have increased much more than that, but they ran out of processing capacity and had to ration supplies.

But storm clouds of dissent were gathering. Fresh fruit packers believed their business was being threatened by the new orange juice, and they were right. Prior to its discovery, it was estimated that most oranges were bought for juicing at home. Now consumers had a less expensive alternative that tasted just as good and was more convenient. And no one

FLORIDA GOLD

could produce and market the new juice for three more years but Jack Thomas. Some of the larger, better capitalized packers mentally kicked themselves for not investing in the new technology when they'd had the chance.

"We're in agreement then?" said Bill Turner, president of the Florida Fresh Citrus Association.

"Yeah," one of the board members said. "We don't sell packinghouse eliminations to Jack Thomas, none of our members accept fruit from growers who sell to him, and we tell the largest grocery chains that if they carry the new concentrate, we won't sell them any fresh fruit." To enforce their intent, one of Tropical juices' evaporators was blown up late one night when nobody was there to get hurt. A note was left on the office entrance that said, *The Florida Fresh Citrus Association doesn't like Premium Select orange juice.*

Jack and Harry met to discuss the situation. "Harry, they're just scared and worried and don't know what else to do," Jack explained.

"Yeah, but blowing up an evaporator? They're expensive. It's a good thing that it's the summer and we're not processing."

"I agree."

"They are breaking the law, you know."

"I know, collusion and illegal restraint of trade, not to mention blowing up our evaporator. But we can't prove they destroyed it. I just hate to get into this. The citrus industry has enough problems with freezes and disease. We need to work together, not try to hurt each other."

"I agree. I just don't think they've left us any choice."

"OK. But I'm going to give them a chance to stop. I'll have our attorney make a copy of the federal law that says what they are doing is illegal restraint of trade and punishable by large fines to the businesses and imprisonment of the company or trade association's officers and board members,

257

and send it to their board. I'll also have him write a letter explaining that in layman's terms, and telling them that if they don't stop what they're doing, we'll have them arrested by federal marshals and they'll have to pay hefty fines. I want to meet with them after they've read our letter. I have an idea that could be good business for everyone."

"What?"

"Why not grant them the license to make bulk FCOJ for packaging? We'll expand only our packaging capacity, and they'll provide the fruit processing and bulk storage capacity to meet our anticipated future needs."

"I like it, Jack. That way our growth will require much less capital, and they will have the opportunity to participate in this new market."

Bill Turner got a phone call from John Morris, one of the packing association's board members, at 8:13 the next Tuesday morning. "Bill, have you read the letter?"

"What letter?"

"The one where Jack Thomas is threatening to have all of us arrested for breaking a number of federal laws!"

"What?"

"I'll have Jenny bring you a copy. You need to call an emergency meeting of the board. And we need to find a good lawyer."

When everyone was assembled and seated, Bill asked, "Has everyone read Jack Thomas's letter?" Everyone had.

"How could we have been so careless as not to check this out with an attorney?" a board member asked.

"We were too emotional about what could happen to our businesses to think clearly," another replied.

"So what should we do, Bill?"

"Just what Jack suggests, go and meet with him." Heads nodded and Bill said, "Are we all in agreement?"

"Yeah," several replied.

FLORIDA GOLD

"OK, I'll try to set up the meeting for day after tomorrow."

The meeting was in Tropical Juices' conference room at nine a.m. "I'm glad you agreed to this meeting and all were able to come," Jack began.

"Jack, on behalf of our board, I want to sincerely apologize for our irresponsible actions," Bill said. "We will pay the cost to replace your evaporator."

"Thanks. Let's put this behind us and look to our future. The market for orange juice concentrate is exploding. We are rationing our supply now because consumption is growing so rapidly, and we are out of capacity. I'd like to propose that you call a meeting of your membership. I checked, and you represent almost seventy percent of the fresh packers in the state. I will offer you an exclusive license to build a bulk citrus concentrate processing plant and manufacture bulk FCOJ. You sell it to me until my exclusive license expires in three years, plus another two years. That makes you our captive concentrate supplier for five years. After that, sell to whoever you choose, although I'd like to think I could be competitive for your concentrate."

"What kind of investment are we talking about and what would it return?" Bill asked.

"We spent $4.1 million to build a six-million-box plant, which is the minimum size to be economically efficient. That doesn't include packaging, or finished goods inventory capacity, which you won't need. That would be for a stand-alone facility, complete with fruit receiving, grading, extracting, finishing, evaporation and bulk storage, and a loading facility. In the future, it could be expanded in six-million-box increments. We divide our business into processing, marketing, distribution, and packaging. Then we use transfer pricing, and on the books, buy our own bulk concentrate and sell it to the marketing division. That ensures

259

that each component is financially competitive. The bulk part of the business earns a nine percent annual return on its capital. It's paid as a processing margin for the fruit processed. We pay 13½ cents a box."

"I'd like our accountant to look at your analysis, but those numbers sound good to me," Bill replied.

"They beat the fresh packing business. Our returns are volatile, but average about six percent," John Morris explained.

"Yeah, we're still in that business," Jack replied.

"How long will it take to build the facility?" a board member asked.

"It took us seventeen months, but then ours was the first commercial concentrate plant. I'd say with our plant manager Ira Long's oversight, about fourteen months."

"So if we get started by the middle of next month, we should be ready to process fruit by the start of the 1950/51 season?"

"That's right," Harry replied.

"Bill, let's call a meeting of our membership and get this project moving," John suggested.

On his way out, Bill stopped and said, "Jack, we really appreciate how you handled this. We came here as lawbreakers and we're leaving with a profitable business opportunity. Thank you."

"It wasn't done as a favor. With your organization to fund our processing capacity growth requirements, we can use our money to invest in marketing."

Jack took a plane to Charlotte, North Carolina, the next week, supposedly on business. He actually planned to buy a vacation home in the mountains and surprise Carolyn with it on their anniversary in August. He found a nice one about twelve miles from Boone on twenty acres with an incredible view, and a clear mountain stream running through the

260

FLORIDA GOLD

property. It would be perfect. He could take Jeb trout fishing in the stream and they could hunt squirrels in the large hardwoods.

The master bedroom was very spacious and had a large bed and large private bath with a deep Jacuzzi tub and shower. Off the master bedroom was a spacious bonus room for the family to listen to evening radio shows. This room also had a bed that could be pulled out if there was a need. The other two bedrooms were downstairs on the main level of the home. One of these had a large bed for two and the other had two twin-size beds. There was one full bathroom with tub and shower off in the hall between these bedrooms. With an additional pullout sofa in the loft area, the main home could accommodate up to eight guests. Over the garage was an attractive one-bedroom apartment, complete with kitchen, living area, full bathroom, and its own washer. The apartment had a full-size bed in the bedroom, and a pullout sofa. An additional four guests could be accommodated with the apartment, for a maximum guest number of twelve.

The fully equipped kitchen had quality appliances and amenities. There was a nice selection of cookware and serving ware, and a good spice cabinet as well. Out on the deck was a barbecue grill and seating for those outdoor meals. The dining area adjoined the kitchen, with a beautiful dining table that would seat a group of up to ten comfortably. There was additional seating at the bar counter.

The living area was off to the side of the dining room and kitchen - the open space of this home was great for gathering after a day of fishing or hiking in the area. Cozy sofas were arranged nicely for conversation, enjoying the views out the windows, or relaxing in front of the beautiful fireplace.

Jack paid cash for the house and returned to Winter Haven.

On their anniversary in August, Jack suggested they go to the mountains for a couple of weeks. "Aren't we too late to get a place to stay?" Carolyn asked.

"I managed to find us a place."

"Good, then we'll plan to leave on Friday."

They arrived in Charlotte at eleven, had a quick lunch, then drove to the vacation home. When they arrived, Carolyn said, "Oh, Jack. This view is gorgeous."

They went inside, and as she went through the house, she said, "My God, Jack, this is the nicest place we've been up here, how were you able to find it on such short notice? Did someone cancel? I bet it costs a fortune!"

"I bought it for us. Happy anniversary!"

"It's ours?"

"Yep."

"Oh Jack!" It's perfect!"

"We have 20 acres, and there's also a trout stream out back that we can take Jeb fishing in. Come on, I'll show you the property."

When they returned to the house, Carolyn said, "This place is beautiful! I've got to call mother and tell her all about it!"

CHAPTER FOURTEEN

The Fresh Citrus Association named their processing business Juice Source. The initial six-million-box-capacity plant started processing the first week of December of 1950, and by March of 1951, Premium Select was no longer rationed. In its first five years, Tropical Juices' sales went from its initial three-plus million cases to thirty-one million. Annual profits reached $2.9 million, a 47 percent annual return on their investment of $200,000 in the research; $4.6 million in processing, storage, and packaging capacity; and another $1.4 million in additional packaging and storage capacity. Jack and Harry became very wealthy men.

In September of 1949, Carolyn said, "Jack, the doctor says that I'm two months pregnant! The baby is due in April!" Jack was ecstatic.

On Saturday, April 15, she woke up at five a.m. with labor pains. "Jack, its time, I need to get to the hospital."

It was a girl - seven pounds, four ounces. As he'd done with Jeb, when the doctor brought her out for Jack to hold, he made the pledge to God and to his daughter to be a good, responsible father. They named her Margaret, after Jack's grandmother, who he still thought was his mother.

In October of 1950, a group of investors from New York that had bought a canning plant in Ruskin, south of Tampa, announced the opening of their processing plant and the launching of their brand, Naturally Orange. They weren't in violation of Jack's agreement with the federal government because they weren't going to make concentrate. Their product would be chilled single-strength juice. They would store it for the off-season as single-strength juice frozen in large two hundred pound cubes, similar to ice at a commercial icehouse but with larger cubes. There was no advertising to support its launch. Jack tasted their juice and it was good. Not quite as good as Premium Select, but still good. However, at three times the weight and volume of concentrate, and packaged in glass bottles, which were heavier than the cardboard-and-tin containers Premium Select was packaged in, it was expensive to store and distribute. The result was a retail price for Naturally Orange that was 27 percent higher than Premium Select. Consumers bought it mostly for the convenience of a chilled ready-to-serve product, but it never expanded beyond the Southeast due to its costly distribution.

In January of 1950, Jack had decided it was time to build another house. He wanted something larger and more elegant than the one he'd built in 1934. Something he could entertain in. Entertainment, particularly of heads of large retail chains and large growers was becoming more important to his business. He told Carolyn, who was elated at the prospect of a new house, and she and her mother immediately began making plans, contacting an architect to design and draw their ideas. The house was finished in October of 1950.

The ten-thousand-square-foot three-story lakefront brick mansion struck awe in whoever saw it for the first time. Quiet elegance was portrayed throughout. Spanish tiles highlighted the entry hall, living room, dining room, and the kitchen. Custom cabinets in the living room, dining room, and kitchen all matched one another. The chandeliers, ceiling fans, and fixtures were exquisite, with gold and antique brass

FLORIDA GOLD

abundant. The curved staircase was made of varnished oak. The large dining room was paneled in mahogany with a buffet, closet, and serving arrangement covering an entire wall. The private library, located on the second floor, was classic for the period, hosting open-shelf bookcases. A billiard room adjoined the library. There were five bedrooms on the second floor, each with its own private bathroom. The master bedroom, on the first floor, had lacquered wood trim moldings, a hot tub, and a fireplace. Its walls and ceiling were covered with a replica of a Botticelli oil painting. All the bathrooms had marble counter-tops and gold-plated fixtures.

Jack decided it was time to pay back their anonymous investor. His dividends had averaged a 47 percent annual return on the $3.7 million he had ultimately invested in Tropical Juices, and now they would return his capital. So he contacted Ben Marvin from Citrus and Chemical Bank.

"Jack, your anonymous investor wants to meet with you before signing the papers," Ben said.

"OK," Jack replied, wondering why he would choose to meet with him now.

"Can you be here on Monday?"

"Yeah."

On Monday, November 6, 1950, Jack went into the Citrus and Chemical Bank, where he was directed back to a conference room. When he walked in the door, there was Ben with a distinguished-looking older man dressed in a blue suit. "Jack Thomas, your anonymous investor, Tommy Lee Dunaway."

"It's a pleasure to finally meet you, Jack."

"Same here, Mr. Dunaway."

"Call me Tommy Lee. Ben, can we be alone?"

"Sure, just have Kathy at the front desk ring my office when you're ready."

"Jack, I don't know any easy way to say this. I'm your grandfather."

265

ROBERT ALLEN MORRIS

"WHAT? MY GRANDFATHER?"

"Yes." Then Tommy Lee told Jack the entire story about the situation surrounding his birth, and Pete and Margaret's decision to claim him as theirs to avoid a scandal.

"So Irma Sue was really my mother?"

"Yes, she was. I'm sure they would have told you when you were old enough to understand. It's too bad about the tragedy that struck the Walkers and your mother and grandmother in Mobile." Then he told Jack about his moonshine business, the loss of Jack's father, and his decision to change his life.

After Jack recovered from the shock he asked, "Is my paternal grandmother still alive?"

"No, she was killed in a train wreck when Jerry was two."

"I'm sorry. You must come visit me at my house - meet my wife and your great-grandson and great-granddaughter. We have a lot to catch up on."

"I would like to do that, but let's schedule it for another time, so you'll have time to break this news to your wife."

"OK. I guess we have some paperwork to sign."

"No, I have already set it up. The $3.7 million plus the $5.2 million in profits you have paid on it are yours."

"Mine? But why?"

"It's the least I can do, for not being there for you."

"Thanks. Thanks so much, Grandfather," Jack said as they embraced.

"You deserve all of it, and more."

After his meeting with Tommy Lee, Jack went home and told Carolyn the startling news. "We've got to have him as our guest," she insisted.

"I agree. How about for Thanksgiving?"

"That would be wonderful."

The visit went great, and both Jack and Carolyn enjoyed getting to know this fascinating man. Carolyn shared the scrapbook she'd assembled about Jack, and Tommy Lee was

266

FLORIDA GOLD

moved by it. "No man could ask for a better grandson," he said. It was also evident that he was taken with little Jeb, his great-grandson, and with baby Margaret.

Jack and Carolyn were also glad that he would now be a part of their lives. He seemed lonely somehow, not just because he was no longer married - like something had been missing from his life. They hoped they could help fill that void.

In November of 1952, when Tropical Juices' exclusive license expired, five new plants opened, all previously fresh packers. Four would market their juice using their fresh fruit labels and the fifth would supply concentrate to retail chains that were starting their own orange juice labels, initially A&P.

Almost immediately the other companies cut their prices and Premium Select began losing market share. Jack and Harry got together to discuss the situation. "Harry, I will not erode our profits to compete with them."

"I agree Jack, but what choice do we have?"

"We'll cut our price, they'll cut theirs in response, and by the time it's over, nobody will be making any money."

"So what should we do?"

"Marketing."

"Marketing?"

"Yeah. How much do we have in retained earnings?"

"A little over $12 million."

"We need to hire a marketing consultant. Design a national advertising program for radio and the new TV as well as magazines. Get any information we can find on what is different about oranges and orange juice, beyond what we know about the nutritional benefits, that we can tell people about."

"Won't our competitors do the same thing?"

"With what? A program like I'm thinking about may cost several million dollars a year. They are just starting up. They can't afford that."

"I'll get right on it, Jack." They hired Benton & Bowles to help them develop a marketing program and create a marketing department. B&B suggested that their advertising message focus on reminding consumers of the health benefits of orange juice, which in addition to containing more vitamins and minerals than other juices, was containing more than the daily requirements of vitamin C, potassium, and compounds that could reduce chances of cancer and heart disease. They should use radio, because TV was too new and in too few households. They should also put half-page ads in magazines, including *The Saturday Evening Post, Life, The New Yorker,* and *Southern Living.* It would cost them $1.2 million a year. In addition, Jack should deliver a tag at the end of the radio message that said, "This is Jack Thomas. We have our own proprietary process that we believe makes our orange juice the healthiest, tastiest orange juice on the market. Do your own comparison to the other brands. True quality doesn't come cheap."

In November of 1953, Jack and his family were at their mountain vacation home. The day after Thanksgiving, Jack took seven-year-old Jeb squirrel hunting in a hardwood hammock at the back of their property, which joined a much larger piece of property that Jack had permission to hunt on. Jeb would use a Winchester single-shot bolt-action .22 rifle that Jack had given him for his seventh birthday and had been taking him to target practice with. As they sat on a stump, Jack whispered quietly, "We'll sit still until we hear or see one."

"OK, Dad."

In a few minutes, Jack heard the distinctive raspy bark of a gray squirrel and searched the tree tops for it. Then he saw the flicker of a tail on an oak limb. "He's in that oak tree about halfway up," he whispered.

FLORIDA GOLD

"I see him," Jeb said. He slowly raised the rifle and pulled the cocking plunger.

"Aim for his chest, just behind his front shoulder." POW. The squirrel tumbled from the tree.

"Good shot, Jeb!"

"Thanks, Dad." "Your shot has them spooked here. Let's ease up and still hunt," Jack suggested. They crept slowly through the oak hammock, stopping every three to four minutes, listening for a squirrel's barking sound and looking for the flicker of a gray tail in an oak tree. Jeb got five more that morning, and they had fried squirrel for lunch.

"Carolyn, could you come with me for a three-day weekend fishing trip offshore from Miami? Jack asked on Tuesday night, March 23, 1954 at dinner. "We'll be hosting Clayton Fairbanks and Jerry Sparks, our two largest growers, and their wives."

"Didn't Harry do that last year?"

"Yeah, but we sort of agreed to take turns, and it's my turn."

"I didn't think the wives went on those fishing trips."

"Not usually, but Jerry is still a newlywed and his wife likes fishing, so we made it a couples' fishing trip this year."

"OK. When?" she replied thinking, *I can think of a lot of things I'd rather do than that.*

"This weekend."

"That's pretty short notice."

"We were planning it for the third weekend in April, but Randy the boat captain had a cancellation and said the fishing has been great."

Carolyn's parents were keeping Jeb and Margaret. Their trip to Miami Beach took about four hours, and they arrived about two thirty p.m. "We're supposed to meet them at this hotel," Jack explained as they drove up to the Fontainebleau Hotel and got valet parking.

269

"Jack, I've read about this place! It just opened. It's supposed to be one of the most luxurious resort hotels in the world!" Then they entered the lobby. "This is an unbelievably beautiful place!" Carolyn remarked as they walked through the exquisite lobby with its fountains, gardens, and art sculptures. "It more than lives up to the article I read about it."

"You really like this place?"

"I sure do, don't you?"

"Tell you what, then," Jack grinned. "Why don't we ditch those old growers and stay here?"

"Really! Wait a minute. Jack Thomas! We were never actually supposed to meet those growers, were we?"

"Guess not," he admitted, grinning. "I just thought you'd like a surprise getaway weekend together."

"Oh, Jack. That's so romantic."

"A rose for the lady," the bellman said as he presented her with a beautiful red rose. Their suite had original paintings decorating the walls, a large chandelier in the living/dining room, a stocked wet bar and a private garden/terrace with a Japanese hot tub. The spacious bathroom had a separate shower and Jacuzzi tub, with marble floor and tabletops, and gold-plated fixtures. The posts and headboard on the king-size bed were hand-carved mahogany. As the bellman showed them the suite, Carolyn gasped, "This is the most beautiful hotel I've ever seen!"

Jack tipped the bellman and he left. Then the phone rang, and after getting it, Jack replied, "That's perfect, we'll see you then."

"Who was that?"

"Your next surprise is being arranged."

"Another surprise?"

"Yep. We need to meet the limousine downstairs in about an hour and a half."

"Do you know how much I love you?"

FLORIDA GOLD

"Not as much as I love you," Jack teasingly replied as he playfully threw a pillow from the couch at her.

"Oh no?" Carolyn giggled as she threw the pillow back at him. Then she dashed into the bedroom saying, "Catch me if you want your special surprise!"

The limo took them to the Miami Beach Marina and Jack said, "How about a sunset cruise on a sailboat?"

"A sunset cruise?"

"Yeah."

They climbed aboard the white twenty-six foot sailboat and their captain said, "Good afternoon, Mr. and Mrs. Thomas, I'm Josh. Mr. Thomas, your champagne is chilled, and I can serve it if you and Mrs. Thomas would like a glass now."

"Yes, Josh, that would be just fine. Here's a toast to another romantic weekend," Jack said, raising his glass.

"To that, and to the best husband in the world."

"And to the best wife in the world."

They soon sailed out of the inter-coastal waterway and into the ocean, and Josh said, "Mr. Thomas, I can bring out your platter of seafood, fruit and cheese now if you'd like."

"Yes, thank you, Josh."

As they sat sipping champagne and munching on shrimp, stone crab, fruit, and cheese, admiring the beautiful sunset, Carolyn knew that even after nine years of marriage, she loved Jack more now than the day they were married. He never took her for granted, and always let her know how important she was to him.

In spite of his busy schedule, Jack was always home by seven p.m. for dinner, unless he was away on business or at a business dinner. If he had additional work to finish, he got up at three or four a.m. and went to the office to finish it then, rather than being late to dinner or missing it.

And at least once a year he planned a romantic weekend for them. Sometimes it was a surprise and sometimes not. They'd been to Puerto Rico, the Florida Keys, Park Avenue in New York, Niagara Falls, and a number of other interesting places. She felt that she was the luckiest woman in the world.

Although all orange juice had the same health benefits, that wasn't evident to the consumer. And only Tropical Juices was talking about its health benefits - the other brands didn't have the financial resources to advertise. In less than a year, Premium Select's market share grew from the 43 percent of the market where it had sunk, to 62 percent and sales were growing at 15 percent a year. Their increase in profits was four times the advertising costs. By 1957, Florida went from processing 15 percent of its oranges in the mid-1940s to 90 percent, and orange production and acreage more than doubled from the1946/47 season.

In June, Jack took his family for a two-week vacation to their mountain home. On Saturday morning, he, Jeb, Margaret, and Carolyn all went on a fly-fishing trip. It was Jeb and Margaret's first time, but not Jack and Carolyn's. They'd taken lessons years earlier on a getaway four-day weekend to Gatlinburg, Tennessee.

It was cool, about fifty-two degrees, and the grass was glistening with dew. Steam was rising from the quiet pools in the stream, and there wasn't a cloud in sight. The water pouring over the rocks had a calming effect that was always relaxing to Jack.

"Watch Dad," Carolyn told them.

"See, pull your leader out with your left hand and work the rod with your right," Jack demonstrated. "It's mostly in your wrist motion. When you have about forty feet of line out, put the fly in a likely spot for a fish, like near a log or bush, then pop it along on the surface of the water."

FLORIDA GOLD

Jeb tried, and ended up in a tree. "Try again," Carolyn suggested as she freed his line.

Margaret worked the rod like a pro, and put her fly next to a stump. As she flicked it on the water, the surface suddenly erupted, and a huge rainbow trout jumped out of the water.

"Nice job! Reel him in, Margaret!" Jack told her. Carolyn got out the Polaroid camera and took a picture of beaming seven-year-old Margaret, holding the trout, standing next to a proud Jack.

"I think I like hunting better," Jeb said.

They caught half a dozen trout and had fresh trout amandine for dinner that night.

"That was one of the finest dinner's I've ever had, Carolyn," said Rob Thompson a week after the Thomas's fly-fishing trip. Rob and his wife, Jean, whose vacation house was on the other side of the mountain, were friends of Jack and Carolyn's.

"Carolyn, you must share your recipe for that potato casserole. It's superb," Jean observed.

"It was her tender, juicy prime rib I was talking about," Rob added.

"Thanks, everyone," replied Carolyn.

"Since we're celebrating Jeb's eleventh birthday, Carolyn made a birthday cake," Jack told their guests. "Let's all go into the family room for cake and coffee or punch."

"And gifts?" Jeb asked wishfully.

"Why, your mother and I thought this wonderful party and meal would be your gift," Jack teased. Jeb didn't say anything, but he knew he would be getting a gift, and he was hoping for a hunting rifle.

"This is what I got you," Carolyn told everyone as she handed Jeb a large gift wrapped in blue paper with a red bow.

273

"This is from me," Margaret said as she handed Jeb a square box wrapped in green paper with an orange bow. "We bought you a gift too, Jeb," the Thompsons' son, Mike, told everyone. "Can I go get it, Dad?"

"Sure, Son," Rob said as he and Jack exchanged amused glances and Mike left to go get Jeb's gift out of their car.

Carolyn was serving the cake while Jack poured coffee for the adults and punch for Jeb, Mike, and Margaret when Mike came back with the rectangular-shaped gift. "Happy birthday!" Mike said as he handed the gift to Jeb.

Jeb tore into the paper. "Wow! A hunting knife!" It was a practical all-around hunter and woodsman's knife with an extra strong 4½-inch curved blade made from the finest Solingen carbon steel sharpened to a razor edge, a special thumb rest, a genuine stag handle and a sturdy dark-brown leather sheath. "Now I have something to field dress that buck, huh, Dad?"

"Yeah, that you do."

Next Jeb opened his gift from Margaret and Carolyn, which was a genuine Alpine rucksack made from the finest quality canvas with reinforced stitching throughout. It had prime leather 1¼-inch carrying straps and two exterior pockets with leather-bound flaps fastened with steel buckles.

Then Jack came out carrying a gift, but it was too small to be a rifle. "Here, Son, from your mother and me," Jack said as he handed Jeb the box. It was a pair of Zeiss Prism 7x35 binoculars. The lenses were of the finest optical quality and fully coated for maximum light transmission. The binoculars were central focusing with a wide field and secondary eye adjustments, and it came with a pigskin case and leather carrying straps.

"Thanks, Dad, Mom," Jeb replied, trying to hide his disappointment at not getting the rifle he had wanted.

Jack looked at Carolyn and winked. "I think we have a problem here, Jack," Carolyn observed.

FLORIDA GOLD

"I don't see a problem here, do you, Jeb?" Jack asked with a comical tone in his voice.

Before Jeb could answer, Margaret shouted, "Jeb has everything he needs for deer hunting but a rifle!"

"You're right, Margaret. He has a hunting knife, binoculars, even a pack to carry his stuff in, but no rifle."

Jack reached behind the sofa and brought out a long red box that said **Winchester** on its lid. "I almost forgot to give you this. Thanks for reminding me, Margaret and Carolyn," Jack teased as he handed the box to Jeb.

"WOW! Is it the Model 70?"

"Open the box and see," Jack suggested as he handed Jeb a knife to cut through the tape holding the lid in place. Considered by many as the finest bolt-action rifle ever built in the United States, the Model 70 Winchester was highly sought after by shooters and hunters. Often referred to as "the rifleman's rifle," its smooth, strong action had no peer. Jeb's was a .30-06, and had a twenty-four inch deeply blued barrel with a select walnut checkered stock, and was mounted with a Leupold 4X scope. "I believe that boy is ready to go deer hunting," Jack teased.

"Thanks, Mom and Dad. Thanks everyone, thanks a lot," Jeb replied, smiling as he ran his fingers over the rifle's deep-brown walnut stock.

In August, Jack joined a new hunting lease. It was located on five thousand acres bordering Lake Hatchineha, only about a thirty-minute drive from where they lived in Winter Haven. It was owned by a car dealer in Orlando, who had ideas of selling it for a combination of lakefront and twenty-acre lots where owners could have horses and ride on common trails he would establish on the property. Since that prospect was years away, he decided to lease it to hunters. With Jack, there would be ten members of what they named the *Turtle Mound Hunt Club*.

275

The hunting lease was some of the most beautiful property with the most diverse terrain that Jack had ever seen in one spot in Florida. There were large oak hammocks with giant oaks that were at least one hundred years old, sandy scrub oak hills climbing to some of the highest elevations in central Florida, pine tree flat woods, open pasture and prairie, and swamps.

The Saturday after he paid the lease fee he took his family to ride on it. They were as impressed with its beauty as Jack was, and with the abundance of game. Large flocks of turkeys, and deer seemed to bound out of almost every thicket. Jeb was ecstatic. Now he had some of the best hunting only thirty-minute drive from home.

Jack bought a Willis station wagon four-wheel-drive jeep so they would not be limited in where they could go on the property, and over the next few weeks Jack and Jeb frequently rode the property getting to know it. Chuck James, the lease manager, held a hunt club workday and cookout for everyone to get to know one another. They built eighteen wooden tree stands fifteen to eighteen feet tall to hunt from.

Chuck designated a spot for their camp in a shady oak hammock and the owner paid for a well to be drilled and for electricity to run to the property. The hunting rules would be bucks only, with a limit of three per member. Wild hogs could be hunted year–round, and there was no limit on how many a member could kill. Turkeys would be three per member.

One group of members from Tampa brought their camp cook trailer over, which became their camp headquarters. Another member and his brother built a screened-in building for relaxing and eating in. A common fire pit with chairs around it was established, and eight of the members brought their own camper trailers to the camp. Jack and Ray Ingram both lived in the area, and didn't need a camper trailer. Later that year a skinning rack and walk-in cooler were set up, and they had a fully functional hunting club. Jack had truckloads

FLORIDA GOLD

of fill dirt dumped on a piece of property he owned that joined one of his orange groves, and had it formed into a tall berm that would stop bullets. Next he had a portable shooting bench built, and marked fifty- and hundred-yard shooting spots from the berm. He took Jeb to their new shooting range, and taught him how to make sure the scope on his new rifle was adjusted properly for the bullet to hit the target spot the rifle was aimed at, which is called "sighting it in." Afterward, he took Jeb to practice on Saturday afternoons until he became a very good shot. Jeb was excited about his first deer hunt, and it seemed like the opening day of hunting season would never arrive. Finally, it did.

Jack and Jeb got to camp about five a.m., and went into the trailer to sign in to a stand. Hunters had to put their name tag on the stand marked on an aerial map, so all the hunters would know where everyone was. Stands were available on a first-come, first-served basis. "Looks like you've got an enthusiastic hunter there," Chuck said as he shook Jack's hand.

"Yes, sir," eleven-year-old Jeb replied. After having coffee with the group, Jack drove to a spot near the stand and parked the jeep behind a bush so it wouldn't be easily visible.

"Don't forget your pack," Jack whispered to Jeb as they quietly got out of the jeep and eased the doors closed, but not latched, to avoid the noise. Jeb's pack contained his new hunting knife, his new binoculars, ten Remington .30-06 pointed soft point Core-Lokt cartridges, a canteen of water, and old rags to clean his hands if they ended up getting - and thus field dressing - a deer. "There's enough of a moon to see without the flashlight," Jack whispered. "Let's stand here until our eyes adjust to the darkness. They soon headed down the trail the two hundred yards to their stand, being careful not to step on branches or otherwise make noise.

"There it is, over there," Jeb whispered as they were searching for the well-hidden tree stand in the nearly dark woods.

"Yeah, I see it now. Tie that cord onto your rifle case and then we'll pull it up once we get into the stand." Jeb tied his gun case handle to the cord that was attached to the top of the tree stand. Jeb climbed up first, followed by Jack. Then Jeb pulled his rifle in its case up into the tree stand.

"Should I load up now?" Jeb whispered as he uncased his new rifle.

"Yeah, put one in the chamber and two in the magazine." Most of the light from the sliver of a moon was blocked by the huge oak tree their stand was in, so the two sat in silence, in almost complete darkness. In the distance a whip-poor-will called, followed by an owl's *who, who, who-whooo*. After what seemed like an eternity to Jeb, but was only about half an hour, dawn began to break, the gray light coming first in the sky. Soon birds were chirping - the musical calls of a mocking bird, the raspy noise of blue jays, crows cawing in the distance.

When Jack could read his watch, he whispered, "Rest the forearm of your rifle across the guard-rail in front of us and take the caps off your scope lenses. You need to set up to shoot where that trail from the right intersects that small clearing about seventy-five yards in front of us." As the sun began to emerge, ground mists began to rise like wisps of smoke from the wire grass in the small clearing in front of them, and the raspy bark of a squirrel in the tree above blended with the sounds of the birds. It was a crisp sunny morning, about fifty degrees, with a light fog. They were surrounded by thick woods except for the game trail.

Jack was glad to be with Jeb on his first deer hunt, many miles into the central Florida wilderness, and realized how special it was. They'd been sitting for about an hour-and-a-half when Jack heard something in the brush. "Get ready,

FLORIDA GOLD

Jeb," he whispered as Jeb nervously took off the rifle's safety and quietly put the stock to his shoulder. Suddenly, two deer, a doe and buck, jumped out and Jack whispered, "Shoot, Jeb!" He shot the buck as it crossed the clearing, the boom of the rifle shot echoing through the deep woods. The buck leaped into the air, and ran into the brush along with the doe. Jack grasped Jeb's arm and said, "I think you hit him, give him time to go down." They waited ten minutes, then climbed down and went after him. Jack showed Jeb drops of blood, and they followed the blood trail. About thirty yards into the brush, they saw him.

"It's an eight point, Dad!"

"It sure is. Good shooting, Son!" Jack said as he shook Jeb's hand.

Jack field dressed the buck with Jeb watching intently, since he had never seen an animal field dressed before. Back at the camp, Ferdinand Rhoden, one of the other hunt club members, said, "Jack, it looks like you're raising a hunter there."

"Trying to," Jack said proudly.

"Congratulations on killing your first buck, Jeb," Ferdinand said.

"Thank you, sir."

In December of 1957 there was a devastating freeze. Old-timers said it was the worst they could remember. All fresh fruit shipments were halted for thirty days until the freeze-damaged fruit would begin to rot, to avoid consumers getting the damaged fruit. Processors also stopped processing, believing that if the fruit couldn't be eaten, it could not be made into juice.

Rules of thumb about the effect of cold temperatures on citrus fruit and trees are that a temperature of twenty-seven degrees Fahrenheit for six hours or more damages fruit, and twenty-four degrees for six hours or more damages limbs and

279

trees. However, if temperatures have been low, with nights at thirty-five to forty degrees for several days before the freeze, the tree builds cold tolerance, and it may take lower temperatures or longer duration of low temperatures to damage the wood. Also, some rootstocks are more cold tolerant than others. The presence of a lake near the grove can raise ground temperatures, as can turning on irrigation and wetting the soil to get it to release heat. Covering the tree with irrigation water that turns to ice can keep the temperatures at thirty-two degrees and minimize freeze damage, although the weight of the ice may break limbs.

Over the days, and sometimes weeks, following a major freeze, many of the cold-shocked trees without damaged fruit would be dropping all their fruit on the ground as a means to survive. Once on the ground, the fruit has to be processed within seventy-two hours, since oranges begin to deteriorate once separated from the tree. However, if the weather stays cold, no warmer than sixty-five degrees, the fruit will hold on the ground for up to a week. The key would be temporarily increasing processing capacity to try and salvage freeze-damaged fruit first, then run the fruit dropped on the ground.

Jack contacted Ed White to get his opinion about processing the freeze-damaged fruit. "We don't know, Jack. But I suspect that if it's processed within a week, any off flavors from the freeze damage will be flashed off by the evaporator. The USDA will have to make the final determination, after the freeze-damaged fruit has been processed."

Jack called an emergency industry meeting at the Florida Citrus Commission headquarters in Lakeland to discuss processing the freeze-damaged fruit. The next morning at eight a.m., two days after the freeze, he addressed a packed meeting room with a garden rake in his hand.

"Fellow growers, take garden rakes and rake the bad fruit from underneath your trees. Then pick the fruit remaining,

FLORIDA GOLD

whether it's freeze-damaged or not. After six days, stop, because any freeze-damaged fruit will not be fit for processing. Then you begin sending us fruit that was dropped on the ground by the cold-shocked trees. We'll cull the freeze-damaged fruit because by then, it will be evident which fruit it is. Those with unhurt fruit will have to wait until the other fruit has been run. I'll pay you thirty-three cents per box for your harvest and haul costs, with a rise to ninety percent of the market price if the USDA OKs the concentrate. If they don't, I eat the harvest and haul costs I've paid you. If they approve the concentrate, we all win in this high-priced supply-reduced market. Are there any processors here that are willing to make the same offer?" None were.

"OK, I need volunteer processors to help process all the fruit that will come in over the next sixty days. I'll pay 13½ cents per box." All of the processors agreed to participate. "We'll all need to run three shifts and process fruit twenty-four hours a day."

"Jack, you do realize that if this doesn't work, we'll be out of business unless we can get a large loan. And I don't know what we'll do for collateral," Harry told him.

"Without fruit we'll be out of business anyway, Harry. Haven't you put enough away to retire on?"

"Yes. I just don't want to see us lose the business."

"I talked to Ed White, and I think this will work."

"Well, one thing's for certain. If it does, we'll own the market and the fruit supply. The growers will adore you for taking such a large risk to save them."

With the added capacity of the other plants, they were able to run four times as much fruit as they would have normally run over the sixty-day period. That, combined with the fact that 60 percent of the fruit still in the field was not damaged, meant that if the USDA approved the juice, not only were they still in business, they would again own the market.

281

ROBERT ALLEN MORRIS

Thirty days later Jack held another meeting at the Citrus Commission offices, and the industry waited breathlessly while the USDA reported their results of sampling Jack's juice from the freeze-damaged fruit. At eight forty-five a.m., the phone on the conference table rang and Jack answered it. "Mr. Thomas, your juice is good. USDA passed the entire sample."

"Thank you. Everyone, the juice passed! We're in business!"

The crowd stood, and clapped and cheered. Jack's bold actions and willingness to risk his business had saved many growers from financial ruin. He was the hero of the industry. Many growers came up to him while they were enjoying coffee, orange juice, and pastries before leaving and said various versions of, "Mr. Thomas, you have my fruit from now on if you want it, at whatever you think is a fair price."

Jack went on national television to explain about the freeze and what was happening to orange juice and fresh citrus supplies. Because it involved a natural disaster to a food crop, the federal government paid for half the air time. "I'm Jack Thomas. I own Tropical Juices, the company that makes Premium Select orange juice. As you may know, there was recently a devastating freeze in Florida. You may have already noticed a scarcity of strawberries and produce in the store because it was damaged by the cold weather. Well, citrus was damaged too. That means a reduction in availability of fresh citrus and orange juice as well. But we're working around the clock to minimize how much your supply of orange juice is reduced. We have hundreds in the field selecting only the fruit that can still be processed, and we're running our processing plants around the clock to process the juice before the fruit begins to spoil from the cold damage. The US Department of Agriculture is inspecting every load of juice, to be sure it meets standards, and we are making sure it meets our own more demanding standards. Tropical Juices is paying

FLORIDA GOLD

the cost of this effort, but because of those costs and scarce supplies, prices will be higher. The juice will be just as tasty and nutritious, and you shouldn't go without it as part of a balanced diet."

"This was a public service announcement brought to you by the US Department of Agriculture and Jack Thomas." That added loads of credibility to what Jack told them. Demand grew even stronger and prices skyrocketed, increasing by 46 percent to $1.53 a gallon.

"I just don't understand it Jack, I never thought the consumer would continue to buy orange juice at these prices," Harry said in a Monday morning meeting.

"It was Jack's advertisement," replied Joe Zigulich, their new director of sales and marketing. Joe, who had been an associate with Benton & Bowles, was a burly man about six feet tall with thick, black curly hair. He'd played football in college and his physique showed that he stayed in shape. "I don't think this will continue when supplies return, but for now consumers are accepting the higher prices because they know why they are so high."

"You know, if you think about it, as a percent of income, and compared to what consumers spend on other beverages, orange juice still isn't that expensive," Jack observed. "Annual per capita orange juice consumption is 4.2 gallons. At $1.53 a gallon, that's $6.43 in fifty-two weeks, which comes to 12.4 cents a week. Sodas are a nickel each, and most people drink at least one a day, which would be 35 cents a week, almost three times the expenditure on orange juice, and orange juice is healthier."

"Your logic makes sense," Joe observed.

"We need to come up with a better way to buy fruit. When supplies are scarce, all the processors bid fruit prices too high, and when there's a surplus, they go too low, below growers' costs of production. And how many times have we paid a competitive price for fruit during the season, then had

283

retail prices drop in the summer and fall so our profits were reduced? Well, I have an idea that might change that.

"We develop a new fruit-pricing mechanism. The fruit price will be determined by the price we sell our juice for, less our costs for sales and marketing, distribution, warehousing, packaging, and processing. We'll also deduct a percentage of sales as a profit margin. The balance will be the grower's fruit price. This calculation will be for a twelve-month period, beginning in November when we start processing, and ending the following October. Payment to the grower will be after we have completed the calculations, probably by December. We will calculate and pay the price per pound of juice solids, not per box like we do now. That way we more closely align fruit prices with juice prices."

"What's the difference in gallons and pounds of solids?" Joe asked.

"Pounds of solids are a measure of the soluble sugar solids in juice. Oranges generally produce from 5.8 to 6.5 pounds of solids per 90-pound box. The concentrate we sell in retail outlets contains 4.135 pounds of solids per gallon, and when consumers reconstitute it into single-strength juice it contains 1.029 pounds of solids per gallon."

"Jack, I don't think most growers can wait until after they've delivered their fruit to be paid," Harry said.

"I agree, so we'll pay them an advance of seventy-five percent of what we think our fruit price will be when they deliver their fruit. We will calculate the price advance by running a continuing calculation of our final price from the selling price data we have."

"I like it," Joe said. "It's fair to the grower and to us."

"How will the grower know we calculated the price fairly?" Harry asked. "We can't let them look at our books."

"We'll have the price calculation verified by a CPA firm. The growers won't be able to see our price and cost data, but the CPA audit will insure that it was done as specified in our

FLORIDA GOLD

contract. I'm going to name this new type of pricing mechanism 'fruit participation,' because the grower participates in our success in the marketplace."

"What if the price calculates too low in some seasons?" Harry asked. "We don't want to lose growers to the cash market."

"As the biggest fruit buyer in the state, our reduction in buying on the cash market alone will reduce its volatility. But the participation price calculation will be a minimum price. We'll always have the right to pay more. I also want to create a captive source of fruit supplies for this new pricing mechanism. They will be our grower partners. Based on the feedback I've gotten since the freeze, many are receptive to a relationship like that with us now."

"We could structure it legally as a grower marketing cooperative. Maybe we name it Juice Orange Marketers," Harry suggested.

Jack and Harry met with a group of growers and discussed the idea with them. They liked the participation price concept, and the fact that only members of Juice Orange Marketers would be paid with the new mechanism. They held meetings, formed a board of directors, became classified as a grower cooperative, and in April of 1958, Juice Orange Marketers was born. It would supply 80 percent of Tropical Juices' fruit requirements. They would buy the balance on the spot cash market. The president of Juice Orange Marketers was Cecil Moore, a big solid fellow with a no-nonsense attitude. He'd been the harvesting manager for a fruit dealer whose growers' groves had mostly been lost to the freeze.

On Wednesday, March 19, Jack got a call from Jim Stewart, president of Florida Citrus Mutual, the citrus growers' trade association. "Jack, its Jim Stewart from Mutual."

285

ROBERT ALLEN MORRIS

"Hey, Jim."

"After your leadership during this last freeze, Florida's growers would like you helping to deal with the citrus marketing and regulatory issues that the Citrus Commission deals with. Our board asked me to approach you about becoming a Florida Citrus Commissioner."

"Jim, I'd be honored, thank you."

The Florida Citrus Commission was a twelve-member board established in 1935 by an act of the Florida legislature as a result of industry request. The act, called the Florida Citrus Code, stated that the Florida Citrus Commission was to protect and enhance the quality and reputation of Florida citrus in both domestic and foreign markets. Commissioners were appointed by the governor of Florida and confirmed by the state senate for three-year terms. Seven were to be growers or represented by grower companies, three members were to represent the processing industry, and two to represent fresh fruit shippers. Under Florida's "sunshine law," all Commission meetings were open to the public and often had two to three hundred attendees.

The Commission oversaw the activities of the Florida Department of Citrus (FDOC). The FDOC, headed by an executive director, carried out Commission policy and acted as the Commission's staff by conducting a wide variety of programs involving industry regulation; scientific, market and economic research; advertising; merchandising; public and industry relations; and consumer promotions. The FDOC and its programs were financed by a tax placed on each box of citrus moved through commercial channels. The Commission set the annual amount of the tax, and quality standards for all citrus grown, packed, or processed in Florida. These were enforced by the Florida Department of Agriculture. The Commission also set rules regulating packaging and labeling of Florida citrus products and licensing requirements for fresh packers, shippers, and processors.

FLORIDA GOLD

Wednesday night at dinner, in March of 1958, Jack asked, "Jeb, would you like to go hunting for a gobbler this Saturday morning?"

"Yeah!" Being in Central Florida, they would be hunting for Osceola turkeys.

On Saturday, March 22, they arrived at the lease camp house at five a.m. Nobody else was there. They hung their tag on the spot where Jack had built a blind earlier in the week, on the edge of a large field where they would blend into the greens and browns of the surrounding cover. Jack had scouted the morning he built the blind, and felt that he'd chosen a good spot because of the gobbles he'd heard there. Then they left for the woods. For decoys, Jack had chosen a full-strut jake (young gobbler) decoy flanked by a hen. The visual attraction would be more than a mature tom could tolerate. He would not allow a jake to keep company with "his" hen during breeding season. Instinct would drive the gobbler to confront the immature jake, positioned only twenty yards away from their blind, putting the turkey in shotgun range.

As the sun rose, a hoot owl called, and a gobble sounded in the distance. Making hoot owl and crow calls was called "shock calling," because it often got gobblers in the distance to sound off, revealing their location. On this property, however, Jack had noticed that the owls and crows themselves usually called out, so there was no need for him to. Then they heard gobbles from three other toms about two hundred yards across the field. They gobbled non-stop from their roosts. Then the tone changed, and Jack whispered, "They've flown down from the roost. Get your shotgun up and in position. Once we see them, don't move until I tell you to shoot." It was a beautiful scene, the sweet smells of spring flowers filling the crisp air on this March morning, a light mist rising from the broom sage in the pasture.

287

The toms gobbled and Jack made a yelping sound in response on his box call, like a hen turkey. With hen yelps, Jack kept the trio of toms interested. Soon, they could see the toms coming through the morning mist about seventy-five yards away. At this point the toms could see his strutting jake decoy and Jack stopped calling. The gobblers began to hurry toward the jake. About ten yards away from the decoy, two of the toms went into full strut while the other headed right for it.

They were soon strutting around the decoy, and one tom was attacking it. "Take the safety off and shoot him when you're ready," Jack whispered. At the shot, the closest gobbler fell to a load of number six shot and began flopping. The distance was eighteen paces.

Jeb jumped out of the blind and ran to the bird. Jack walked over and said, "Great job, Son." Then he took Jeb's picture with the gobbler. They weighed and measured it back at camp. It had a twelve-inch beard and weighed nineteen pounds. Lunch was fried turkey breast, mashed potatoes and gravy.

CHAPTER FIFTEEN

In October of 1960, Dave Castle, the citrus commissioner from Naturally Orange, proposed that Florida's generic orange juice advertising emphasize the phrase "made only from Florida oranges." This was supposedly to protect Florida growers from the price impact of imported juice from Mexico, Costa Rica, or elsewhere. In reality, it was to protect Naturally Orange, whose chilled single-strength juice couldn't be economically sourced from anywhere but Florida. Jack took issue with Dave's proposal.

"Fellow commissioners, if we place that limitation on processors and prevent obtaining juice from other countries, in a severe freeze Florida orange juice could price itself out of the market."

"But how do we know the juice from these other countries will always be of good quality?" asked Commissioner Alexander, chairman of the FCC.

"I know I would require that a foreign processor meet the same specs as we do," Jack replied.

"Yeah, Jack, that's you. But what about other processors or dairies that supply private labels?" Commissioner Huff asked.

"OK. Why don't we create a Florida-quality seal of approval to be displayed on packages of juice?" It can say on them that the juice was processed and packaged according to specifications required by this commission."

"That works for me," Commissioner Huff said.

"I move we bring this to a vote," Commissioner Alexander suggested.

"I so move," Commissioner Huff said.

"All in favor?"

Most said aye.

"Opposed?"

"No," said Commissioner Castle.

"The ayes have it, motion carried," Commissioner Alexander said.

Jack had hired Ed White years ago as a consultant. Jack wanted Ed to keep up with new technological developments in citrus juice processing and advise him of ways that Tropical Juices could capitalize on these developments. Ed was a thin, quiet man, about five foot eight with sandy hair, who often stuttered when he got excited.

"Jack, Ralph Cook, who founded Cook Machinery Company in Clearwater, Florida, has designed a new, better type of evaporator," Dr. White explained in a meeting he'd called with Jack in December of 1960. Jack had also asked Harry to join them.

"Tell us about it," Jack said.

"It is called a TASTE evaporator, which stands for *Thermally Accelerated Short Time Evaporator*. It exposes the juice to higher heat for a shorter time than the evaporators now in use, producing a better-tasting concentrate with little heat damage. It is also simpler and lower in cost to operate. But most importantly, it enables evaporating the juice to sixty-five degrees Brix instead of forty-five like current evaporators. This results in a more biologically stable juice, and lowers storage costs since the concentrate is a six-to-one ratio to single-strength juice versus one that is a three-to-one.

FLORIDA GOLD

"But doesn't cut-back still require storage of the concentrate at forty-two degrees Brix?" Jack asked.

"No. Cut-back isn't required. The TASTE evaporator recovers the oil and water-phase flavor essences lost in steam during the evaporation process in a unit mounted near the top of it."

"So we could add these essences back to the concentrate to restore its fresh-squeezed taste instead of using cut-back?" asked Jack.

"That's correct. They would be added during the packaging of the concentrate."

"That would definitely reduce our storage costs," Harry added.

"And since you won't be using cut-back, the sixty-five degree Brix concentrate can be stored in large tanks instead of 55 gallon drums, which will reduce storage costs even more," Dr. White added. "Jack, I can develop an essence package for Premium Select if you'd like that will make it taste much better, and practically undetectable from fresh-squeezed juice in blind taste tests."

"Great, then we'll have a better-tasting product at a lower cost," Harry concluded.

"Yeah," Dr. White replied, "until other processors switch to TASTE evaporators."

"At least we'll get a head start. When can you have it ready?" Jack asked

"In about four to five weeks."

"Great, do it."

Jack and Carolyn decided that since Jack was spending time on the hunting lease with Jeb, he should take Margaret on a pheasant hunt. She and Carolyn had each gotten twenty-gauge Browning Superposed double-barreled over-under shotguns for Christmas in 1960, and the whole family had begun shooting about one Saturday each month at the Polk

291

County Trap and Skeet Club ever since. Margaret had become a pretty good shot.

In October, Jack and Margaret flew to Sioux Falls, South Dakota, rented a car and drove to Harrold. The lodge was about five miles south of there. They were greeted by owner and operator Arturo Candler. The eighteen-thousand-square-foot lodge had a cherry wood self-serve bar, billiard room, and library. Native American painted buffalo skulls, mounts, and antiques dating back from the days the West was settled were blended with creature comforts including the Wild Bill Hickok cigar room, a steam bath, and Jacuzzi. Chef Joe Foster treated the taste buds of guests with sirloin steak, barbecue brisket, slow-cooked ribs and mandarin-glazed pheasant breast.

Their rooms were comfortable and spacious. The first day began with a hearty breakfast of bacon, scrambled eggs, hash brown potatoes, biscuits, and jelly. After breakfast there was a safety briefing, then off to the fields to hunt. They rode on a hunting buggy with elevated seats on the back, and a dog box below with four eager pointers. It took about fifteen minutes to get to the first field they were going to hunt. While the dogs were let out of the box and ran wildly about, Jack and Margaret climbed down from the seat, put shotgun shells into their hunting vest pockets, and took their shotguns out of their cases.

The guide, Tony, said "Let's go this way." In about five minutes, one of the dogs went on point and the other one honored it from behind. Jack and Margaret crept forward, and the brush suddenly erupted with a half dozen pheasants. Jack decided to watch Margaret shoot. She smoothly mounted her gun, swung with the flying bird, and fired. It crumpled in midair and tumbled to the ground. "Good shooting, Margaret," Jack congratulated her.

"Thanks, Dad. That was fun!" The pointer nearest the bird retrieved it and took it to the guide, who put it in his vest

FLORIDA GOLD

game pouch. The dogs soon went on point again, and this time both Jack and Margaret shot. Both got a pheasant. By noon they had seven of them, and decided to go in for lunch. While the guide was cleaning their birds they had Caesar salad and turkey breast sandwiches for lunch. "Dad, I'm having a wonderful time. Thanks for bringing me," Margaret said as she touched his arm.

"I'm having a good time too. Tell you what, we'll try to come every year, just the two of us."

"Really? Oh, Dad, that would be great!"

They got six on the afternoon hunt. Dinner that night for the eight hunters, many of which had their sons with them, was a gourmet feast consisting of amuse-bouche with caviar and quail eggs for an appetizer, guava-glazed pheasant breast with foie gras ravioli and pineapple confit for the entrée, and bouchée of chocolate bread pudding for dessert. Following that were cigars and brandy for the adults.

Jack and Margaret left for the airport the next morning after breakfast. Both realized how much they had enjoyed this time together.

At dinner one night in May of 1962 Jack asked, "How would everyone like to go on a hunting trip in Maine this September?"

"What would we be hunting?" Jeb asked.

"You and I would be hunting black bear, and Mom and Margaret would be hunting grouse and woodcock. After three days of hunting, we'll drive around the coast of Maine and visit fishing villages and sample the local seafood. We would be gone eight days."

"I think that makes a wonderful vacation, Jack," Carolyn said.

"Me too," Margaret added.

"Of course we'd have to get Jeb and Margaret out of school," Carolyn observed.

293

"Oh, I think that would be OK. We'll write a paper about the trip," Margaret suggested.

"I think that's a great idea," Jack replied.

They planned to fly from Tampa to Boston on Saturday, September 22, rent a station wagon, and drive to Freeport, Maine, where they'd spend the night. They would drive to the bear/grouse camp on Sunday. Their black bear hunt was scheduled from Monday through Wednesday, September 26. The grouse and woodcock hunt would be on that Tuesday and Wednesday. The following Sunday they'd drive back to Portsmouth, New Hampshire, which was close to the Boston airport, and fly back to Tampa on Monday, October 1. They were all excited about their approaching trip.

Carolyn spent most of Friday packing for the trip. Jack woke up at five thirty Saturday morning full of anticipation about their upcoming trip and hunts. Carolyn and Margaret fixed a light breakfast for everyone, while Jack and Jeb loaded their baggage into the van. They were parked and had their luggage checked at the Tampa airport by nine thirty a.m.

Their flight was uneventful. They arrived in Boston just after two p.m., got their rental car, and were off to Maine. As they drove into increasingly rural terrain with large conifers and mountains in the background, Carolyn thought how special it was to be headed to the north woods of Maine on a hunting trip and vacation with Jack and their two children. They made it into Freeport just after six p.m. Jack chose Freeport to spend that night because it is where the corporate headquarters of L.L. Bean, the famous outdoor outfitter, had been located for over forty years.

They went to the Harraseeket restaurant for dinner. They were a rustic place down on the fishing docks. They got 2½-pound steamed Maine lobsters, steamed clams, boiled red-skin potatoes, and boiled sweet corn, and ate on paper plates outside at a picnic table on the waterfront. It was about fifty

FLORIDA GOLD

degrees and chilly - a stark contrast to the eighty-plus-degree weather they'd left in Florida. L.L. Bean's impressed them. They had never seen so much hunting, fishing, camping, and outdoor clothing in one store. Jack and Jeb bought some tackle to fish for brook trout. Since they would bear hunt only in the afternoons, the mornings offered an opportunity for fishing in the numerous mountain streams and lakes that were in the area where they would be hunting. After a cup of chowder at a fifty-plus-year-old pub, it was back to their hotel for a good night's sleep.

They went to a rustic little café in Freeport for breakfast. The breakfast was a buffet, and Jeb and Margaret marveled at the baked beans on it, supposedly to eat with eggs the way Southerners eat grits with eggs. They met ten other bear hunters eating there too, headed for Canada. The air was filled with the sweet aromas of Yankee breakfasts, and they could overhear the other hunters discussing their plans as their excitement continued to build.

They arrived at the bear camp about eleven thirty Sunday morning. Just past the entrance was a huge skinning rack made of two upright logs, each about twenty-two inches in diameter, with a third log across the two upright ones. Just beyond were the guide's house and a barn, where Jack had been told to meet him. "Jack Thomas," he said as he shook Wayne Gorski's hand. The master guide and owner of the camp and guide service, Wayne was a burly man in his late fifties, about five feet ten inches, with a long white beard. He had been guiding bear hunters for over thirty years.

"Good to meet you, Jack."

"This is my wife, Carolyn; our daughter, Margaret; and our son, Jeb."

"I take it you and Jeb will be bear hunting and the ladies will be bird hunting?"

"That's correct," Jack replied.

295

"Good, we need to get everyone registered and licensed. Since you have your family with you, you won't be staying in the camp. You'll be in a nice three-bedroom house on Sebec Lake, about thirty minutes away. People in Boston own these summer vacation homes and I rent them out in the fall to hunters who bring their families along. I think you'll find the house quite comfortable."

They followed Wayne to the house. It sat on the bank of the crystal-clear glacier lake, which was about a mile across, and there were snowcapped mountains in the distance. The leaves had turned to yellow, red, gold, orange, and colors in between, and were breathtaking. It was a good example of the wilderness beauty of Maine. The house had a large picture window that looked out on the lake. It was stocked with everything they would need but food.

"Remember, you need to check your rifles to make sure they are still sighted in correctly before you hunt. Our range is out behind the barn. Other than that, you and Jeb need to be at the barn at seven tomorrow morning. I'll be in Canada at my other camp. Bob Bettle will show you and the other hunters your stands in the morning. Ladies, my wife, Nancy, will be taking you bird hunting. She'll pick you up here at eight Tuesday morning."

After unpacking, Carolyn and Margaret dropped Jack and Jeb off at the camp's make shift rifle range to check their rifles to be sure they hadn't changed point of aim since they were zeroed in Florida several weeks earlier. Carolyn and Margaret took the station wagon and went grocery shopping about fifteen miles away in Dover-Foxcroft, a small town just large enough for one traffic light. Margaret cooked that night, and fixed fried pork chops, creamed corn, and collard greens for an excellent dinner. That time of year in northern Maine the days were in the low seventies and the nights in the mid-forties, a welcome change from Florida's hot, muggy climate.

FLORIDA GOLD

Carolyn was up early and fixed sausage, grits, biscuits, and eggs for breakfast. Jack and Jeb met Bob, along with the other hunters, at the barn at 6:50 a.m. There were three other hunters - one from Texas, one from Pennsylvania, and one from Canada. After going over the hunt procedures and rules, they followed Bob in their station wagon about forty miles from camp to the entrance to the Katahdin Iron Works wilderness area, a 3.8-million-acre area in the North Woods region of Maine. Their stand was fourteen miles from the entrance to the wilderness area. Since Jack and Jeb were hunting together, they had a ground blind. It was a three-sided wooden structure with two folding stools and a square hole in the front wall about six by six inches to shoot through. They were about seventy yards from the bait can, which held stale doughnuts and peanut butter. They would not hunt until three p.m., since bears only fed in the late afternoons.

They went back to the house for lunch, and were back to their stand by three thirty p.m. They didn't see any bears, and were back to their place by eight.

On Tuesday, Jack and Jeb were up early, and left to go fishing about seven. They went to a stream near Guilford. Jack caught four medium-size brown trout and Jeb caught three. They brought them back to the house and cleaned them to have for dinner.

At eight that same morning there was a knock at the door, and when Carolyn answered it, a woman in her mid-fifties with short brownish-gray hair and hazel eyes said, "Good morning, I'm Nancy Gorski, your hunting guide. You must be Carolyn."

"That's correct. Margaret, Nancy's here to take us bird hunting."

"Hey, Mrs. Gorski," Margaret said.

"That's Nancy. Are you ready to go?"

"Yes."

297

"May I see your guns?" Nancy asked when they'd parked at an old abandoned farm house.

"Certainly," Carolyn replied.

"Browning twenty-gauge Superposed. I'm impressed." Nancy turned the dogs out and they entered the thick brush behind an old, falling-down barn. In about twenty minutes one of the dogs went on point. "He's yours, Carolyn," Nancy said, since Carolyn was closest to the dog on point. She crept toward the dog, and suddenly a grouse erupted into the air. She swung just past the bird and fired. It crumpled to the ground. "Nice shooting," Nancy congratulated her. She retrieved the bird and they continued. By noon they had shot at nine birds, and killed three grouse and two woodcock.

"Mom, walking through all that thick brush has me exhausted. I'm ready to go in and come back tomorrow," Margaret explained at noon.

"That suits me. We'll go and clean these birds for dinner."

"Mom, Dad and Jeb must have caught these trout this morning," Margaret said as she looked at the fillets in the refrigerator.

"Great. We'll have trout, grouse, and woodcock for dinner tonight."

The next morning, Bob agreed to take Jack and Jeb to a new stand. It was another four miles into the wilderness area. They had lunch at a small diner in Milo and were on the stand by 3:20.

Beyond the bait in the distance was a tiny hanging basin tucked into an embrace of rocky peaks. Below was an almost perfectly circular meadow of grass surrounded by dark timber, and above it was a smattering of gold hardwoods. A beautiful mountain lake was tucked behind the meadow, its flawless reflections of the peaks broken only by the ripples of feeding trout.

FLORIDA GOLD

Taking in the view reminded Jack of why he loved the rural outdoor hunting and fishing lifestyle. It also reminded him of how lucky he was to be in the wilderness hunting again with his son, and off on a wonderful vacation to a special place with his family.

About four thirty, a large bear silently crept to the bait can. "Jeb, there's a bear hitting the bait," Jack whispered. Jeb nodded and eased the safety of his rifle off. The bear was facing them, about seventy-five yards down a hill where the bait was. Jeb put the cross hairs of the scope on the area at the base of the back of its neck, and squeezed the trigger, sending a 180-grain Nosler Partition toward the bear at 2,650 feet per second. The bear dropped where he stood as the roar of the rifle shot broke the stillness. Since he was flopping around, Jeb put another shot into his shoulder as insurance, as instructed by the guide.

"It's the ones you think are dead that get you," Bob had explained.

"Nice shot, Jeb."

"Thanks, Dad."

They went to the bear and made sure he was dead. "He looks huge, Dad!"

"He sure does." They put the game tag in his ear, but had been told not to field dress the bears. It was so heavy they could barely move him, much less get him up the 150-plus-yard steep hill to the road. It would soon be dark anyway, so they decided to go in. The cold nighttime and early morning temperatures would keep the bear meat from spoiling.

They left with Bob the next morning, Wednesday, at seven to get Jeb's bear. Since Bob had to re-bait some stands on the way in, they agreed to meet him at the bear. He got there about nine, and they all hauled the bear out to the road on an old four-man army stretcher that Bob brought, and loaded him into the back of Bob's truck. Jeb rode with Bob since he was hauling the bear, as required by law. They

299

checked him at the Sebec check station and took him to camp.

After hanging the bear up, they weighed him. "He's a good-sized bear - 372 pounds," observed Wayne, who had returned from his Canada bear camp. Wayne and Bob skinned and quartered him. They put the hide and quarters in the freezer, and planned to debone the quarters that afternoon. After a lunch of bacon sandwiches, Jack and Jeb separated the back strap, deboned the four quarters, wrapped the meat, and put it back in the freezer. The taxidermist came by about seven, and they agreed to make a rug out of Jeb's bear. Of the other three hunters in their group, only the one from Pennsylvania had killed a bear. The other two had not even seen one.

Carolyn and Margaret didn't have much luck the second morning. They only got two shots. But since they were in extremely thick brush, and one flushed before Margaret was ready, they didn't kill any. They had fried bear back strap for dinner.

They were up the next morning at six a.m. packing. There was a light rain falling, and it was cold and damp. While Carolyn, Margaret, and Jeb finished packing, Jack went to the hardware store, bought two ice chests to put the bear meat in, and got ice at the ice house. They packed the meat on ice, loaded their stuff into the station wagon, and after saying good-bye to Wayne, Nancy, and Bob, left camp about eight-thirty a.m. headed for Bar Harbor. They arrived just in time for lunch.

"This is fabulous!" Margaret said. They were sitting at an ocean-side table with a beautiful view, and the waitress had brought them four lobsters, clams, steamed sweet corn, and boiled red-skin potatoes. Jack and Carolyn were having a Chardonnay, and Margaret and Jeb had Coca-Colas. It was sunny and the temperature was seventy degrees. Over the next three days they visited Portland, Kittery, and

FLORIDA GOLD

Kennebunkport. The ocean-side towns were picturesque, and the seafood excellent. In Portland they were able to take a boat tour and see whales.

They drove to Portsmouth, New Hampshire on Sunday, and went to Warren's Lobster House for dinner. It was famous for its large salad buffet, and for its Maine lobster. After waiting forty-five minutes for a table, they stuffed themselves on the lobster and other seafood delights. They were off the next morning at six forty-five, and in the airport by nine. They arrived back in Tampa at two thirty, and were home by four fifteen. A good time was had by all.

On December 12 and 13, 1962, another severe freeze struck Florida citrus. This one was more damaging than the one in 1957 had been. Months later when fruit production statistics became available, they showed that Florida orange production had been reduced to half of its pre-freeze level. Jack called a meeting with Harry, Ira Long, Joe Zigulich, and Cecil Moore.

"Jack, this one is really bad," Cecil explained. "Our growers are finding ice in over half of the fruit they cut. And now that the other processors know the USDA will pass fruit salvaged from the freeze, you'll no longer get other plants willing to contract process for you." Finding ice in fruit means that the juice has frozen, rupturing the juice cells, which makes the fruit spoil if temperatures don't remain cold. Ice in fruit is also an indicator of the severity of a freeze.

"This is serious," Harry observed.

"Cecil, you, Joe, and Harry handle the sales, procurement and financial issues this situation creates. Ira, get the plant ready to run three shifts a day, seven days a week. I'm heading for South America."

"You're taking a vacation at a time like this?" Ira asked incredulously.

301

ROBERT ALLEN MORRIS

"I wish I was. I'm going to see if I can find additional oranges. Brazil produces a sizeable crop, but it mostly goes to the fresh market. There is one small processor in Araraquara, though, that runs packinghouse eliminations."

"Why not go to Mexico? It's closer," Ira asked

"Central Florida Processors tried that in the 1957 freeze and it didn't work out. Mexico's government-supported ejido land-tenure policy prevents the large commercial acreages required to support a processing sector."

Jack's plane landed in Araraquara on Tuesday morning, and Alberto Silva met Jack at the airport. On the ride to Alberto's processing plant, he asked, "Just how bad was this freeze, Jack?"

"Many are saying the worst of the twentieth century."

"That's too bad."

Alberto toured Jack through the plant, which was clean and well organized. "You know how to process oranges," Jack observed. "When does your season run?"

"June through January."

"May I have a sample of your orange juice?"

"Of course, let's go into the lab. Everyone, this is Mr. Jack Thomas, the owner of Tropical Juices in Florida. Gilberto, would you prepare us a sample of orange juice?"

"Yes."

Jack tasted the juice, and it was good - not as good as Premium Select, but still good. When they added their essence package it should taste as good as the juice they made in Florida.

"How much could you sell me?" Jack asked.

"We'll have over three million gallons we could sell you when we finish processing in January, if the price is right," Alberto replied, thinking, *I will need at least $2.25 a gallon to cancel the contract with my European buyer.*

302

FLORIDA GOLD

"How about $2.50 per concentrate gallon, delivered to the Port of Tampa?"

"You just bought yourself some orange juice."

"For that price, I also want the option to take all you produce next season, to be exercised by May 31. I suspect that this freeze killed a lot of citrus trees, which will have supplies down for a number of years, until trees can be planted and they reach the fruit producing age of five-to-six years old. We should know by May. And if that's true, I will probably want to buy all of your juice for a number of years."

"If the price is right, that can be arranged. Now that our business is concluded, let us go to my *fazenda* and have a nice relaxing lunch out by the pool. You simply must try Fernando's pingas."

"What are *pingas*?" Jack asked

"An alcoholic beverage made from fresh sugarcane juice that is fermented and distilled. Very popular in São Paulo. Be careful when you drink them, though, because they are very high in alcohol – 100 proof."

"I'll consider myself warned."

"After naps, we'll feast for dinner. Roast suckling pig, fried bananas, beans and rice, fried cassava. Fit for a king!"

"Lead the way."

When Tropical Juices' essence package was added to the Brazilian concentrate, it tasted as good as Premium Select. The added supply from Brazil gave Tropical Juices enough supply to grow Premium Select more than any other orange juice in the supply- starved market, and Tropical Juices' profits were projected to set a new record in 1963 - $11 million.

In May, at the end of the shortened freeze-impacted season, Jack called a meeting with Harry, Joe, Cecil, and Ira. "The Brazilian concentrate really worked out well," Ira told them.

"Yeah, but our members are not happy about Tropical Juices using Brazilian juice," Cecil explained.

303

"They need to understand that without it Florida orange juice would have priced itself out of the market, and everyone would have switched to juice drinks like citrus punch," Joe explained.

"I know, it's just difficult to get Florida growers to understand that."

"Cecil, what percent of the trees does it look like we've lost?" Jack asked.

"Our estimate is about twenty-five to thirty percent."

"That much?" Harry asked.

"Yeah."

"That's a twenty-five to thirty percent reduction in fruit supplies for over five years, until growers can replant damaged groves," Jack observed. "Ira, I'm going to need to buy concentrate from Alberto Silva again. I reserved that option when I was there in December. I'd like you to go to his plant in Araraquara and check out his processing practices. He should just be starting to run fruit. Also, I'd like to get your estimate of what it would cost to double its capacity, and how long that would take. I'll probably need to take twice as much as he can produce now, for at least five years. Call me when you get that done, and I'll join you in Araraquara."

"Jack, we might want to consider buying from him on a permanent basis. Their juice is available during most of our off-season, June through December. That means we'd have less juice to store for off-season use and for blending early fruit at the start of the season. That lowers our costs."

"Good point, Harry. I'll try to put something permanent together when I'm in Brazil.

Joe, I want you to start doing some market research on what type of juice beverage consumers would like as a substitute for orange juice. It needs to be citrus based. Hire Benton & Bowles if you need to. I'd like to see preliminary information by the end of June."

FLORIDA GOLD

Jack then left and headed with his family to their home in North Carolina for two weeks of vacation. He flew directly from Charlotte to Miami, on to São Paulo, and finally Araraquara. Carolyn, Margaret, and Jeb were planning to stay in North Carolina for another two weeks, and Carolyn's mother and father were joining them.

Alberto and Ira met Jack's plane just before noon, and they all went to lunch. "Jack, these guys know what they're doing," Ira said. "I'm even learning some things from them."

"Good. Alberto, how much concentrate can you sell us this year?"

"At what price?"

"$2.25 a gallon."

"What's wrong with what you paid last year?"

"We were in a crisis then."

"But your industry must have lost a lot of trees, otherwise you wouldn't be exercising your option."

"Oh, well, Ira, I guess we head to Mexico and meet with Carlos," Jack bluffed.

"OK, OK. You've got a deal. At $2.25 you can have all my production, four-and-a-half million gallons." After lunch, they went to the plant and inspected the fruit and the juice. That night at Alberto's fazenda, Jack asked Ira what it would cost to double the plant's capacity.

"Labor is about a third what it is in the U.S., so my estimate is $2.5 million, and it can be done in the off-season and ready to run at the start of next season."

"Great."

The next morning, Ira and Jack had breakfast with Alberto at the fazenda. "Alberto, we'd like you to double the capacity of your processing plant and have it ready to run by a year from now. Since you are building onto an existing plant, that time frame should be easily achievable. We will take all of its output for ten years."

305

"It is difficult to get financing here, particularly for a new venture like citrus processing. For groves, coffee, or sugarcane, yes, because the land is collateral, but a plant is only as good as the market for its products, and you are strangers from Florida. Also, there are not enough packinghouse eliminations in Araraquara to support a doubling of our capacity."

"That means you will need to buy fruit directly from growers for processing that doesn't go to a packinghouse."

"We have never done that before. How do you price it? We cannot afford to pay fresh fruit prices for processing fruit."

"You won't have to. The grower will make more money selling his fruit to you for processing than he will selling it to the fresh packinghouse at a higher price."

"But how is this possible?"

"Your processing costs are lower than fresh packing costs, and you will use ninety-nine percent of his fruit. The packing house must discard twenty to thirty percent of his fruit as culls, then they make a profit selling them to you that the grower never sees."

"How will my processing costs affect the price I pay for fruit?"

"By using participation pricing to pay for the fruit. To do this, your fruit price would be determined by taking your concentrate price per gallon of concentrate sold, minus your shipping cost, storage cost, and processing cost, minus a percentage of sales as a required profit. That would result in a price per gallon of concentrate still to be made. The price per ton of fruit would be the price per concentrate gallon multiplied by the number of concentrate gallons in a ton of oranges. For Brazilian oranges, there would probably be about nineteen concentrate gallons per ton of fruit. If a twelve million box plant with an asset value of $5 million sold 9.3 million gallons of concentrate at $2.25, a five percent return on sales would be $1 million a year. A $1 million return

FLORIDA GOLD

on a $5 million plant is a twenty percent annual return on the asset value of your plant. Not a bad return on investment."

"Jack, I really like how you think. You are very smart. We will make very good business partners."

"If you would like, when it's time to go explain participation pricing to the growers, either me or my chief financial officer, Harry Osborne, will go with you to help."

"That solves the fruit procurement problem, but what do I do about financing?"

"How about if Tropical Juices loaned you the money at no interest? You'd pay it back over the next ten years."

"Would you do that?"

"Yes. Again, for all the output of your expanded plant."

"Like I said, we will make very good business partners. You have a deal, Jack."

"Great. I'll have our attorney begin drafting a contract immediately for you to review."

"Can I interest you and Ira in being my guests in Rio for the rest of the week?"

"Thanks, Alberto, but we must be getting back to Florida."

Joe set up a meeting of the management committee on Monday, June 17, which consisted of himself, Jack, Harry, and Ira. He'd hired Benton & Bowles to conduct the market research Jack had wanted and they were ready to present their preliminary findings. "Jack, our research relied exclusively on focus groups."

"What are focus groups?" Harry asked.

"Those are small groups of consumers that are asked their response to a number of questions about a specific topic, or asked to give their opinion of a new product. The most preferred substitute for orange juice by adults would be a juice blend with orange juice in it, since it would still be one hundred percent juice. The most preferred substitute by consumers aged eight to eighteen would be a juice beverage, because it would be a fruity soda pop. The consumers twelve to eighteen suggested that vitamin C be added to replace that lost by not drinking as much orange juice. When input from the mothers was included about the juice beverage, the overwhelming preference was to make it low calorie - to reduce the sugar the children were consuming and to give the adult women a nutritious diet juice drink."

"Great work, Joe. Pass that on to the Benton & Bowles consultants as well," Jack said. "What's next?"

"We need to formulate the juice blend, and come up with a tasty drink base for the beverage. The Benton & Bowles consultants said that Arthur D. Little was one of the best at those tasks."

"OK, let's get them down here and get them going. What's going on in finance, Harry?"

"Not much. Our projected $11 million in profits looks like it will hit $14 million. That Brazilian concentrate really helped out."

"We had a productive trip to Brazil, and I think we will have a reliable supplier of substantial volumes of quality concentrate for at least the next ten years," Jack reported. "If nobody has anything else, I guess that about wraps it up."

"One thing?" Joe asked. "We need a name for the two new juice products."

"That's easy," Jack replied. "For the juice blend, Tropical Blend, and for the juice beverage, Tropical Light. It's why I chose Tropical Juices for our name. For the time we would expand beyond orange juice."

In June of 1962, Jack hired Martin Beasley as director of personnel. Martin, who was tall and awkward looking, had a way of putting people at ease. He had a bachelor's degree in psychology and a law degree from the University of Florida. He had most recently been part of the senior management of the Teamsters union, and before that had been a personnel manager for a California fresh citrus packing business.

FLORIDA GOLD

The Arthur D. Little consultants recommended a blend of 30 percent orange juice, 20 percent tangerine juice, 25 percent white grape juice, 10 percent mango juice, and 15 percent pineapple juice for the blend. It would have the same amount of vitamin C as orange juice. The juice beverage would have the same juices as the blend in its base, but consist of 35 percent juice blend and the other 65 percent artificial sweetener and water. It would have half the calories of orange juice, and the same amount of vitamin C. The blend was priced 10 percent below Premium Select, and the beverage was priced 20 percent below, which with much lower cost ingredients, gave both products a larger profit margin than Premium Select.

The advertising surrounding the new product launch said, "Tropical Juices is bringing you two new products - Tropical Blend and Tropical Light. Tropical Blend is a unique blend of orange juice and exotic tropical fruits to excite your taste buds. Tropical Light is the same, but with half the calories of orange juice. Both have the same vitamin C as orange juice. These products are brought to you at prices below orange juice, which recently suffered supply-damaging freezes. Why these bold new products? Because our customers deserve a choice." The footage with the blend shows a housewife happily pouring Tropical Blend from a glass bottle into an elegant crystal glass and drinking it down, saying, "I love my nutritious Tropical Blend." The footage with the beverage shows Mom at a cookout in the backyard pouring a glass for her son, daughter, and herself, raising it and saying, "To our health."

On June 12, 1964, Jeb graduated from Winter Haven High School as class valedictorian. It was seven p.m., and the auditorium was filled with parents and siblings of graduating seniors. Jeb went to the podium and began his graduation speech. "Fellow students, good evening. First of all, thank you. Thank you to the faculty and administrators who have taught and cared about each of us. Thank you to our guests who have taken time to recognize our accomplishments. Perhaps the biggest thank you goes to parents and family who have supported us, both financially and emotionally.

"Class of 1964, today is our day! Four years ago we entered Winter Haven High scared, full of anticipation, yet excited. Today, diplomas in hand, we will go our separate ways, seeking our way in the world. Many of us will stay close to home, while others will move to different parts of the state, and still others will move to other states or countries. It is a big, exciting, and sometimes scary world out there. But we have something that is rare and valuable, that many others don't have. We have the morals, character, and fortitude that growing up in Polk County and going to Winter Haven High School gave us. This will be one of our most valuable assets.

"Some of us will enter the professions such as physician, teacher, economist, lawyer, accountant, engineer. Others will become supervisors, managers, or administrators. Some of us will become skilled craftsmen or craftswomen, and others will start our own business or assume responsibilities in the family business.

"Is it time to be scared again? I think fear can be a positive thing. It can keep us focused and motivated. Unlike President Roosevelt, I don't think the only thing we have to fear is fear itself. What we have to fear is giving in to it. Not using it to help us avoid mistakes and become complacent. Using it as an excuse to avoid taking smart risks. For only by taking risks can we enjoy rewards. It's OK to be afraid to lose...afraid to fail. But do not let that fear become self-fulfilling. Let it motivate you to always be your best.

"Our biggest challenge may not be to achieve great things, but to gain the wisdom to be able to balance failure with caution and forethought. If it weren't a big challenge, I

FLORIDA GOLD

could just tell you how to do it...but I don't know how to do that. We are each going to have to find our own way to turn our failures into successes.

"Good luck, class of 1964!"

Jack and Carolyn were very proud of Jeb and his accomplishments. He would be starting college at the University of Florida in September.

Tropical Blend and Tropical Light were launched in June of 1964. Sales took off like a rocket. By 1966, their second year, Tropical Blend and Tropical Light together were almost as big as Premium Select, which, with the help of the added supplies from Brazil, had continued to grow. For fiscal year 1966, sales hit $400 million, and profits were $43 million. They now had 1,984 full time employees, with 188 people in white-collar jobs in the corporate offices. Their senior management structure consisted of Jack as president and chief executive officer, Harry as the executive vice president and chief financial officer, Ira as vice president of operations, Joe as vice president of sales and marketing, and Martin as vice president of personnel. Juice Orange Marketers was still their primary fruit supplier. They had three bulk plants that contract processed fruit for them in Florida, and Alberto Silva - his company now named Citro-Tropic - as their Brazilian supplier.

Martin called a meeting on Monday morning with Jack and Harry. "Jack, we need a new office building," he said.

"Yeah, we've seriously outgrown this one," Harry added. "We can't just keep adding on house trailers to accommodate additional employees."

"I guess you're right. How many employees do we have now, Martin?" asked Jack.

"If you include the plant, about 2,000. About 200 of those are white-collar employees in offices."

311

"I agree, it's time to build new offices. Harry, find a good architect," Jack requested.

Jack decided to go with a new design concept. Instead of the traditional hallways with offices located on both sides, the floor plan for the two-story office building would be shaped like a rectangle, with concentric rectangles creating five zones. At the center would be file and workrooms, which would be directly accessible by support staff in adjacent workstations. Just beyond would be the file cabinets and walkway, and at the perimeter, private offices in three different sizes. With every executive requiring quick access to their support staff and files, these functions would be evenly dispersed instead of consolidated.

There would also be four conference rooms, two large and two small, and a large break room with refrigerators, two sinks, a stove and oven, three large stainless steel coffeemakers, and two large tables where employees could eat a lunch they'd brought to work. The offices, conference rooms, and reception area would be wood paneling, and the furniture in the offices and conference rooms, mahogany. A cafeteria offering breakfast, lunch, and dinner – at cost - that would serve both office and plant employees was built adjacent to the processing plant and another large break room was added in the plant.

The construction was completed on August 5, 1966, and everyone was in their new offices and the cafeteria was in use in a week. The old ones were torn down, except for the original cinder block building that had housed Sun Sweet Citrus' offices. Jack could not bear to tear that down, so it became a storage space for old files.

One night at dinner in October of 1965, Margaret said, "Mom, Dad, I've met a boy at school, Josh Henderson, and he's asked me out. I want to go." Margaret had grown into a

FLORIDA GOLD

real beauty like her mother, and she was the romantic fantasy of many of the teenage boys in her school.

"But Margaret you're only fifteen. I don't want you to start dating until you're sixteen," Jack explained.

"But he's one of the most popular boys in school. If I don't accept, nobody will ever ask me out."

"Jeb, do you know this boy?" Carolyn asked. Jeb was home from college for the weekend.

"Not very well. He was not in my class. He's a junior. But he's doing well in track meets and I never heard anything bad about him."

"Tell you what, Margaret." Jack said. "Invite him here for dinner on Friday, and if we think he's ok, you can go out with him."

"Really?"

"Yes," Carolyn agreed.

"Thank you, Mom and Dad!"

On Friday night at six thirty the doorbell rang, and when Jack answered it a nervous, skinny boy said, "Mr. Thomas, I'm Josh."

"Come in, Josh, welcome to our home," Jack greeted him warmly.

"Hi, Josh," Carolyn said. "Margaret will be down shortly." Jeb was out on a date, and wouldn't be joining them for dinner. "Let's sit in the living room," Carolyn suggested.

"Josh, I hear you're quite a track star," Jack said.

"Yes, sir. I really like it. I'm hoping we can make the state finals next spring."

Then Margaret came in and said, "Hi, Josh." She was tall, about five feet, eight inches, and svelte, with flowing blonde hair, limpid blue eyes, delicate facial features, and a flawless complexion. She had on a black wool skirt dress. It had three-quarter-length sleeves, and was fitted through the bodice and hips with a full-pleated skirt and zipper in the back. She wore stylish high-heeled pumps. Her light makeup was just enough

313

to bring out her innocent beauty. Jack couldn't believe that this beautiful young woman was his daughter.

For some reason, Josh appeared unaffected by Margaret's beauty, and it made Jack wonder why. Dinner was pleasant, and afterward Josh explained that he planned to take Margaret to a barbecue at one of his friends' family's farm near Bartow the next day. "We should be home before dark," he told them.

As they were preparing for bed, Jack said, "Carolyn, I think I like Josh. He didn't ogle Margaret when she was dressed so well and looked so beautiful, and he's taking her out during the day with other people. He won't even have her out after dark."

"I agree, but something just doesn't seem right. He doesn't seem at all interested in her romantically."

Josh picked Margaret up at her house the next day at eleven thirty a.m., and they drove to the farm. They pulled up in the yard, and there were half a dozen pickup trucks in a line. There was no barbecue, but seven boys were standing in a group drinking beer, and all appeared too young to be drinking legally. She was the only female there. "Josh, I'm not so sure..."

"Come on, we'll have fun," he told her. They got out of his car and walked to the group. The boys spread out, and one had a double-barreled shotgun. Then she recognized a hand-operated machine for throwing clay targets.

"I hear you like to shoot and hunt," Josh said spitefully. "You must be a real tomboy. Why don't you show us what a good shot you are, tomboy?" His voice had a mean sound to it. The other boys were snickering.

"Sure, I'd love to," she replied. "But first, you have to give me each of your names. I want to go out with each of you and show you a real good time, but I need your names and phone numbers so I can call you." Someone got a piece of paper and pencil from his truck and each boy eagerly wrote down his

FLORIDA GOLD

name and phone number, thinking, *Man, she's good-looking. I never thought I'd score with a beauty like her.*

Once she had all their names and phone numbers, she took four shotgun shells out of the box and loaded two. "Put two clays on the throwing arm," she told the boy who was going to operate the clay thrower.

"A double. I'm impressed," Josh told the crowd sarcastically.

"Pull!" she shouted. Two clays soared into the air. She smoothly mounted the gun, pointed, and shot twice. Both clays shattered. Then she loaded the other two shells, pointed the shotgun above the boys' heads, and fired once. She lowered the gun and pointed it at Josh's crotch. "Now Josh, unless you are not interested in ever getting married or having children, I suggest you go inside and call my father to come and get me. We'll all wait out here."

"Y-y-yes, ma'am," a cowering Josh said nervously

Jack soon arrived, and walked over to the group. "What did you think you were doing?" he asked. Nobody said anything, so Margaret told him.

"Well, I think this is something your parents will love to hear about."

"I got all their names and phone numbers, Dad."

"Great, let's go." Margaret unloaded the shotgun and tossed it on the ground. "Nice shotgun. I really like the balance. Shoots good too."

The boys just stood there, too astonished to speak. Finally, one said, "Josh, what in the hell were you thinking, you shit head?"

"Yeah, get a date with a looker like that and pull this stupid stunt. Hell, you must be a queer or something."

On the trip home, Jack said, "I'm proud of you, Margaret. It took courage to stand up to them like that."

"Thanks, Dad. You always taught me not to let anyone push me around."

315

ROBERT ALLEN MORRIS

In 1967, Jack made the cover of *Fortune* magazine when he was chosen as one of the one hundred wealthiest men in North America. The story about him described his childhood, his helping shut down the illegal child labor camps, the events that earned him the Congressional Medal of Honor, and how he built the largest juice company in the world. On the cover he was wearing a blue suit and a hardhat out in their plant, and fruit was being unloaded from large trailers in the background, under the caption "The Orange Juice King."

Almost immediately, investment-banking firms began coming around trying to see if Jack would consider selling his profitable, rapidly growing company. He referred them all to Harry, who was emphatic that the company was not for sale. However, Harry suggested they get together to discuss the situation in detail. Jack suggested they go to his vacation home in the mountains. They flew up on the new company plane, a Model 23 Learjet. On the way, as they were enjoying lobster and Oysters Rockefeller, Harry said, "Man, Jack, we've sure come a long way from the Amalgamated labor camp." They looked at each other, then burst into laughter.

"Here's to the United States of America, the best country in the world," Jack said, raising his glass of champagne in a toast.

"I second that," Harry said, raising his glass.

At breakfast the next morning, Harry said, "Jack, I would like us to sell."

"I could sense that. But why?"

"I'm fifty-five, my health isn't the best, and I'd like to retire and spend time with my grandchildren."

"Do we have any good offers?"

"Most are bottom-feeders. But the Global Soft Drink Company seems to be seriously interested, and with their worldwide distribution capabilities, they can successfully take us international."

316

FLORIDA GOLD

"Why are they so interested?"

"One reason is because our juice products are having an impact on their soft drink sales. They see health and fitness as a coming trend, and our products offer that, while theirs don't. Plus, they really admire your entrepreneurial and management skills, and would like to get you into their company."

"What type of money would we be talking about?"

"In my opinion our company is worth $500 million. And if they're smart, I think they'd let you continue to run Tropical Juices, with a base salary and percent of the profits."

"Set up a meeting," Jack told him. "Now I'm going fly fishing," he replied as he began to put on waders, then took a fly rod out of its rack.

"Fly fishing!"

"Yeah, I've been trying to catch old Flyslinger for over a year now. But he's one wary trout, and big too. Probably weighs over five pounds."

"I'm game, if you'll teach me."

CHAPTER SIXTEEN

Jack and Harry's initial meeting with the Global Soft Drink Company would be at their offices in Memphis on August 11, to avoid arousing suspicions at Tropical Juices. From GSDC were several financial analysts from the business development department, and Doug Altman, their director of finance. After everyone was seated and names and responsibilities had been exchanged, a young man stood - Dennis Kemper, who looked to be about thirty. "I just want to take this opportunity to welcome our guests from Tropical Juices to Memphis," he began. "I think we are going to have a productive meeting. If everyone will open their proposals, we'll begin."

The proposal began with a section titled "External Business Environment," and was a description of the Florida citrus industry. Next was a brief description of the history of Tropical Juices, then its status today - procurement and marketing strategies, operating costs, analysis of its strengths and weaknesses, and five years of financial statements. Dennis did a good job of going through the material.

Then Doug Altman took over the meeting. Doug was a slightly plump man who appeared to be in his mid-thirties, wore thick eyeglasses, and was already balding. His eyes never really made contact with whomever he was talking to, and he had a superior attitude, like he was better than

319

everyone else. "Mr. Thomas, we're prepared to offer you $350 million for Tropical Juices, and we'd like to retain your services for three years as a consultant, to help teach our people the business. After that, if you wish, you could finish your career at GSDC, depending on what the opportunities are at that point in time."

Jack quietly stood and said, "Thank you, Mr. Altman. Harry, I believe we have business elsewhere," and headed toward the door. Harry quietly followed. As they were leaving the room, Doug jumped up and said, "Wait! What's wrong?"

Jack stopped and looked at the short, chubby man in front of him, holding back a desire to slug him. "You bring me up here, put me in a room with a bunch of kids who don't know anything about running a business in the real world, then insult me with an offer nowhere near what my company is worth! Take your kids and go play somewhere else. I don't have time for this nonsense. Harry, contact the International Beverage Company and tell them we'll take them up on their offer to reconsider."

"Wait, Mr. Thomas!" Doug shouted desperately. But Jack and Harry had left.

"Boy, we sure screwed that up," Dennis observed.

"Yeah," Edwin, another one of the financial analysts, agreed.

"What went wrong?" Dennis asked.

"You didn't take the time to understand the man who owned the company you wanted," replied George Davis, the senior vice president of finance, as he entered the conference room. "Jack Thomas is a war hero, who built his company from nothing. He's a man of principal, integrity, and pride. He won't negotiate something as important as the value of his company. You simply must put your best offer on the table and get his response. If he says no, you apologize and move on. If he says yes, you've been successful. More important than understanding the business and the numbers is

FLORIDA GOLD

understanding the man who owns the company you are trying to buy. I know that GSDC is new at acquisitions, but if our strategic plan is implemented we have several in front of us. So take this as a learning experience. Maybe with Bob Singleton's help, I can bring Jack back to the table. I don't know, but I'm willing to try."

He had a meeting with Bob later that day to discuss the failed acquisition attempt. "Do you think we can get him back to the table?" Bob asked.

"I don't know, but I think we need to try."

"What's your strategy?"

"Contact Harry Osborne and apologize. Meet with them on their turf, and make them our best offer."

"How much is Tropical Juices worth?"

"The business and industry they are in is volatile, and profits fluctuate, although they've stabilized their business more than any others in the citrus industry. I'd put their current value somewhere between $400 and $600 million."

"What should we offer?"

"I say $500 million, and retain Jack as the company's president, with a $175,000 base salary and twenty percent of their profits as a bonus. Jack is the key to the success of this business. Without him, I'm not so sure I'd recommend buying it."

"Set up another meeting."

"Harry, what happened in there?" Jack asked as they were heading to the airport.

"They don't know much about acquisitions. In fact I believe we're the only sizeable company they've ever tried to buy."

"Should we just walk away?"

"Probably not. They'll see that today was a mistake and I believe they'll get back in touch with us to try again. We're

ROBERT ALLEN MORRIS

such a good strategic fit that they're not going to want to lose us."

"OK."

The following Monday, August 14, George Davis called Harry Osborne. "Harry, this is George Davis, the senior vice president of finance for GSDC. I'd like to extend our sincere apology to you and to Jack Thomas for what happened last Friday. Would you give us another chance?"

"I don't know. Jack is pretty mad about what happened. I'll see if I can convince him."

"OK," Jack reluctantly agreed. "But I don't want to meet with those kids again. I want someone who can accept or reject the acquisition."

"Where do you want to meet with them?"

"Let's go to the Citrus Club in Orlando on Friday."

Harry called GSDC back and relayed Jack's request to George Davis, who said, "You'll be meeting with me and Bob Singleton, GSDC's president."

"Fine."

On Friday at noon, Harry and Jack went into the elegant lobby of the Citrus Club, and George Davis and Bob Singleton were waiting on them. After introductions, they were escorted to the private dining room Jack had requested. "Mr. Thomas, would you like to see menus now, or later?" the waiter asked.

"Later, say in about fifteen minutes."

"Yes, sir."

"Jack, we both want to apologize for what happened last week," Bob began.

"Yeah, we're new to acquisitions, and our people don't know what they're doing," George explained.

"Apology accepted, now let's move on," Jack replied.

"We don't want to waste your time again. So here's our offer," George began. "Its $500 million, and Jack, if you stay on as president of Tropical Juices at a $175,000 annual salary,

322

FLORIDA GOLD

you get a fifteen percent share of Tropical Juices, which means you get fifteen percent of the annual profits and fifteen of the selling price should we ever sell Tropical Juices."

"Make my share twenty percent and you've bought yourself a juice company." "Done!" Bob said. "Of course our offer is subject to verification of the numbers we were given." "Certainly," Harry Osborne replied. "Waiter," he called. "Oh, there's one other thing," Jack remembered. "I get to run Tropical Juices as I want to. No interference from GSDC unless I ask for it. GSDC is simply an owner/investor. If our performance is ever below expectations, you can be as involved as you choose to be." "Agreed," Bob said.

Over the next several months, GSDC auditors and financial analysts examined all aspects of Tropical Juices' books, procurement contracts, advertising agreements, etc. to verify their initial analysis. This due diligence showed the information they had to be correct and accurate. George Davis called Harry Osborne and said that the offer stood.

The acquisition was finalized in late November. Harry's share came to $165 million and Jack's was $335 million. On Friday, December 8, there was a large retirement party for Harry at the Lake Region Country Club in Winter Haven. In addition to employees, guests included a number of large growers, Florida bulk concentrate suppliers, presidents of supermarket chains, the head of Tropical Juices' advertising agency, and Alberto Silva from Brazil.

A number of employees and guests came up and told their own unique stories of their experiences with Harry over the years. Then Jack went to the podium and said, "Harry, come up here with me." Harry climbed onto the stage and stood next to Jack. "Harry Osborne is my oldest and dearest friend," Jack began. "We first met in 1922 in a child labor camp in North Florida, where we were slaves. Harry helped

323

me to survive those first few months, and taught me how to read, write, and do arithmetic because there was no schooling for us." The crowd was silent, as most of them knew none of this about their past. "We both escaped at different times, and were reunited here in Winter Haven in 1936. I owned the Sun Sweet Citrus Company and Harry accepted my offer to come and be in charge of finance and accounting and whatever else we needed. We planned the birth of Tropical Juices together, from a government invention and ambitious ideas. Together, we have steered its growth and success. Harry, old friend, may you enjoy your well-deserved retirement. You will be missed. And I will always cherish the memories of our times together." Then they embraced. There was a standing ovation, and both Carolyn and Jean, Harry's wife, began to cry.

On December 21, Jack got a call from Bob Singleton. "Jack, your new chief financial officer will be there on Wednesday, January 3. He's very bright, and I think you'll like him. In fact I believe you've met Doug Altman."

"Doug Altman?"

"Yeah. Jack I know you had a bad first impression of him, but Doug's very good at what he does. He learned the orange juice business when he prepared for the acquisition of your company and I believe he has something to offer Tropical Juices. I think he'll make a good CFO for you."

"OK, point made." ▯e ▯ ▯▯▯e▯ ▯en▯e▯ Jack thought. ▯▯er▯▯o▯▯ ▯ ▯▯e▯▯ ▯▯▯▯e▯▯▯nee▯ to ▯▯▯e ▯▯▯ ▯not▯er ▯▯▯▯n▯e▯

"Carolyn, let's spend Christmas at our house in North Carolina," Jack had suggested at dinner on Friday night after Thanksgiving. Jeb and Margaret were both out on dates. "We'll invite your parents to join us. With Margaret graduating from high school and Jeb from college in June, it's going to become more and more difficult to get both of them with us at the same time."

FLORIDA GOLD

"I agree. Jeb has already been talking about going skiing in Colorado with his friends over the holidays, but I don't think he's made any definite plans yet. And with my parents both in their seventies, it won't be much longer before they won't want to travel. Plus, you need to get away for a week. I can see all the stress you've been under lately with GSDC buying the company."

"Great! We'll all fly up on the Learjet."

"Will Tropical Juices still have it after the acquisition?"

"Yeah. For personal travel I'll just pay GSDC a charter fee the way I pay Tropical Juices now."

It snowed, so they were able to enjoy a white Christmas.

On Wednesday morning, January 3, at nine, Jack's phone at Tropical Juices buzzed. "Mr. Thomas, Mr. Altman is here," Jack's secretary, Rhea, said.

"Good, bring him in. And have Ira join us."

There was a tap on Jack's door.

"Come in," Jack replied.

"Hi, Jack," Doug said as Rhea escorted him into the office.

"Welcome aboard, Doug," Jack said as he stood and shook hands. "Would you like some coffee or orange juice?"

"No, I'm fine."

"Mr. Long is on his way," Rea said.

"Thanks, Rea," Jack replied as she left his office. "Have a seat, Doug. Have you had a chance to look for a place to live?"

"Not yet, what with the holidays and all. I'm staying at the Terrace Hotel in Lakeland. My wife, Cathy, will be down this weekend and we plan to house hunt."

"Good morning, Jack," Ira said as he entered Jack's office.

"Mornin', Ira. I believe you've met Doug Altman. He's going to be our new chief financial officer." As they shook hands, Jack said, "Doug, Ira will give you a plant tour, then

325

ROBERT ALLEN MORRIS

Cecil Moore, president of Juice Orange Marketers, our main fruit supplier, will take you on a grove tour, and Joe Zigulich will schedule you some time with Leo Marsh from our advertising agency."

"Doug, we'll start in my office," Ira explained. "I'll give you an overview of all the plant operations, then we will go and observe them in the plant."

"Sounds good to me," Doug replied as he and Ira were leaving Jack's office.

"Mr. Thomas, the applicant to be your new secretary is here for her interview," said Rhea just before three that afternoon. Rhea was retiring when Jack hired her replacement.

"Good, bring her in," Jack replied, thinking, *▢▢o▢e t▢▢ ▢ t▢e one ▢ro▢ ▢ utu▢▢t▢▢t ▢▢our ▢ro▢ er▢ r▢▢e ▢▢out▢*

"Mrs. Gerry Brown, Mr. Jack Thomas," Rhea said.

"Hi, Mr. Thomas."

"Have a seat, Mrs. Brown."

"That's Gerry," she corrected. She looked to be in her mid-forties, was overweight, and wearing a pale-blue blouse with a ruffled collar, white skirt, white heels and a minimum of jewelry. Her hair was brown with strands of gray and starting to thin. Her inquisitive eyes were hazel.

"And that's Jack for me. Tell me about yourself."

"I prefer Mr. Thomas, if that's OK."

"Whatever you prefer, Gerry."

"I'm recently widowed, have two children, both in their twenties and married so I live alone. I'm currently the executive secretary for Florida Citrus Mutual, and have been for the past eleven years. Prior to that, I was the secretary for the senior partner of Ernest & Davis, the accounting firm. I started there right out of college in 1944. I have a bachelor's degree in English with a minor in business administration from Florida State."

"Why do you want to leave Mutual?"

FLORIDA GOLD

"I want to work in the private sector. Mutual is a trade association, not responsible for making a profit. I think the private sector would be much more challenging and rewarding."

"Would you have a problem working late sometimes, or coming in on a Saturday?"

"Absolutely not."

"What is your current pay?"

"I make $2.70 an hour."

"Let's see, that comes to just over $5,600 a year," Jack said as he did the calculations. "Would you be OK with becoming salaried?"

"That depends on the salary."

"How about $7,000[11] a year plus a twenty percent bonus tied to personal goals and company profitability?"

"If that's an offer, then I accept."

"Great, when can you start?"

"How about two weeks?"

"That works for me."

About a month later, Doug scheduled a meeting with Jack and Joe on a Monday morning. "I've come up with a way to considerably lower our costs of making concentrate," Doug began.

"How will you do that without compromising our quality?" Jack asked.

"I've studied our flavor oils and our evaporator costs, and I think my ideas will work."

"Do you have a sample of the juice for us to taste?" Joe asked.

"I figured you'd ask that, so yes, the lab has samples. I'll have them brought in."

"I want Ira in this meeting also," Jack said. "Have him bring us the samples." Joe gave him a call.

---

[11] The same as $46,859 in 2013.

327

A sheepish-looking Ira came in with a pitcher of juice and four small paper cups. The juice was poured, and everybody tasted it.

"This is crap, Doug. Ira, what's wrong with this juice?" Jack asked.

"The amount of peel oil added to the concentrate before storage has been reduced and the evaporator vacuum was lower."

"Is the lower vacuum what gives it that cooked flavor?"

"Yeah. But that's probably due to a leak from a maintenance oversight on Doug's reduced maintenance budget. We are in the process of fixing that. It didn't affect all of the juice made this way."

"What about that oxidized flavor?"

"That's from the reduced volume of peel oil."

"There's no way we're going to sell this crap," Jack said.

"But Jack, the costs to make this are sixteen percent lower," Doug explained.

"After they taste it, nobody will buy it."

"I thought you'd think that, so I've implemented the changes, and beginning next week, the cost-reduced juice will be shipped. Then you'll have proof that the consumer will accept it. With the strength of the Tropical Juices and Premium Select brands, the consumer will accept the changes. That's what they teach us in business school. It's the strength of the brand, not the product, that counts."

"WHAT? Ira, did you know about this?"

"Yes, sir."

"And you implemented it without checking with me first?"

"Doug said you were on board, plus my bonus is based on controlling manufacturing costs."

"How much of this crap have we made?"

"About a month's supply of juice with the reduced amount of peel oil," Ira replied.

FLORIDA GOLD

"Joe, sell it to someone to use as a drink base where sugar and water can be used to offset the bad taste. I WILL NOT SELL THAT CRAP TO OUR CUSTOMERS!"

"But how will we supply our market after we lose a month's supply?" Joe asked.

"Let me worry about that. Doug, Ira, you're both fired! I want you out of your offices by close of business today."

"But Jack, just give it a..."

"OUT, NOW!"

"Joe, call Brent," Jack requested. Brent Champlain, a mechanical engineer in his early forties, was a genius with machinery and designing efficient citrus processing systems. He was about five foot eleven, with brown hair and hazel eyes, and always had a pleasant expression on his face. He made a point to reward loyalty from his employees. Brent was in charge of the sourcing program of bulk concentrate supplied by Florida bulk processors and Alberto. In that role he frequently had to modify a processing plant or make changes in processing practices to improve the quality of the product it supplied to Tropical Juices. He also coordinated their shipments, communicated the amount of juice needed from them each season, and insured their juice was continuously being made to Tropical Juices' standards. He had been the plant manager for one of Tropical Juices' bulk concentrate suppliers before Jack had hired him three years ago.

"Yes, sir?" Brent replied about ten minutes later when he came into the meeting.

"Brent, were you told to change our juice specs?" Jack asked.

"No, was I supposed to?"

"No. How much additional juice could we get from our suppliers over the next month?"

"I don't really know without running some numbers, but probably not very much. We're in the peak of the early-mid

329

fruit season and all of the plants are running to the max already. What doesn't come to us is committed to other customers. And of course Brazil's season has ended, and they already sell us all of their juice."

"That's what I thought. Brent, I just fired Ira and Doug."

"WHAT?"

Jack explained what had happened.

"I can't believe Ira didn't come to you before making such major changes in the juice manufacturing," Brent said.

"Well, he didn't. And now that's history. Would you be interested in assuming his responsibilities?"

Brent looked surprised, but said, "Yes, sir, it would be a privilege to have that job."

"Good, it's yours. You start now."

Late that afternoon, Jack called Bob Singleton. "Jack, I was just getting ready to call you. I can't believe you fired Doug."

"He wanted me to sell inferior juice."

"So if you disagreed with him, just refuse to sell it, don't fire him."

"It wasn't that simple." Then Jack told him what had happened. "If he hadn't made those changes without informing me, I just would have considered it a mistake. But now we've lost a month's supply of juice in the peak of our processing season, and we can't replace it until later in the season."

"Doug didn't tell me all that," Bob admitted. "What should we do?"

"I'll need to go on prime-time national television and explain to our customers what happened. Otherwise, we'll lose a lot of them, and it will be expensive to get them back. We will lose some anyway."

"What will the airtime cost?"

"Our estimate is about $100,000, but it doesn't really matter. We have to do it."

FLORIDA GOLD

"I agree. And I'm not going to give Doug a job here. I agree with you, he was dishonest and untrustworthy."

A few days later, Jack went on national TV and explained that due to a manufacturing problem, Premium Select would be in scarce supply for several months. But rather than sell juice that wasn't of the highest quality, Tropical Juices would ration its juice supply. He urged customers to try their Tropical Blend until supplies of Premium Select could be restored. Sales of Premium Select dropped, but not by much more than their supply had. And increased sales of Tropical Blend more than made up for the drop.

"Harry, I need a new CFO," Jack said when he called his old friend.

"What happened to Doug?"

Jack explained, then Harry replied, "I never did like that guy."

"Do you know anyone who I could interview?"

"My son, Derrick."

"That's right. If I remember, he has a degree in chemical engineering."

"Yeah, and he also got an MBA from Stanford."

"What is he doing now?

"He's the CFO for a winery in California, but they're up for sale and he figures the new owners will want their CFO in there, so he's quietly looking for a job."

"Have him give me a call."

Jack asked Derrick; his wife, Janice; and their daughter, Susan, to join him and Carolyn at their home in Winter Haven for a weekend. Jack preferred to get to know somebody for a job as important as CFO over a couple of days in a social setting.

Carolyn met Derrick and his family's plane at the airport in Orlando.

"It's good to see you again, Derrick, Janice," said Carolyn. "And who is this?" she asked, pointing to Susan.

ROBERT ALLEN MORRIS

"I'm Susan and I'm five years old."

"Well, welcome to Florida, Susan."

Derrick looked a lot like his dad, including the red hair and shrewd-looking eyes. As they walked through Jack and Carolyn's house, Janice said, "Oh, Carolyn, I really love your house!"

"Thank you. Let's go out by the pool. I believe Carlota has fixed us some snacks."

About an hour later, Jack came out to join them. "Mr. Thomas, it's good to see you again, sir!" Derrick said enthusiastically.

"That's Jack. And the sir isn't necessary. Janice, you're looking good. California must agree with you."

"I can't complain."

"I take it this little lady is Susan?"

"Yeah, and I'm five."

"So what's Jeb up to these days?" Derrick asked, as they continued to munch on the snacks and Carolyn opened a bottle of Cabernet Sauvignon.

"He's just finishing his degree in mechanical engineering from the University of Florida," Carolyn explained. "He graduates in June."

"After graduation, he'll be joining the army to fight in the Vietnam War," Jack explained. "When he returns from military duty he wants to work for a large citrus grower. After a few years there, he plans to go for his MBA."

Later, Jack and Derrick were preparing to grill steaks, and the women were inside fixing baked potatoes and steamed sweet corn. "These steaks come from a steer one of our growers pen fattens. Its prime beef, not choice like you get in the grocery store," Jack explained as he put five New York strips on the hot grill.

"I can't wait to try one."

Jack prodded one of the steaks and asked, "Derrick, what do you think Tropical Juices' key strengths are?"

332

FLORIDA GOLD

"Talented, motivated managers and employees, a consistently high-quality product, an aggressive marketing program, and a constant focus on cost efficiencies." Jack took a sip of wine. "Who are our major competitors and their strengths?"

"You are your own biggest competitor, because you are the leaders in product innovations, ingenious procurement strategies where both sides always win, and a marketing program that effectively delivers a compelling message. No one else is in that league, so your biggest challenge is making the best better."

"What if a competitor has a problem with their juices that they do not inform their consumers about? Should we point it out to consumers in our advertising?" Jack asked, turning the steaks with tongs.

"No. If there were health hazards with their juice, the USDA wouldn't let it be sold. So let the consumer taste and compare."

"Should we leverage our size as a fruit buyer to reduce the prices we pay for fruit on our contracts?"

"No. Oranges are a commodity and supply and demand sets the price, not the size of the buyer," Derrick replied, taking a sip of wine.

"Derrick, I like your thinking. Now let's go have some great steaks."

The weekend went well, and on Sunday at lunch, Jack offered the job to Derrick, who happily accepted. They called Harry together to tell him.

"I couldn't be happier," Harry said. "I know it's going to be a great relationship for both of you."

Derrick would start in three weeks, on April 8, 1968.

Margaret was the valedictorian of her 1968 senior class at Winter Haven High, the same as Jeb was in 1964. As when Jeb gave his speech, the auditorium was filled with the families of graduating seniors. She went to the podium and began her speech. "I feel very proud to graduate today. Thanks to our principal, Mr. Talbot, and to the teachers and support staff. All of you have helped us reach this milestone in our lives. Love to my family and close friends, Mary, George, and Amelia. Graduation brings a rush of benevolent feelings, and we should rightly be proud of everything we have achieved. We've loved, laughed, cried – we've lived life.

"It's said that 'Every new beginning comes from some other beginning's end.' We welcome this new beginning with a mix of excitement, fear, and anticipation - the same emotions we felt four years ago when we were freshmen at Winter Haven High. A very wise and accomplished man - my father, Jack Thomas - taught me that self-confidence is the most important, the most indispensable characteristic of success.

"A quiet self-confidence – not cockiness, not conceit, not arrogance – is the key to winning, to excelling, no matter what you do in life. Some of us already have the beginnings of this confidence from academic, athletic, or social success. It must be increased. Others of us must still develop it, if we want a life that will thrill us, rather than scare or bore us.

"Henry David Thoreau once said, 'The mass of men lead lives of quiet desperation.' I don't believe that most do – but I do believe that quietly desperate people are the ones who never quite found their self-confidence.

"So how do you get it? What is the secret of developing your own brand of self-confidence? Again, my father taught me. First, you must resolve to grow intellectually, morally, technically, and professionally every day, through your entire school, work, and family life. While there is nothing that builds self-confidence more than winning against the odds, believe it or not, losing against great odds builds it as well. So take big swings, take smart risks, even if you have to go back to the dugout on occasion and sit down. Seek out the

FLORIDA GOLD

challenges that others are afraid to touch. The world will soon get to know you, and more important, you will get to know yourself.

"We are driven, passionate, and determined. We are accomplished high school graduates. We are the Class of 1968. Congratulations, everyone. Good luck and God bless."

As with Jeb, Jack and Carolyn were very proud of Margaret and her accomplishments. Margaret was starting as a freshman at the University of Florida in September, majoring in agricultural economics. "Well, Jack," Carolyn said as she put her arms around him. "Both are grown now, and the last one is leaving the nest. I don't think we did too badly with them."

"I think we did very good. Both are smart, accomplished, responsible young adults. They have bright futures ahead of them."

On Saturday, June 15, 1968, only one week after Margaret graduated from high school, Jeb graduated from the University of Florida with high honors, and a bachelor's degree in mechanical engineering. He was third in his class. He also won the "Outstanding Senior Leader" award, for his accomplishments as president of Theta Tau, the engineering fraternity; in Florida Blue Key, the leadership fraternity; and as president of the student body in his senior year. Jack, Carolyn, Margaret, Martha, and Don all came to the ceremony and cheered when he was presented with his diploma. Afterward, they all went out to a seafood restaurant in Cedar Key, a small fishing town on the gulf, and celebrated.

On Monday, June 24, Jeb reported to the US Army inductee center in Orlando for his physical. During the exam, the doctor detected a heart murmur. "How long have you had this condition, son?" the doctor asked.

"What condition?"

"You have a heart murmur."

335

"What's that?"

"Your heart isn't beating the way it's supposed to. You will not be able to serve in the military with this condition. Beyond that, you should see your family doctor and get his advice."

"Jeb, the only advice I can give you is to eat wisely and do not smoke," his doctor explained. "There is no cure, but most people that have heart murmurs live long, productive lives."

Jack was able to help Jeb find a job as a grove supervisor for one of the grower members of Juice Orange Marketers. Medusa Fruit Farms consisted of 3,700 acres of groves located in Highlands County near Sebring. Jeb would begin his new job on Monday, July first, giving him two weeks to move and find a place to live.

CHAPTER SEVENTEEN

After Brent took over operations, Jack hired Allen Adams as vice president of procurement, to be responsible for the fruit procurement relationship with Juice Orange Marketers, any additional fruit procurement Tropical Juices engaged in, and the bulk juice relationships in Florida and Brazil. Allen stood five foot nine, had dark-brown hair, and was overweight but solidly built. He had a master's degree in agricultural economics from the University of Georgia, had been a plant processing supervisor for Juice Source, and most recently had been director of grower relations for Florida Citrus Mutual, the grower trade association. On Monday, July 9, 1969, at the regular monthly meeting of the executive committee, which consisted of Jack, Derrick, Brent, Martin, Joe, and Allen, Joe said, "There's a lot of consumer interest in grapefruit juice. People believe it helps them lose weight, and market sales are up thirty percent in only a couple of years. I believe we should consider adding grapefruit juice to our product line."

"Does grapefruit really help people lose weight?" Jack asked.

"The researchers haven't been able to prove that it does or that it does not, but doctors are prescribing it as part of a diet program," Joe replied.

"Several plants are now processing grapefruit that didn't before," Brent added.

ROBERT ALLEN MORRIS

"Where did the extra supply come from?" Jack asked.

"It was diverted from the fresh market," Allen replied. "Before this added interest in grapefruit juice, about seventy percent was sold fresh. Now it's about half and half between fresh and processed."

"Do we have the capacity to process grapefruit?" Jack asked.

"Not during most of the season, but in the gap between early-mids and Valencias during March, we would have about a four-week window to run grapefruit. We could probably run about two million boxes then," Brent told them. "Then as we grow we can source the additional concentrate from bulk processors."

"Jack, there's one more thing. There is a strong trend toward ready-to-serve chilled juice. More housewives are getting jobs outside the home, and chilled juice is gaining market share because it is more convenient," Joe explained.

"I don't disagree with that. The chilled juice section in my store has increased in size in the last few years," Jack said. "I'll contact Ed White and see if there's anything we need to know about processing grapefruit. And Brent, since this will be a chilled ready-to-serve product, I want it to be sold in cartons, not glass."

"But Jack, cartons leak. That's why nobody uses them for milk or juice."

"Distribution in cartons would be much less expensive because of the reduced weight, so we need to find out a way to design a carton that doesn't leak."

"Jack, processing grapefruit is no different than processing oranges," Ed told him. "But you will need a grapefruit essence flavor package."

"Can you develop one for us?"

"Certainly. Do you want it toward the bitter side or the sweet side?"

FLORIDA GOLD

"What do you recommend?"

"Sweet. And even though most of the market is shelf stable juice in cans or glass bottles, don't make a shelf stable product. The heat to make it shelf stable increases the bitterness of grapefruit juice because of the naringin and limonin in it. And that heat kills off the vitamin C. A frozen product, or ready-to-serve chilled juice made by reconstituting and bottling frozen concentrate, is definitely tastier and healthier."

"Jack, there's a researcher at Georgia A&M who may be onto something about designing cartons that don't leak. I think we need to meet with him," Brent said.

"OK set it up."

About a week later, on a Friday in September, Jack and Brent met with Dr. Richard McAfee. He was a small thin man, with a short graying beard and wire-rimmed glasses. Except for the tattoo of an anchor on his forearm from his days in the navy as a submariner, he looked like the typical member of a college faculty.

"It's all in the heat seal that closes the gable top on the carton," Dr. McAfee explained. "The leak occurs where the four pieces of carton are folded together and glued to two other pieces of carton on the top. But I've developed a machine that keeps the carton from leaking. If you'll allow me to demonstrate, I'll be back shortly."

He went to his rental car and brought back an ice cooler. Then he took a carton out of it. "Gentlemen, this is a carton I put reconstituted Premium Select in thirty days ago. See, no leakage. Let's taste it." Joe got cups and Dr. McAfee shook the carton, then poured everyone a sample.

"This tastes like it was just made," Jack observed.

"I agree," Brent said.

"So why isn't this technology being used?" Jack asked.

"Politics and lack of research funds have kept it from being developed. Since Georgia A&M is in a state with a lot of

339

pulp wood supplies and paper mills, it is logical for us to be trying to solve this problem. However, the money to fund packaging research, and thus its focus, has been on development of lighter cans by replacing tin or steel with aluminum, and development of light plastic bottles made from polyethylene terephthalate to replace heavier glass, particularly for carbonated soft drinks. There have been no funds to research the cardboard packaging problem. It's the same for the other research institutions."

"Why did you proceed to solve it anyway?" Jack asked.

"Because, I thought it was important to make cardboard cartons useable as a lighter package for non-carbonated beverages like juice and milk. And I thought if I could solve the problem, I could find a company that would be interested in obtaining the patent rights. I've done all of this work secretly in my home lab. The only way Brent found out about it is that his son John has been helping me in my lab."

"Richard, how would you like to come to work for Tropical Juices as director of R&D?" Jack asked. "At double your current salary."

"Really? That would be great. Finally, I could see my ideas put into action, not die in some political or bureaucratic morass."

"Good, when can you start?"

"In a month."

Ed had to wait for the start of the processing season to develop the essence flavor package, but by early January it was done. They opened one line, test ran grapefruit for one shift, added the essence package, and took samples for the executive committee to taste.

"This is really good!" Joe said.

"Yes, it is," Jack observed. "Ed really knows his stuff."

After he was hired, Dr. MacAfee went to visit a number of companies in Georgia, finally chose Georgia Tool and Die to

FLORIDA GOLD

make the heat-sealing machine to his specifications, and then applied for a patent on it.

"Richard, when the patent is approved, I will pay you $1 million for it," Jack told him.

"Why? Even if I had been able to patent it at Georgia A&M, I would not have collected any royalties."

"Because I believe in rewarding talent and hard work."

"Thank you, Jack. I agree with what I've been told - you are a rare man."

Jack negotiated a contract with National Paper to supply the new cartons, and Joe hired Orlando Art and Graphics to design the artwork for them. It had a yellow background and showed a grapefruit being juiced in a home juicer with the caption "Premium Select Grapefruit Juice. For Your Health."

The grapefruit were processed in March as planned, and the product launch was scheduled for April 6. A new grapefruit juice advertisement was aired on the day of the launch. It showed two women in a supermarket checkout line. The one in front had a carton of Premium Select Grapefruit Juice in her cart. The woman behind her says, "June, is that Premium Select Grapefruit Juice you have?"

"Yes, you should try it. Its tastes great, and I've lost ten pounds since I began including it in our diet." Then a male voice says, "Try Tropical Juices' new Premium Select Grapefruit Juice, for your and your family's health."

Due to the lower distribution costs, Premium Select grapefruit juice was lower priced than the juice packaged in cans and bottles, and because of Ed's flavor package and the fact it was chilled and not shelf stable, it tasted much better. They also sold it as concentrate, but the advertising only showed the chilled carton product. They were also the only company advertising grapefruit juice. Sales took off, and by January, they were rationing supply. Allen negotiated contract processing agreements with two bulk processors, and

341

developed a grapefruit participation agreement with Juice Orange Marketers.

At an executive committee meeting in April of 1972, Tropical Juices was reviewing sales performance. "Premium Select grapefruit is still growing in double digits," Jack observed.

"Yeah, even though the grapefruit diet fad is mostly over," Allen observed.

"It's the convenience. Consumers like the convenience of a ready-to-serve product," Joe offered.

"I agree, we consume more of it than orange juice now because Carolyn likes the convenience," Jack reflected. "So I think it's time for Tropical Juices to offer a ready-to-serve orange juice."

"I think our co-packers that are packaging Premium Select Grapefruit would also be happy to get our business for a reconstituted orange juice," Brent said.

"We're not going to make a reconstituted product. We're going to make it into chilled juice without concentrating it."

"Why?" Joe asked.

"Better taste. Pasteurization only heats the juice to 190 degrees, while evaporation heats it to 220. As a result of the lower heat, a better-tasting juice can be made with pasteurization," Jack replied.

"How will we store it for the off-season?" Brent asked.

"Richard and Ed White will come in and explain that," Jack replied. "This is a project the two of them have been working on together. Gerry," Jack said as he picked up the phone, "will you ask Richard and Ed to come in now?"

Gerry sent them in, and Jack asked Richard to tell the group about the project. "The juice will be frozen in blocks for storage, similar to what Naturally Orange does," Richard replied.

FLORIDA GOLD

"I don't think their juice tastes as good as Premium Select, and it's much more expensive to store and distribute," Brent observed.

"That's because of the way they freeze their juice for storage," Ed explained. "They copied icehouse technology, and freeze the juice in large cubes. When they freeze it, the center freezes last, which enables enzymes and bacteria to build in the core. The freezing and later pasteurization before packaging eliminate any health problems, but the juice has a distinctive off-flavor."

"So how are we going to freeze our juice?" asked Brent.

Richard replied, "We're going to build molds, or buckets, that constitute a twenty-gallon block of frozen juice that is four inches thick, six feet long and four feet wide. The thinner block will freeze and thaw in much less time than the large ice cubes, so the enzymes and bacteria will not have time to build. We will freeze it in about two hours, immersing the buckets in a brine solution to speed the freezing process. The bucket will be exposed to 212 degree steam, which will loosen the frozen juice and the block can be dumped out of the bucket. It will be stored at -5 degrees, and stacked on wooden pallets where the blocks can be handled with a forklift. When we are ready to use the juice, we will thaw it by running it through crushers that consist of a rotary drum with spikes which will make it into a slurry. Then, juice heated to 100 degrees will be circulated through it to melt the ice crystals. From there, it will be pasteurized and packaged."

"Also, using cartons instead of glass will reduce distribution costs," Jack explained.

"Not-from-concentrate will still be more expensive to distribute than chilled ready-to-serve reconstituted juice, which is shipped to the packagers as concentrate and then reconstituted with water before packaging," Brent explained.

"That means we will have to have a good enough product and marketing program to overcome that," Jack replied. "Brent, you and Ed develop a list of additional equipment we will need to install. Derrick, work with Brent to estimate the additional capital this will require and also how much higher the cost of the delivered juice will be.

"Joe, contact Orlando Art and Graphics and get them onto carton graphics design. I want this to be a white carton, to signify purity. Also, get in touch with Benton & Bowles and get them going on an advertisement."

"What will the product be called?" Joe asked.

"Premium Natural. And I want the advertising to emphasize the fact that this juice has never been made into concentrate, thus it's closer to fresh-squeezed. Let's get back together to discuss our progress in two weeks."

They reconvened as scheduled. "Jack, here is a list of equipment that will be required. It's pasteurizers, chillers, additional chilling capacity, peel eliminators, freezing capacity, storage, and frozen block crushing capacity," Brent explained.

"What are peel eliminators?" Jack asked.

"Devices that prevent peel from getting into the finisher. When pressed in a finisher, peel gives the juice a slightly bitter aftertaste. It doesn't affect the flavor of concentrate because the off-flavor is flashed off in the evaporator. But that will not happen when making not-from-concentrate."

"How long will it take before we are ready to run fruit into NFC?" Jack asked.

"About five months from when we begin construction," Brent replied.

"Allen, can you buy the additional fruit?" Joe asked.

"How much will be required?"

"I'd assume about two to three million boxes for this first season," Joe answered.

"Buy three. I don't want to have to ration supplies again," Jack suggested.

"I can get that if I start now."

FLORIDA GOLD

"Derrick, how much will it cost to install the additional equipment?" Jack asked.

"Roughly $4.5 million for six million boxes of capacity."

"And what will it add to the costs of the delivered juice compared to reconstituted?"

"On average, about twenty cents per half gallon for markets east of the Mississippi."

"Price it at a twenty-five-cent per half gallon single-strength equivalent premium to our Premium Select, and make sure our advertising supports its higher price," Jack requested.

"Why twenty-five cents instead of twenty?" Derrick asked

"Because, it will affect sales of Premium Select concentrate, and I want to be sure we are exchanging lost Premium Select sales for a more profitable product," Jack explained. "Let's get started."

The advertisement showed several growers carrying boxes of ripe oranges to a truck and loading them. One of the growers is hand-squeezing an orange into a clear glass on a table. He raises the glass of juice and says, "Nothing comes closer to this" – then he raises a carton of Premium Natural – "than this." A voice-over says, "Tropical Juices Premium Natural Orange Juice. Naturally pure, tasty, and nutritious. It has never been made into concentrate." The scene goes back to the grove where all the growers are pouring and drinking Premium Natural NFC. They all raise their glasses and say together, "Premium Natural. To your health!"

On Saturday, June 17, 1972, Margaret graduated with a bachelor's degree in agricultural economics from the University of Florida. She was first in her class in the College of Agriculture, and was presented the J. Wayne Reitz Medal of Excellence and the Outstanding Senior Award. She'd also been president of the Sigma Gamma Rho sorority in her

345

senior year, and had received a commendation letter from the president of the university for starting a popular dove shoot that raised thousands of dollars for orphans. Much like for Jeb's graduation, the family came to the ceremony, applauded when she was presented with her diploma and other awards, and went out to a restaurant and celebrated afterward.

Margaret accepted a job as a financial analyst for the National Agribusiness Company, which was based in Lakeland, Florida. The NAC was a large family-owned diversified firm with farms in Florida, California, and Texas, and annual sales of about $150 million. The company produced and marketed fresh and processed vegetables, fresh citrus, bulk orange concentrate, sugarcane, and cattle. Margaret's job would be helping to analyze the feasibility of expanding, changing or selling off operations; forecasting commodity prices; and developing cost budgets and profit plans for new farming operations. She started on Monday, June 26, and moved back in with her parents while she looked for an apartment in Lakeland.

They launched Premium Natural on Monday, January 24, 1973. Sales started slow at first, then suddenly erupted. Everyone wanted the fresh-squeezed-tasting NFC, and out-of-stocks began to increase. An out-of-stock occurs when an item is not available for sale as intended and is missing from the retail shelf, in this case because production couldn't keep up with demand. Sales of Premium Select concentrate declined by about a third, but not as much as sales of Premium Natural grew while customers switched to Premium Natural, a process known as cannibalization. But that didn't matter because the profit margin on Premium Natural was higher than that for Premium Select. The fresh-squeezed-tasting product was also bringing new consumers into the market.

FLORIDA GOLD

It was soon evident that they would exceed the 3 million boxes of fruit they had bought for Premium Natural, but reduced fruit requirements for concentrate gave them the extra fruit they needed. They finished the season using 5.6 million boxes for Premium Natural, with plans to add another 6 million boxes of capacity. Profits soared to new heights, and Tropical Juices became the most profitable business owned by the Global Soft Drink Company.

In April of 1975, Bob Singleton asked Jack to come to the next GSDC stockholders meeting and banquet in Memphis, and let Tropical Juices be recognized as the star in GSDC.

"I would love to come, Bob. But I want to bring my senior management team with me. They are what really enabled us to do what we've done."

"That's fine. In fact I think it's a good idea."

Jack, Derrick, Martin, Joe, Brent, Allen, and their wives all came to Memphis. At the meeting, Bob went over GSDC's financial performance for the past year. "So Tropical Juices has made more profits per dollar of our investment than any other business unit within GSDC," Bob explained. "One reason for that is that GSDC has not interfered with them at all, except to provide support, and then only when asked. Tropical Juices is run as if it was a stand-alone company, and it has not needed any financial resources from GSDC. It just returned lots of profits and cash. I want to bring the man and his management team up here to recognize their success and contribution. Jack, bring up your team."

Jack brought them up on stage and they stood, facing the crowd of about 150 people.

"Everyone, this is Jack Thomas, president of Tropical Juices, and his management team." There was a low murmur in the audience as some of them recognized Jack - "Isn't that the World War II hero?" "Yeah, I think so," etc.

ROBERT ALLEN MORRIS

Jack went to the podium and introduced each one of his management team, explaining their responsibilities. When he was through, the stockholders gave them a standing ovation.

In September of 1972, Jeb entered the Harvard Business School, declaring his specialties as marketing and international trade. He graduated in June of 1974, and accepted a job with Tropical Juices, working in the processing plant as juice production manager. He was on Jack's form of a management training program, which would entail him working in the plant and in finance for two years each before moving into marketing in 1978.

In February of 1975, Margaret announced that Don Barron, the grandson of the founder of the National Agribusiness Company, had asked her to marry him, and she'd accepted. They planned a June wedding. "Oh, Margaret, that's wonderful!" her mother replied excitedly. "We've got to start planning the wedding right away!"

"Congratulations, honey," Jack offered. "Don's a fine man, and he comes from a good, hardworking family. He'll make a good husband."

In 1977 there was a devastating freeze. It actually snowed in Orlando. It wasn't as bad as the one in 1962, but it was bad. Tropical Juices exercised its option to take all of Alberto's concentrate and diverted oranges destined for concentrate into NFC in their plant, which now had a capacity of thirty million boxes. Jack had Derrick and Allen do the analysis to determine how high to raise their selling price to reduce sales volumes in line with reduced supplies. When he called Bob at GSDC, he was told that he was away in Europe, and that he should explain the situation to Lee Gold, the new executive vice president of marketing.

"What can I do for you, Jack?" Lee asked.

348

FLORIDA GOLD

"I just wanted to give you a run down on the freeze and its impact on citrus."

"Yeah, I hear it got cold down there. Snowed in Orlando."

"That's right. Lee, we estimate that based on the reduction in fruit supply, we'll need to raise our selling prices for orange and grapefruit juice by about thirty-five percent."

"WHAT? No way. That will kill our market."

"Lee, our competitors will be doing the same thing. It's part of how this industry responds to a freeze."

"Aren't your fruit prices tied to what you sell the juice for?"

"Yes, but if our fruit prices aren't competitive with other processors, we'll lose our fruit supply base."

"Nonsense. Tropical Juices is the best thing that has ever happened for them. They'll support you in this. And your lower prices will build market share."

"Lee, most of our growers will probably lose between a fourth and a third of the fruit in their groves. They will need higher fruit prices to cover their higher production costs per box."

"Well, I'm not buying it. Do not increase your prices."

"OK, then we'll lose our fruit supply, and we'll be out of business."

"Jack I just think you're overreacting to this whole thing because you're too close to it."

After two days of trying, Jack was finally able to get in touch with Bob Singleton, who approved Jack's price increases. "I'll explain things to Lee," Bob promised.

Once the 1977 freeze was behind them, Jack met with Allen Adams to discuss fruit supplies and procurement. "Jack, with the amount of tree damage this freeze has done and as big as our needs have grown, Juice Orange Marketers will only be able to supply about a third. We'll need to take the rest as Brazilian concentrate and from the cash market."

349

"I'm OK with buying fifteen to twenty percent of our fruit needs annually on the cash market because it gives us flexibility in case our sales forecast is not accurate. But buying more than that year-to-year is risky with the amount of fruit we need."

"Maybe we should consider buying groves."

"To meet half of our fruit needs would require about thirty-eight thousand acres. That would cost over $300 million. With the larger asset base, our return on investment would be reduced, and our financial performance below standards."

"How else will we get the required fruit?" Allen asked

"Long-term contracts."

"What?"

"We will select large, well-capitalized growers, some of whom may not be growing citrus, but other crops like vegetables or sugar cane. They will all be located south of Lake Placid, down in the LaBelle area where it doesn't freeze as often. We'll negotiate fifteen-year contracts with them for all of their fruit. About half of this will be new plantings specifically for us. The contracts will have a guaranteed minimum, or floor price, in them that covers the grower's costs and provides a profitable return on his investment. That floor price will be adjusted annually for inflation. The market price will be the higher of their floor price, or ninety-five percent of Tropical Juices' participation price. The five percent discount on our participation price will be in exchange for the floor price. That way when prices are low, we protect them with the strength of our brand, and when prices are high, we get a discount to help us in the marketplace. In five years, Tropical Juices will have its grove division without investing anything in groves."

"But won't floor prices be risky?"

"If we owned our own groves, we'd have the same requirement to cover our costs and make a profit to justify

FLORIDA GOLD

the investment. So we'd have to, in effect, pay ourselves the floor price plus the rise to our participation price. With long-term contracts, we avoid the $300 - $350 million investment."

"I like it, Jack. It's a brilliant procurement strategy."

"Get me on the agenda of the next Southwest Florida Growers Association meeting. I want to describe this long-term contract to the members, and encourage those interested to contact you or me."

"Dad," Jeb began as he and Jack were riding to the lease to go spring gobbler hunting. "I asked Natasha to marry me and she's accepted."

"That's wonderful, Jeb. She's real smart, and also very beautiful. I'm sure she will make a wonderful bride. Have you set a date?"

"Yeah, Saturday, October 18. And I wanted to ask you something."

"Sure, Jeb."

"Would you be my best man?"

"Of course. I'd consider it an honor. Sure you want your old man? Most fellas choose their best friend."

"Dad, you are my best friend."

"Thanks for telling me that, Jeb. It means a lot. You're my best friend too."

On Saturday, October 18, 1977, Jeb was married to Natasha Happel at the First United Methodist Church in Winter Haven. They went on a seven-day Caribbean cruise for their honeymoon.

On Friday, July 21, 1978, Margaret had a baby boy. He weighed seven pounds, fourteen ounces. They named him Ferdinand, after his grandfather, Ferdinand Barron. All the family was there at Lakeland Regional Medical Hospital to see the new baby.

On Wednesday, October 3, 1979, Natasha had a baby boy. He weighed eight pounds and three ounces. They named him Jeff. Jack and Carolyn were standing with Jeb when the doctor brought the newborn baby out for Jeb to hold.

By 1980, Jack and Allen had secured thirty-eight thousand acres of groves under long-term contracts. At full maturity, that would be about fifteen million boxes of fruit annually - three million grapefruit and the balance oranges. About half of the acreage was mature groves already producing fruit.

On Sunday, August 16, 1981, Margaret had a baby girl. She weighed seven pounds, fifteen ounces. They named her Martha, after Carolyn's mother. Again, all of the family was at the hospital to see the new baby and enjoy this special occasion with Margaret and Don.

In December of 1983 there was another freeze worse than the one in 1977. But Tropical juices was protected by its long-term contracts, which, even though they wouldn't be producing fifteen million boxes of fruit for another five to seven years, given the mature groves in the mix, were producing 8.2 million boxes of oranges. That, combined with fruit from Juice Orange Marketers, and bulk concentrate from Florida bulk plants and Brazil, enabled Tropical Juices to have ample supplies during the freeze. And for the 27 percent of their fruit now coming from long-term contracts, they had a 5 percent price discount. They watched as the other processors and brands struggled to survive, while Tropical Juices, with ample fruit and juice supplies and the lowest cost of goods in the industry, saw market share and profits soar. Once again, Jack had navigated the risky, treacherous citrus business waters safely and profitably.

"Mr. Thomas, Mr. Singleton is on the line for you," Gerry said.

"Hey, Bob. How are things in Memphis?"

FLORIDA GOLD

"Fine, Jack. Great job in mitigating the impact of the freeze."

"Thanks."

"Jack I'm going to retire in July, and the board has asked me to approach you about taking my place as GSDC's president."

"I'm not sure I'm qualified for a job like that."

"With the management challenges you handle in the risky citrus business? I think you are more than qualified. And with a bigger company to run, there's no telling how big and successful GSDC would become."

"Bob, tell the board I'm honored that they asked, but my heart will always be with the Florida citrus industry."

"I'm not surprised. But would you be willing to help us select someone?"

"Of course."

At a Citrus Commission meeting in April of 1984, Commissioner Harris proposed that orange juice advertising be eliminated until fruit supplies returned. "We can't supply the market we have, why continue to advertise?"

"If we eliminate the orange juice advertising, how much would that reduce the tax?" Commissioner Paxton asked.

"By about a third," replied Steve Robinson, executive director of the Florida Department of Citrus.

"Advertising is done primarily to increase prices," argued Jack, who was now chairman of the commission. "Are you saying you will accept a lower price for your fruit, Bill?"

"No, I just.."

"Well that's what will happen in a year or two without our advertising program. Because juice blends and beverages, which are cheaper than orange juice, will begin to replace orange juice, demand will decline and so will prices," Jack explained.

353

"Jack, Tropical Juices sells a juice blend and a juice beverage. Why would you care if orange juice demand declines?"

"Because, as a commissioner, my responsibility is to look out for the welfare of the citrus industry, not the welfare of Tropical Juices."

"That's enough for me. I move we continue the advertising programs," Commissioner Bell proposed.

"So moved," Jack replied. "Do I hear a second?"

"Second."

"All in favor?"

"Aye."

"Opposed?"

"Nay," three commissioners replied.

"The ayes have it," Jack said.

"We need to be able to sell Premium Natural west of the Mississippi, to make it a national brand. We're missing too much market out there," Jack told the executive committee on Monday, February 4, 1985.

"The problem is that our shelf life for NFC in cartons is only about thirty-five days," Brent explained. "With the distribution time, if we were to go west of the Mississippi, it would have to be in glass."

"Too expensive," Jack replied. "Brent, ask Richard to join us."

"What's up?" Richard asked when he'd arrived.

"We need to get more than a thirty-five day shelf life on Premium Natural so we can take it national," Jack explained.

"That means you need a better oxygen barrier carton," Richard replied.

"What does that do?" Joe asked.

"It reduces the oxygen that comes in contact with the juice, thus increasing shelf life. How much do you need?"

"Fifty-six days should be adequate," Brent replied.

FLORIDA GOLD

"Can you design something like that?" Jack asked.

"As a matter of fact, I have been working on that problem for almost a year now. I figured that with the success of Premium Natural in the eastern markets, you would want to take it national."

"Have you developed anything yet?" Brent asked.

"No, but I'm close. If I devote full-time to it, I should have something in about a month."

"Devote full-time to it," Jack said. "I would like to be ready to roll Premium Natural to the west by July 15. Allen, buy three million boxes of additional fruit on the cash market for processing into NFC. If Richard can't get the carton developed in time, we'll just concentrate the juice and sell it."

On March 22, Richard called the executive committee together. "I think I have the oxygen barrier carton perfected. Its two layers of ethylene vinyl alcohol. I had these three of the oxygen barrier cartons filled with juice about half an hour ago. Let's wait fifty-six days and see if the juice is still good. We'll store it at forty-five degrees, the same as should be in a refrigerated truck or supermarket juice cabinet."

On May 17, the group met. Richard poured juice samples for everyone, and they tasted the juice. "Richard this juice is great! You've done it!" Jack said.

"Yes, I agree. And the process is patentable, so our competitors can't copy it."

"Great, Richard. If our roll westward is successful, once it is patented, Tropical Juices will give you a million dollars for the patent rights."

"Thank you, Jack."

"I'll expand National Paper's contract for the non-leaking cartons to include exclusive manufacture of the oxygen barrier cartons for Tropical Juices, and modify their confidentiality agreement to cover these cartons also," Jack explained. "Joe, our launch west of the Mississippi is critical. I want to put what I'll call 'The Taste Challenge' in our

355

advertisement. We will ask consumers to buy fresh oranges at the supermarket and buy a carton of Premium Natural. Juice the oranges and compare the fresh-squeezed juice to Premium Natural. If Premium Natural isn't better than the fresh-squeezed orange juice, we'll give them coupons for free oranges. And if it is, we'll give them coupons for a free half gallon of Premium Natural."

"But what if the fresh-squeezed juice is better?"

"It won't be, because our roll westward will begin in mid-July. There will be no Florida oranges in the stores, only California navels and Valencias, and they're not as juicy as Florida oranges, which is why the only oranges made into juice there are packinghouse eliminations."

The taste challenge was a huge success. Tropical Juices had to add two people to the switchboard to handle all the congratulatory calls. They were in 100 percent distribution within weeks of rolling into major markets such as Houston, Dallas, Denver, Phoenix, Los Angeles, etc.

In October of 1985, Jack got a call from the office of Doyle Connor, the commissioner of Florida Agriculture. "Jack, you've been selected for the Florida Agriculture Hall of Fame."

"Really? That's a special honor."

"Your award and induction into the Hall of Fame will be at the state fair in Tampa on January 23 at the Hall of Fame banquet at seven p.m."

"Ok, I look forward to seeing you there."

Carolyn had provided the selection committee with Jack's biographical information, accomplishments, and photos for a narrated slide show. When it finished, Commissioner Connor said, "Ladies and gentlemen, Jack Thomas; his lovely wife, Carolyn; and their two children, Jeb and Margaret."

Then, in an unscheduled appearance, Florida governor Bob Graham came to the podium. "Ladies and gentlemen," he began. "I was in the audience in Lakeland in 1945 in a

FLORIDA GOLD

ceremony to celebrate Jack winning the Congressional Medal of Honor when then Governor Caldwell told the audience that 'When you're in the presence of Jack Thomas, you're in the presence of greatness.' Well, the state of Florida has been blessed with greatness to have Jack Thomas as a citizen, and as the entrepreneur that built the largest juice company in the world, based here in Florida. Jack, I admire you and what you've done."

"Thanks, Governor Graham."

There was a standing ovation. Carolyn, Jeb, and Margaret were very proud, and Margaret's eyes became glassy with emotion as she again heard what a fine man and how admired her father was.

A few weeks later, Jack received a letter from the Florida Citrus Showcase, informing him that he had been selected for the Citrus Hall of Fame.

"Both in one year," Carolyn observed. "Not bad for a country boy," she teased.

Jack was given a plaque and inducted into the Citrus Hall of Fame at a banquet held at Nora Mayo Hall in Winter Haven on April 3. They used the same narrated slide show. Again, his family was there. They went to the stage with him to accept the award, and he got a standing ovation.

In May of 1986, at an executive committee meeting, Jeb said, "I think Tropical Juices should move into Europe with our juices. It's a huge untapped orange juice market, with more consumers than in the US. It is supplied mostly by Brazil to store labels. It would probably have to be reconstituted concentrate, since NFC would be too expensive to ship. We'd probably ship the concentrate to Rotterdam, and package into ready-to-serve and distribute it from there."

"I like the idea," Jack said. "It gives us a new market and an opportunity to make Tropical Juices into an international

357

brand. Jeb, this will be your project. Manage it how you see fit."

Jeb took Joe and Brent with him to Rotterdam to meet with Claus Saft Verpackung, one of Citro-Tropic's customer companies. The meeting went well, and CSV agreed to reconstitute Premium Select ready-to-serve, package it, and distribute it. It would be called Tropical Premium Select. They would also pack and distribute Tropical Light as a low-calorie juice nectar.

The advertising around the product launch said, "Too busy to juice your own oranges? Try Tropical Premium Select orange juice and Tropical Light nectar from Tropical Juices." Then Jack went on, saying, "The last time I was in Europe was during World War II. But I helped fund the development of this wonderful juice as part of the war effort to get a nutritious beverage here for starving war victims. Now I'm back, and our juice is even better. Try it!"

"There you have it first hand," a voice-over said, meant to sound like a newscaster. "Jack Thomas, World War II hero, winner of the American Medal of Honor and the Legion of Honor, here to provide you with this tasty, nutritious beverage."

Sales erupted, and in a year, they were 35 percent of the Premium Natural sales in the US, and growing at a 21 percent annual rate. At a meeting of the executive committee, Jack commended Jeb, Joe, and Brent on such a successful introduction of their products into Europe.

The following Saturday night, Jack and Carolyn held a small banquet with their closest friends at their home for Jeb. At dinner, Jack stood and raised his glass of wine in a toast. "Here's to Jeb, for a successful launch of Tropical Juices into Europe, and to his bright future with the company."

FLORIDA GOLD

"Jeb, we're out of milk. Let's stop at that convenience store and get a jug," Natasha suggested as they were headed home on a Monday evening.

"OK," Jeb said as he turned into the convenience store parking lot.

"Can I go in with Mommy? I want a coke," said little Jeff.

"OK, come with me," Natasha said.

"I'll wait in the car," Jeb said.

About fifteen minutes passed and they were still in the store. *I wonder what's keeping them,* Jeb thought. *I'd be better to go in and check on them.*

When he was about to enter the store he saw three men with guns. One was taking cash out of the register, the second held a gun on the store clerk, and the third was holding Natasha and Jeff, his gun pointed at the boy's head. They did not wear masks, which told him nobody was likely to escape alive. "Don't nobody do nothing stupid," the one holding his wife and son said to three customers being forced to lie on the floor. "If you do, I shoot the boy and then his mother."

Jeb squatted down and crept slowly through the door. Their backs were to him, so he hadn't been detected so far. Natasha saw him but didn't let on. Jeb made it to within about eight feet from the one holding the gun on Jeff, and leaped onto him, knocking him down. The gun slid onto the floor and Natasha grabbed it and tossed to Jeb, who quickly shot the attacker. The man holding the gun on the store clerk turned, but Jeb was too fast and he killed him also. But the third man at the register shot Jeb in the chest a split second before Jeb's shot hit him fatally in the head.

"Jeb!" Natasha screamed. He was lying lifeless on the floor.

"Daddy! Daddy!" Jeff cried.

One of the people lying on the floor got up and said, "I'm a doctor, let me look at him." He put his hand to Jeb's jugular vein, and a few seconds later shook his head and said, "I'm sorry." He noted the time of death was 6:23 p.m.

Natasha and Jeff were sobbing, and the doctor went over and tried to comfort them. "Did you know the deceased, ma'am?"

"He was my husband and Jeff's father," she sobbed.

"I'm so sorry. He was a true hero. We'd probably all be dead if it wasn't for what he did." The store clerk had called the police, and they arrived shortly. They took Natasha's and the other people's statements while Jeb's body was taken to the city morgue. A female officer brought Natasha and Jeff home, while another officer followed in their car. When Natasha was inside, she called Jack and gave him the tragic news. In spite of his own intense agony, his immediate concerns were for Natasha and Jeff. He told them he and Carolyn would be right over.

"Carolyn, there's been a terrible tragedy," Jack began, and then he told Carolyn the horrible news. "Carolyn, he was a hero, and his actions saved the lives of others."

"I know," she sobbed, "but it cost him his life!" Then Jack caught her as she fainted. Jack called their doctor, shared the news with him, and got her a prescription for a sedative. Then he called his secretary.

"Gerry, I need a favor."

"Sure, what?"

"Jeb was just killed in a convenience store robbery."

"My God! How did it happen?"

"I'll share the details later. Carolyn is taking it hard. I just got a prescription for a sedative for her. I don't want to leave her alone, so would you come by my house and pick it up, then get it filled and bring it back? I would also appreciate it if you'd stay with her while I go see Natasha and Jeff."

"Of course, I'll leave right now."

"Also, when you get to work in the morning, set up a meeting of all the management for one thirty p.m. in the

FLORIDA GOLD

upstairs meeting room. I want to personally tell everyone what happened."

"Of course, Mr. Thomas."

Around midnight, after Jack had returned from consoling Natasha and Jeff, and Carolyn had been asleep for several hours, he went out back to the pool and sat down. He was sitting in the dark by the pool, lost in his thoughts, when he heard the distant rumble of thunder. A violent thunderstorm soon began. He walked out of the pool area to watch the storm. The rain smelled fresh and sweet as the lightning sent flashes of light into the darkness, followed by deafening thunder. Jack walked out into the yard and into the rain, not caring as it soaked his hair, face and clothes, not concerned about the lightning.

Then he fell to his knees and looked upward as he prayed to God and wept, the storm raging around him in the darkness. "Oh, God, my father in heaven," Jack prayed. "You've given me many challenges in my life. I never questioned them and I did my best to deal with them. I believe they made me stronger. But I don't understand losing my son," he sobbed. "This challenge is so devastating. Jeb was a good man, with a bright future. I know his act of bravery saved lives and I'm proud. But why, oh Lord? Why?

"Jeb," he sobbed. "I'll be the father you can't be to Jeff. I'll spend time with him, and teach him to be an honorable man. I'm going to resign and retire, so I'll have the time to do just that, and spend time with Margaret's children as well. I love you, Son. In Jesus' name, I pray. Amen."

And then Jack wept uncontrollably, his body shaking with sadness and despair as he cried and cried the tears of his lost hopes and dreams for Jeb. He fell asleep on the wet grass in the wooded backyard. It was the first time the Medal of Honor winner and CEO of the world's largest juice company had cried since his first night in the child labor camp.

ROBERT ALLEN MORRIS

The sun woke him up the next morning, and he realized that it was going to be a beautiful day. He went in and took a shower, shaved, and dressed. He checked on Carolyn and she was still sleeping. As Jack was having his breakfast, he felt better. Somehow the emotional release from the night before had cleansed him and rid him of his depression. He knew that no matter what the future held, he'd be able to deal with this challenge the way he'd always dealt with challenges. He had much to be thankful for. A lovely and devoted wife, a wonderful daughter, and three special grandchildren. Everything would be alright.

The news about Jeb's death and his act of bravery was all over the front pages of the ▒▒▒e▒▒n▒ ▒e▒▒er and the ▒ r▒▒n▒o ▒ent▒▒e▒the next morning. Calls poured into Jack's office and into their home. Gerry and their maid, Jenny, handled them all. Carolyn stayed in bed.

The funeral was held on Saturday morning, October 17, 1987. Jeb had turned forty-one in June before he was killed.

"Jeb Thomas was a special man," the minister told the enormous crowd at the funeral in the First United Methodist Church. "He was a responsible and loving husband and father, a devoted son, a cherished brother, and a valuable part of the senior management team at Tropical Juices. The police believe the act of bravery that led to his death saved the lives of those in the store. But most of all, Jeb Thomas was a man of God. And we must believe that God had a plan for Jeb on the tragic day he went into that store. Jeb's in a better place now, continuing to watch over his loved ones. He will be missed by many. Let us pray."

CHAPTER EIGHTEEN

"Roger Woods is on the line for you, Jack," Gerry told him a few days later. Roger was now the CEO of the Global Soft Drink Company.

"Hey, Roger."

"Jack, I just wanted to offer my and the GSDC board's deepest sympathies for the loss of your son, Jeb."

"Thanks, Roger."

"His leadership moved Tropical Juices into Europe, and its huge success is a credit to his management talent. I also understand his act of heroism saved lives at that convenience store."

"Yes, Roger, Jeb was one of a kind. I believe he's in a better place now, though. I was going to call you, so it's good that you called. I'm finally going to retire. I turned seventy-two last February, and it's time. I have some grandchildren that need my time more now than Tropical Juices or GSDC does. So I'm giving you a year's notice. I'll be glad to help you train my replacement."

Silence on the other end. "Roger, are you there?"

"Yeah. I just can't believe you're retiring. You'll certainly be missed."

"Well, I am. And like I said, I'll stay for another year and help train my replacement."

"OK, and thanks."

The next month, at a meeting of the GSDC board, Roger announced Jack's plans to retire. "Roger, we knew this would happen soon, because of Jack's age," Irving Shapiro, the chairman, replied.

"I know. I just wanted to get approval to get a search company employed to hire his replacement."

"Roger, there is nobody that can replace Jack," James Clayton observed.

"I agree," Linda Goldman said.

"Now that Jack's son is gone, he has no successor. I think it's time to consider selling Tropical Juices," James suggested.

"Yeah, it takes unique management talent to prosper in an industry as risky as citrus. How many times has this board disagreed with Jack's decisions or actions, but kept to our promise to leave him alone, only to find out we were wrong and he was right?" Irving explained.

"I agree," Roger said. "Plus, Tropical Juices has just moved into Europe. That offers huge growth potential for a buyer."

"So do we get an investment banker involved?" Linda asked.

"No. Only Jack can explain this business and the citrus industry accurately enough to convey its potential value. Let's have our mergers and acquisitions department prepare the prospectus and let Jack sell it," Irving replied.

"OK, let's vote. Everyone in favor of Irving's suggestion signify by saying aye."

It was unanimous.

"Jack, we need to meet," Roger said when he called him.

"Is it about my successor?"

"Something like that."

"I sold our place in North Carolina and just bought a twenty-seven-thousand-acre ranch in Colorado that has great fly fishing. Why don't we meet there for a weekend?"

FLORIDA GOLD

"That sounds good. I've been waiting for you to show me some good fly fishing ever since you invited me to your place in North Carolina and I couldn't come."

"The fly fishing is better in Colorado. When do you want to go?"

"How about the Friday after next?"

"Great, I'll meet you at the Denver airport. Just let me know what time."

At dinner in the ranch house in Colorado, Roger said, "Jack, GSDC has decided to sell Tropical Juices."

"Really?"

"Yes. Since Jeb died you have no likely successor, and quite frankly, without you to run Tropical Juices, we doubt that it will be anywhere near as successful. Besides, the citrus business is too volatile and risky for us."

"I'm not surprised. Who is going to handle the sale, Goldman Sachs?"

"No, we want you to, Jack. You know the business best. Hell, you created it and turned it into the largest and most profitable juice company in the world."

"I agree, I can probably do the best job of selling it. How much does GSDC think it is worth?"

"Our financial analysts say $1.8 billion."

"Yeah, but that's just based on the numbers."

"Jack, an average return on stock holders' equity of twenty-seven percent is not bad numbers."

"I agree, but you want to find a buyer where Tropical Juices offers strategic value above the numbers."

"I agree, and that's why we want you to sell it."

"I think its worth at least $2.2 billion."

"It will take a vote from the board to raise our minimum to that amount, so I'll get this on January's agenda."

"Fine. Also, I want a small fee."

365

"With the twenty percent you'll walk away with in this sale? I'm surprised."

"The fee will be divided among my five senior managers, to protect them if the new owners dismiss them."

"Understandable. How much?"

"Two and a half percent of the selling price."

"That's fair, and it's less than an investment banking company would charge for services that will not get as good a price as I'm sure you will be able to get. But we need to be sure your management does not resign before the new owners have a chance to learn the business."

"Each one of my senior management team getting the money will sign a contract that says they will stay in their jobs until the new owners either ask them to leave or offer them a job. If they are offered a job, they can accept or refuse it, but will agree to stay on for six months after their replacements are on board to help train them."

"That's fair. It's a deal. Now tell me where we will be fishing in the morning. I also want to show you my private collection of flies."

Jack arrived at the International Liquor Company's Park Avenue offices on schedule. "Jack Thomas to see Mr. Edgar Goldberg," Jack told the receptionist in the impressive lobby.

"Jack, how are you?" the CEO of the International Liquor Company asked as he walked up and shook Jack's hand.

"Fine, Edgar."

"Great. Our people are assembled and waiting on you."

Ben Hack, the CFO, went over the offer. "So the net amount will be $1.7 billion."

"Not good enough, gentlemen. We need $2½ billion."

"We aren't authorized to pay..."

"I understand. That's why I have an appointment with National Wines this afternoon. Thanks for your time. I won't waste any more of it," Jack replied as he stood to leave.

FLORIDA GOLD

"Wait, Jack," Edgar said.

"We'll raise our offer to 1.9."

"Make it 2.2 and you have a deal."

"Done! Jack, I understand that you own twenty percent of Tropical Juices."

"Yes, that's correct."

"You'll be a much wealthier man after this sale."

"I agree, but I am already wealthy in ways not defined by money."

"Ben, get Laura to bring us some champagne in here to celebrate."

On the way back to Winter Haven, Jack called his office.

"Gerry, is my senior management team in the conference room?"

"Yes sir, they have been for about ten minutes waiting on your call, as you requested."

"Gerry, I want you to come to the airport and meet my plane along with the senior managers".

"Certainly, Mr. Thomas."

"OK, now put me through on speaker."

"Hello, Jack?"

"Derrick is that you?"

"Yes."

"I've got great news. The International Liquor Company has just agreed to buy Tropical Juices for $2.2 billion."

"OK that's good," Joe said half-heartedly.

"I don't detect any excitement," Jack said, knowing why.

"Jack, you know how things go in an acquisition, none of the jobs at our level are secure now," Martin said.

"That doesn't matter."

"Why?"

"Because, as part of the deal, each of you gets $10.5 million. Didn't you know I'd protect you in this sale?"

"Not like that! What can we say, Jack? We owe you everything," Derrick said.

367

ROBERT ALLEN MORRIS

"Each of you has earned every penny as far as I'm concerned. You just have to agree to stay in your current jobs until the new owners ask you to leave or offer you a job. If they offer you a job, you can accept or reject it, but you must be willing to stay for six months and train your replacement if you elect to leave."

"Again, Jack, thanks."

"Derrick, would you and the rest of the senior management team meet my plane at the airport?"

"Of course."

"Derrick, I need to talk to you alone."

"Sure, Jack," Derrick replied as the others left.

"Derrick, cut a check for $2.5 million. It will be paid back from the proceeds of the sale."

"I take it that $2.5 million is for Gerry?"

"Yeah. Would you bring her to the airport with you?"

"Sure, Jack."

As Carolyn was driving to the Bartow airport to meet Jack's plane, she thought back over the forty-three years that she and Jack had been married. He was finally retiring, and with his share of the profits he'd made over the years, particularly over the last twenty, and what he'd get from this sale of Tropical Juices, their net worth was pushing $2 billion. With the investments Jack had most of it in and the resulting profits, their family and its subsequent generations would be financially secure into perpetuity. But that wasn't what impressed her the most. Jack had been the perfect husband and father, more romantic than most men, always giving her love and support when she needed it, paying attention to the little details of their relationship, his love unconditional. He'd also spent a lot of his valuable time with their children and with her. In spite of his horrible childhood, or maybe because of it, he'd been a leader and an inspiration to all who knew him.

368

FLORIDA GOLD

She'd never heard him complain about anything, and never met anyone who didn't admire him. And when you were around him, he had this way of making you feel good about yourself. She knew she'd been married to a rare and great man for forty-three years. As she pulled into the airport she saw Jack's plane touching down. She knew he'd be successful in his negotiations, even before he'd called and told her. And now she and her family would have him all to themselves for the rest of his life. As she drove out onto the tarmac, she silently thanked God for bringing this wonderful man into her life, as she had so many times before.

The Gulfstream landed at Bartow Airport at 4:19 p.m. Margaret and Natasha were there to meet him with their kids. "Grandpa, Grandpa!" the girl and two boys shouted running toward Jack as he stepped off the plane. 𝟤𝟤 𝟤𝘶𝟤𝘵 𝟤𝘦𝟤𝟤𝘩𝘯𝟤𝘩𝟤 𝘵𝟤𝘦 𝟤𝘦𝟤𝘵 𝟤𝟤𝘳𝘵 𝘰𝟤𝟤 𝟤 𝟤𝘵𝘦𝟤Jack thought as he hugged them.

"Who wants to ride horses and go camping on the ranch?" Jack asked.

"We do, we do!" they shouted.

"Well then, get aboard our plane." Their mothers were already handing the luggage to the attendant to load as Carolyn came up and hugged him.

About that time, the officers from Tropical Juices drove out on the tarmac and got out of their cars. They formed a circle around Jack and Carolyn.

"Guys, I want to tell you how proud of you I am for your hard work and dedication, and that certainly includes you, Gerry. In fact, to show you how much I appreciate your hard work and faithful service, Gerry, I have a bonus for you."

"Sir?"

"Derrick, do you have the check?"

"Yeah," he replied as he handed Gerry the $2.5 million check.

She looked at it and staggered. Derrick caught her.

"Oh, Mr. Thomas, I - I don't know what to say." Then she began to cry.

"Gerry, you've been a wonderful, productive, and devoted assistant to me for twenty years. Your hard work enabled all of us to be more productive, and I just wanted to show how much you are valued and appreciated," Jack said as he hugged her.

"Thank you, sir," she said through her tears. "God bless you." Carolyn was crying too.

The group from Tropical Juices got into their cars and left, and Carolyn put her hand on Jack's shoulder. "That was a fine thing you just did for Gerry."

"Well, she deserved it."

"I know, but most bosses would have given her a plaque and a meal at her favorite restaurant, not $2½ million."

"She deserved to be meaningfully rewarded."

"I agree. Now, do we finally have you to ourselves?" she asked as she gazed lovingly at him.

"Actually, I'm getting ready to run off with Demi Moore. I just haven't had the nerve to tell you."

"What? Jack!"

"Just kidding. After 43 years you should know you're the love of my life."

"Damn, I guess that means I have to call Don Johnson and turn him down."

They both looked at each other and began laughing.

"What are you two up to?" Margaret asked.

"Just keeping humor in our marriage," Carolyn replied.

"Carolyn," Jack said as he looked lovingly at her, "I'm ready to begin this chapter of our life."

"I think it will be the best."

"I know it will," he said as he walked toward the plane, holding the hand of his soul mate of forty-three years.

About the Author

Robert Allen Morris, a Florida native, is an agricultural economist with over thirty years of experience in the citrus industry. He is currently Vice-President of Sales and Marketing for Blue Lake Citrus Products, Inc., the company that produces and markets the Noble brand of high end specialty citrus juices as well as bulk citrus juices sold to other brands and retail chains. From 2007 until 2012, Allen was on the faculty of the University of Florida, stationed at the Citrus Research and Education Center in Lake Alfred, FL. His responsibilities included both educational programs and research. Prior to that, he held managerial positions with various companies including Cutrale Citrus Juices USA, the North American subsidiary of Sucocitrico Cutrale, one of the world's largest citrus growers, processors and exporters, based in Araraquara, Brazil; Tropicana, one of the largest citrus juice brands, and the Coca-Cola Company. He has also done consulting for many citrus growers, processors, and branded citrus juice firms. Allen has published over thirty articles on citrus in trade and professional journals and has given numerous presentations about citrus world-wide. He wrote this novel because he wants to explain the intricacies of the birth and growth of the orange juice industry to the public, while making it an interesting story. And, he wants to give readers an opportunity to experience the old Florida, the way it was before all of the theme parks and condos. Allen currently resides with his wife Kate in Winter Haven, FL, and can be contacted at AllenMors@aol.com. Visit www.AllenMorrisOnline.com for more literary works by Allen.

Made in the USA
Charleston, SC
11 June 2015